Advance Praise for *Enhancing Architectural Drawings and Models with Photoshop*

Scott Onstott has a way with Photoshop and CAD—plain and simple. In fact, his ingenious insight is somehow always presented "plain and simple" so that the average user can fully comprehend the techniques he is trying to get across. Scott's years of teaching come into play here as he masterfully takes the reader from novice to expert as they traverse the pages of this book. His years of CAD experience and insight shine through as he has truly been there—just as the reader is now—and whether you are working in 2D or 3D, Scott has the answers. Scott Onstott's books are the first ones I pick up when I need to master a new software product—and he never lets me down!
    —Lynn Allen, Autodesk Evangelist

This Photoshop book is unique because it specifically focuses on the use of Photoshop by architects, particularly the new 3D capabilities in the last few releases of Photoshop Extended—information that is hard to find elsewhere, even in the Photoshop documentation. It was illuminating and exciting to see what is now possible to do with 3D models in addition to 2D drawings in Photoshop! Scott Onstott brings together his extensive expertise and skills as an architect, technologist, artist, and author in crafting this book, which is written in a clear, concise, and engaging manner and amply supported by numerous illustrations. It starts from the basics of how to prepare a drawing or model within its native application for enhancement in Photoshop and goes on to cover all of the relevant features and functionalities that can be used, including the latest CS5 capabilities such as Content-Aware removal, enhanced selection controls, Puppet Warp, HDR Toning, Mixer Brush, the new Materials library, Repoussé, and image-based lighting. Everything that you want to know about how to use Photoshop for enhancing architectural drawings and models is in this book.
    —Lachmi Khemlani, Ph.D., Founder and Editor, AECbytes

Enhancing Architectural Drawings and Models with Photoshop®

Scott Onstott

WILEY

Wiley Publishing, Inc.

Senior Acquisitions Editor: Willem Knibbe
Development Editor: Denise Santoro Lincoln
Technical Editor: Ian le Cheminant
Production Editor: Eric Charbonneau
Copy Editor: Sharon Wilkey
Editorial Manager: Pete Gaughan
Production Manager: Tim Tate
Vice President and Executive Group Publisher: Richard Swadley
Vice President and Publisher: Neil Edde
Media Associate Project Manager: Jenny Swisher
Media Associate Producer: Josh Frank
Media Quality Assurance: Shaun Patrick
Book Designer: Franz Baumhackl
Compositor: Maureen Forys, Happenstance Type-O-Rama
Proofreader: Candace English
Indexer: Ted Laux
Project Coordinator, Cover: Katie Crocker
Cover Designer: Ryan Sneed
Cover Image: © Peggy Chen / iStockPhoto

Library of Congress Cataloging-in-Publication Data

Onstott, Scott.

  Enhancing architectural drawings and models with photoshop / Scott Onstott.—1st ed.

    p. cm.

  ISBN 978-0-470-91656-8 (pbk.)

  1. Adobe Photoshop. 2. Architectural drawing—Computer-aided design. 3. Architectural models—Computer simulation. I. Title.

  T385.O573 2011

  720'.285—dc22

                         2010045652

ISBN: 978-0-470-91656-8 (pbk)
ISBN: 978-1-118-03506-1 (ebk)
ISBN: 978-1-118-03505-4 (ebk)
ISBN: 978-1-118-03507-8 (ebk)

Dear Reader,

Thank you for choosing *Enhancing Architectural Drawings and Models with Photoshop*. This book is part of a family of premium-quality Sybex books, all of which are written by outstanding authors who combine practical experience with a gift for teaching.

Sybex was founded in 1976. More than 30 years later, we're still committed to producing consistently exceptional books. With each of our titles, we're working hard to set a new standard for the industry. From the paper we print on, to the authors we work with, our goal is to bring you the best books available.

I hope you see all that reflected in these pages. I'd be very interested to hear your comments and get your feedback on how we're doing. Feel free to let me know what you think about this or any other Sybex book by sending me an email at nedde@wiley.com. If you think you've found a technical error in this book, please visit http://sybex.custhelp.com. Customer feedback is critical to our efforts at Sybex.

Best regards,

Neil Edde
Vice President and Publisher
Sybex, an imprint of Wiley

Acknowledgments

I wish to personally thank you for taking the time to learn more about using Photoshop in an architectural context. It will give you great personal satisfaction to master such an amazing program and use it in ever more creative ways. Mastering any software is a difficult task that requires many hours of study and commitment, but learning how to enhance your architectural drawings and models in Photoshop is worth the time and effort. In addition to improving the presentation of your professional materials, knowledge of Photoshop opens to you the opportunity to participate in the vibrant community that has grown up around Photoshop, not just in architecture, but also in many other fields and disciplines.

A team of people has been instrumental in making this book the reality you are holding in your hands or reading on the screen. First, I'd like to thank Chris Main, who is a key figure in the Photoshop universe (managing editor of *Photoshop User* and former managing editor of *Layers*) for writing the foreword to this book.

I would also like to express my sincere gratitude to the professional team at Sybex (an imprint of Wiley) for making possible such a technically and linguistically correct, readable, and polished book. It has been a pleasure working with senior acquisitions editor Willem Knibbe and editorial manager Pete Gaughan again, having worked with them both long before Sybex was part of Wiley. I couldn't be more pleased to have this book published through Wiley, as their team is truly top-notch. Many thanks go to Denise Santoro Lincoln for her superb work as this book's development editor. Thanks also to my good friend Ian Le Cheminant, who has done a stellar job keeping me on track in his work as technical editor. Many thanks also to copy editor Sharon Wilkey, production editor Eric Charbonneau, and last but not least, editorial assistants Jenni Housh and Connor O'Brien.

About the Author

Scott Onstott has a degree in architecture from UC Berkeley and has worked in several prominent architecture, engineering, and interiors firms in San Francisco. In addition, he has taught AEC software to thousands of students at several Bay Area universities. Scott has written and edited scores of books, magazine articles, and video tutorials, including the video series "Photoshop for Architects."

Contents

Foreword

As the former managing editor of *Layers: The How-to Magazine for Everything Adobe* (2005–2010) and the current managing editor of *Photoshop User,* the official magazine of the National Association of Photoshop Professionals (1999–2004, 2010–present), I've worked with many talented, incredibly bright writers and educators. So I was honored when Scott Onstott asked me to write the foreword for the book that you're now holding because I count Scott as one of those top talents whom I've had the privilege to work with. His knowledge of Photoshop, architecture, 3D, and digital imaging always amazes me.

Scott is a regular contributor to *Photoshop User,* and I look forward to editing his column every issue because I know that I'll always learn something new. Just glancing at Scott's resume will tell you that he's extremely knowledgeable and a true master at his craft. The list of books, DVDs, and CDs that he has worked on as technical editor, revisor, compilation editor, contributing author, author, and self-publisher makes me feel like I've been standing still for the past 10 years.

Of course, that's not true, as I've edited quite a few Photoshop articles in my time. And that's the main reason I'm so impressed with Scott's new book. Even with all the Photoshop knowledge that I've accumulated over the years from some of the top graphic artists and trainers in the world, I still walked away from Scott's book learning an abundance of new Photoshop techniques and tricks. Scott reveals some hidden gems in Photoshop that you would be hard-pressed to find on your own (or even in an entire course on Photoshop). In fact, I'd love to tell you about some of them right here, but I don't want to steal Scott's thunder. And best of all, Scott tells you *why* the many techniques that he shares with you in the book are so important to real-world professionals who use Photoshop every day to create and manipulate amazing architectural drawings, photographic images, and 3D models. You'll also find a lot of tips and tricks for using digital cameras to capture the images that people in this industry use every day.

And don't worry if you're new to Photoshop. Scott clearly guides you every step of the way, and the many practice files he provides on the DVD make it even easier to learn these techniques, keeping you focused on learning Photoshop and not out trying to gather or capture your own image files with which to practice. He even provides multiple versions of the same file as it progresses through a series of tutorials. That way, if you want to skip ahead, you can just open the version of the file that you need—that's a very nice touch.

As you work your way through this book, you'll learn a lot about Photoshop. And I mean a lot. To enhance architectural drawings and models in Photoshop, there are many tools and features that you need to know how to use. From smart objects to layer styles to filters to 3D tools to animation and video, you'll learn it all right here in this book. Even if your main focus isn't on creating or editing architectural renderings or 3D models, there's a ton of information that you can easily carry over to other aspects of digital imaging and manipulation.

As with any profession, the more proficient you are with the tools of your trade, the more efficient and productive you'll be. But the real advantage is that you'll spend more time being creative and spend less time trying to figure out which is the best tool for the job at hand. This book will be a giant leap forward in making you a more productive and creative professional.

CHRIS MAIN
Managing Editor
Photoshop User *magazine*
www.photoshopuser.com

Introduction

This book is for architects, designers, engineers, builders, real estate developers, web designers, students, and anyone who communicates with drawings and 3D building models in their work. Adobe Photoshop can be used for so much more than resizing and printing images; Photoshop is an indispensable tool for enhancing the level of your graphic communication.

The Extended version opens up whole new vistas of creative possibility, including 3D imagery, animation, and video editing capabilities. You'll need the Extended version for assorted tutorials in Chapters 3, 5, and 8–12.

Each chapter of this book exposes you to concepts and techniques that show you how to integrate Photoshop into your digital workflow in conjunction with other software such as AutoCAD, Revit, 3ds Max, SketchUp, and NASA World Wind. You will find step-by-step tutorials that reveal a wide variety of techniques built on many years of real-world experience. You'll also learn how to enhance your graphic presentations and gain important marketing benefits for your practice.

This book assumes basic familiarity with Photoshop's essential concepts. If you are an absolute beginner to Photoshop, I recommend reading the first edition of this book: *Enhancing CAD Drawings with Photoshop* (Sybex, 2005).

How to Use This Book

The first two chapters of this book are related and should be read in sequence. Chapter 1 is about preparing computer-aided design (CAD) and/or building information models (BIM) for enhancement, and Chapter 2 teaches you how to add the enhancements (such as color, pattern, shadow, and lineweight) in Photoshop.

All of the other 10 chapters are self-contained and organized by subject, so feel free to read them in any order. I recommend flipping through the book's color section to get an idea of what's possible. After deciding on what type of imagery you are interested in creating, you can select the relevant chapter and dive right in. Each chapter features tutorials that take you step by step through many complex procedures. The goal of performing these steps on your own is to aim for an understanding that you can abstract into skills you can apply to many different real-world situations.

While every project presents different obstacles and opportunities, I urge you to focus on the concepts and techniques presented, rather than memorizing the specific steps used to achieve the desired result. The best way to build skills is to perform the steps on your computer exactly as they are presented in the book during your first reading. After you achieve the desired result, start over and experiment using the same techniques on your own project (whether invented or real). After you have practiced, think for a moment about how you have achieved the desired result, and try to abstract the steps performed into concepts that you will remember. Only then will you really begin to own the knowledge and get the most out of this book.

Hardware and Software Requirements

You'll first need to make sure your computer can handle Photoshop and a host of additional software to get the most out of this book. Here are the requirements for both hardware and software:

Mac

- Multicore Intel processor
- Mac OS X v10.5.7 or v10.6
- 1 GB of RAM
- 2 GB of available hard-disk space for installation; additional free space required during installation (cannot install on a volume that uses a case-sensitive file system or on removable flash-based storage devices)
- 1024×768 display (1280×800 recommended) with qualified hardware-accelerated OpenGL graphics card, 16-bit color, and 256 MB of VRAM
- For some GPU-accelerated features, graphics support for Shader Model 3.0 and OpenGL 2.0
- DVD-ROM drive
- QuickTime 7.6.2 software required for multimedia features

Windows

- Intel Pentium 4 or AMD Athlon 64 processor
- Microsoft Windows XP with Service Pack 3; Windows Vista Home Premium, Business, Ultimate, or Enterprise with Service Pack 1 (Service Pack 2 recommended); or Windows 7
- 1 GB of RAM
- 1 GB of available hard-disk space for installation; additional free space required during installation (cannot install on removable flash-based storage devices)
- 1024×768 display (1280×800 recommended) with qualified hardware-accelerated OpenGL graphics card, 16-bit color, and 256 MB of VRAM
- For some GPU-accelerated features, graphics support for Shader Model 3.0 and OpenGL 2.0
- DVD-ROM drive
- QuickTime 7.6.2 software required for multimedia features

Additional Software

This book uses the following software in workflows with Photoshop:

- Autodesk AutoCAD 2011 or Autodesk Revit Architecture 2011
- Autodesk 3ds Max Design 2011
- Google SketchUp 8
- Garden Gnome Software Pano2VR

Although none of this software is required, it is recommended to get the most out of this book's tutorials. The companion DVD contains trial versions of some of these software packages. Google offers a free version of SketchUp.

What You'll Find in This Book

Chapter 1, "Preparing Drawings in CAD or BIM for Enhancement," goes into the complexities of formatting and outputting scaled raster data from the vector world of CAD and BIM programs such as Autodesk AutoCAD, and Revit.

Chapter 2, "Enhancing Drawings in Photoshop," teaches you the skills to enhance the technical drawings output from Chapter 1 with the power of Photoshop. You'll add tone, color, pattern, gradient, and shadow to line drawings that pop the presentation up to a new level.

Chapter 3, "Stretching the Photographic Truth," gives you techniques to stretch the literal truth and shift focus in the visual story you are selling your clients. From removing unwanted objects, to replacing the sky, to adjusting color, to subtly altering content and expanding the dynamic range, you'll be able to paint the picture you desire.

Chapter 4, "Crafting Interactive Panoramas," provides detailed steps to help you pick up a number of skills ranging from properly shooting panoramic images and merging them into a composite whole, to blending all the seams and outputting full 360-degree interactive experiences for the Web.

Chapter 5, "Exploring Multiple-Exposure Tricks," details tricks that become available when you shoot multiple exposures of the same subject. Techniques include removing objects in motion, rendering time-lapse video from a series of stills, artistic processing of video clips, and expanding dynamic range by using exactly two bracketed images.

Chapter 6, "Creating Texture Maps," shows you how to work with texture maps for use in Photoshop or other 3D programs. You will create textures from scratch, make seamless textures, harvest objects from photos to use as textures, and gain the skills needed to extract people from photos for reuse in your building elevations and perspective projects.

In Chapter 7, "Compositing Imagery from 3D Applications," you'll learn the art of compositing, whereby you transfer renderings of various visual components (diffuse, specular, shadow, and so on) from 3ds Max into Photoshop for blending into a final composition. The same process can be adapted to working with other high-end 3D packages. In addition, you'll learn how to narrow the depth of field in Photoshop to focus the viewer's attention on an area of interest.

Chapter 8, "Working with Imported 3D Models," covers the mechanics of working with 3D models inside the Extended version of Photoshop. You will gain the skills necessary to successfully transfer 3D models into Photoshop, navigate in 3D space, adjust materials and maps, illuminate with virtual light, cast shadows, and render the model within Photoshop.

Chapter 9, "Illustrating 3D Models," offers artistic methods for illustrating 3D models other than photo-realistic rendering. From illustrating with smart filters, to hybrid uses of 3D render settings, to painterly approaches to illustrating models, the artist in you will find expression.

Chapter 10, "Integrating 3D Models with Photos," blurs the border between photographs and 3D imagery. You'll learn to integrate 3D models as entourage in architectural interiors, as well as integrate entire buildings into street photos so that the virtual appears to be almost real.

In Chapter 11, "Playing with Depth Perception," you'll experiment with depth perception to create richer visualization experiences. Techniques include extruding a logo into a 3D object with Photoshop CS5's new Repoussé feature, harnessing vanishing point to replace textures in perspective, measuring in perspective, and shifting the entire perspective. In addition, you'll explore the world of stereographic and anaglyphic imagery that extends the illusion of depth to novel modes of perception.

Chapter 12, "Working with Animation and Video," opens the door to working with animation and video within Photoshop. Tutorials include animating one frame at a time, animating using the timeline, altering videos the smart way (with smart objects), and finally, animating 3D models in the timeline.

What's On the Companion DVD

The DVD-ROM that accompanies this book includes all the files you'll need to use in the tutorials and exercises throughout the chapters. The sample files include native drawing, model, and Photoshop files plus various types of image formats and video files. The companion DVD also contains videos captured off my screen that briefly describe techniques from each chapter.

Free trial versions of Adobe Photoshop CS5 Extended, Autodesk AutoCAD 2011, Google SketchUp 8, and Garden Gnome Software's Pano2VR (the panoramic utility used in Chapter 4) are also included on the companion DVD.

How to Contact the Author

Wiley strives to keep you supplied with the latest tools and information you need for your work. Please check their website at www.wiley.com for additional content and updates that supplement this book. Enter the book's ISBN—978-0-470-91656-8—in the Search box (or type **enhancing models**), and click on the product to get to the book's update page.

If you have any questions or comments about this book, I encourage you to contact me by visiting my website (ScottOnstott.com) and using the web contact form there.

Preparing Drawings in CAD or BIM for Enhancement

Communicating design ideas with plans, elevations, and section drawings is second nature to architects, engineers, builders, and designers in related disciplines. Many professionals subconsciously assume that everyone is aware of what is actually an obscure set of graphic conventions surrounding measured drawings. These conventions are either learned in design school or integrated through osmosis early in one's career.

1

Chapter Contents

Making drawings readable by everyone
Preparing drawings in CAD or BIM
Working with AutoCAD 2011 drawings
Working with Revit Architecture 2011 models

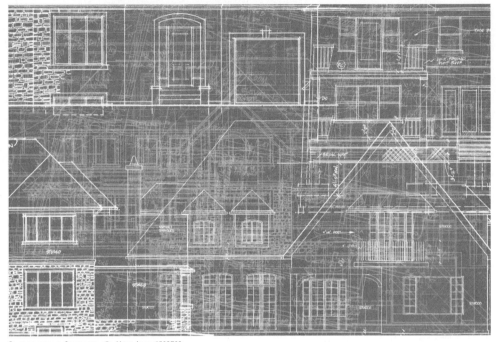

Photo courtesy of iStockphoto, © Vasko, Image #502782

Making Drawings Readable by Everyone

Does the average man or woman on the street know what a section drawing is, let alone how to read a section tag referencing a drawing? What do dashed lines represent to someone not in the design world? How do centerlines appear, and what do thicker lines indicate? More important, who cares?

For those working with design principles every day, it might be surprising to hear that some members of the general public, and maybe even some of your clients, don't fully understand 2D computer-aided design (CAD) drawings; they remain an abstraction for many people and, more important, these people might not verbalize this fact. After all, although we all inhabit 3D architecture every day of our lives, most of us do not have to correlate that experience with 2D drawings on a regular basis.

Whether or not you choose to create 3D building information models (BIMs) or show 3D imagery to your clients, at the end of the day you're still required to generate 2D drawings as legal construction documents. This chapter teaches you how to begin the process of enhancing your drawings, whether you start in CAD or BIM. In Chapter 2, "Enhancing Drawings in Photoshop," you'll learn how to add color, gradients, textures, and shadows to enrich technical line drawings and render them comprehensible by technical and nontechnical people alike.

Preparing Drawings in CAD or BIM

CAD and BIM programs are primarily vector tools. Software engineers have programmed intelligence in these programs in the form of numerous parameters that control the appearance of building components for most conceivable real-world situations. Modern CAD and BIM programs include a few raster features, such as the ability to do the following:

- Assign pixel-based textures to objects and bounded spaces

- Print or export images directly

- Access 3D rendering features that calculate pixels based on geometry, lighting, and materiality

Photoshop, on the other hand, is primarily a pixel-manipulation tool, with a few notable exceptions (such as the Pen tool and 3D toolset). When it comes to enhancing drawings, what we are really talking about is rasterizing, or softening, hard-edged objects and bounded spaces with pixel-manipulation techniques, which is where Photoshop truly excels.

Although it's possible to enhance a single-layer line drawing exported from CAD or BIM, my preference is to import multilayered drawings so that line thickness and anti-aliasing can be managed in Photoshop. The ability to transfer multilayered drawings from CAD or BIM into Photoshop is complicated by fundamental differences between vector and raster data.

On this book's accompanying DVD I've included a LISP program I wrote to automate the transfer of drawings from AutoCAD to Photoshop. (LISP is the LISt Processing interpreted programming language that has been part of AutoCAD for decades.) Such automation is theoretically possible in other CAD programs, but not provided in this book.

There is no way to transfer multilayer drawings from Revit Architecture directly into Photoshop without using AutoCAD as an intermediate step. We therefore need to enhance single-layer drawings coming directly from Revit (see "Working with Revit Architecture 2011 Models" later in this chapter).

Working with AutoCAD 2011 Drawings

I'm working with AutoCAD 2011 in this book, but the LISP program and techniques presented will work in versions of AutoCAD going back more than a decade, to AutoCAD 2000. There are various steps to working with AutoCAD drawings, which I cover in detail in this section.

The game plan for transferring any CAD drawing into Photoshop is to first clean up the CAD drawing you're interested in enhancing. Cleanup will be necessary for every drawing you transfer from AutoCAD into Photoshop.

The first time you go through this procedure, you'll need to create a raster print driver in order to export single-pixel-width lines from AutoCAD. In addition, you'll create a custom "paper size" (actually specified in pixels) and create a custom plot style to properly export lines as pixels. Once these drivers are set up, you can use them indefinitely to convert vector drawings into raster images.

You'll also need to make a test plot in order to configure the LISP program to automate the creation of images from each layer in your CAD drawing. The last preparatory procedure is reassembling all image layers exported from the LISP program within AutoCAD into a smart object in Photoshop (see Figure 1.1).

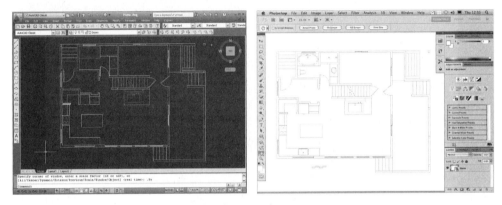

Figure 1.1 Converting an AutoCAD drawing to a Photoshop smart object

Cleaning Up Drawings

The data of CAD drawings must be in a suitable form before it can be used successfully in Photoshop. It is therefore important to follow a few basic cleanup guidelines when preparing CAD drawings for use in Photoshop:

- Follow "clean" drafting practices so that end points of entities snap together precisely.
- Verify that entities are on the correct layers.
- Simplify layers into human-readable form; the layers you transfer into Photoshop are for your reference and do not need to adhere to a standard CAD layer-naming convention.
- Purge any unused layers and blocks (because blocks can trap layers).
- Cut away and erase any nonessential areas of the drawing that you won't be enhancing in Photoshop.
- Erase any filled or hatch areas, symbols, title blocks, or dimensions you don't want to appear in Photoshop.
- Simplify the drawing as much as possible to maximize readability.

> **Note:** If you do not follow "clean" drafting practices in CAD, your job in Photoshop will be much harder. It is best to spend some time in CAD cleaning up legacy drawings before working on them in Photoshop.

Setting Up a Printer Driver and Paper Size in AutoCAD

AutoCAD is fundamentally a vector program, meaning it stores entities as mathematical objects by using a spatial coordinate system. Lines are stored as end points that are located by their x-, y-, and z-coordinates in space. To convert this vector data to pixels, you need to set up an image printer driver. After you "print" the drawing, the entities from CAD end up as black pixels on a white background in a raster image.

The following procedure doesn't actually print on a real device; you are merely setting up a virtual "printer" to export raster data from AutoCAD. These steps need to be performed only once. After you configure the image printer driver and its associated custom paper-size file, you can use these steps as often as you'd like to export images from AutoCAD. If you are a CAD manager, you can copy the driver files you set up here onto your file server and have all AutoCAD users in your organization reference them.

To set up a virtual printer, follow these steps:

1. In AutoCAD, type **PLOTTERMANAGER** and press Enter to open the folder containing plot drivers.

2. Double-click the Add-A-Plotter-Wizard (as shown in Figure 1.2).

Figure 1.2 Plotter driver folder

3. On the Introduction screen, click Next to open the Begin screen.

4. Leave the My Computer radio button selected and click Next, as shown in Figure 1.3, to open the Plotter Model screen.

5. Click Raster File Formats in the Manufacturers list, and then select the Portable Network Graphics PNG (LZH Compression) option in the Models list (Figure 1.4).

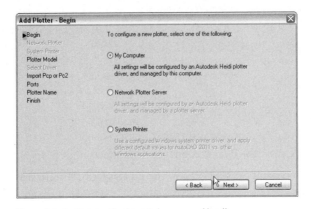

Figure 1.3 Configuring the driver to be managed locally

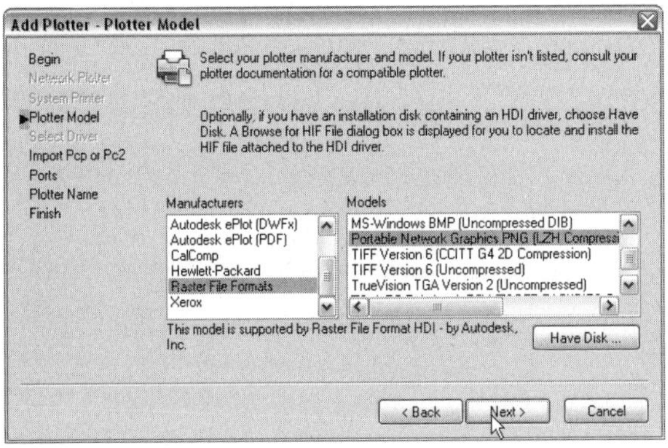

Figure 1.4 Selecting the PNG image format

6. Click Next and Next again to accept the defaults on the Import PCP or PC2 and Ports pages.

7. Click Next again and type **ImagePrinter** as the Plotter Name (Figure 1.5).

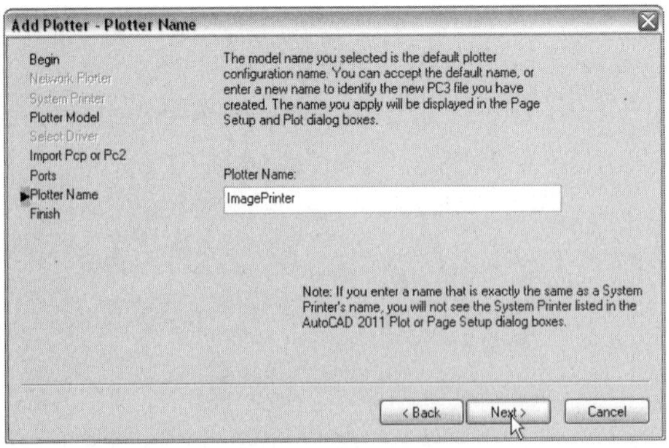

Figure 1.5 Naming the plot driver

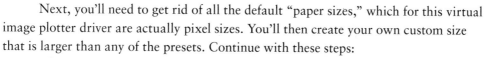

Note: The name *ImagePrinter* is used in the AutoLISP file on the accompanying DVD. Please use this name so that the LISP program functions properly later in this chapter.

Next, you'll need to get rid of all the default "paper sizes," which for this virtual image plotter driver are actually pixel sizes. You'll then create your own custom size that is larger than any of the presets. Continue with these steps:

8. Click Next and then click the Edit Plotter Configuration button.

9. Click the Device And Document Settings tab in the Plotter Configuration Editor that appears and expand the User-Defined Paper Sizes & Calibration node in the driver hierarchy.

10. In that expanded list, click Filter Paper Sizes. Then click the Uncheck All button.

11. Select the Custom Paper Sizes node and click the Add button (Figure 1.6).

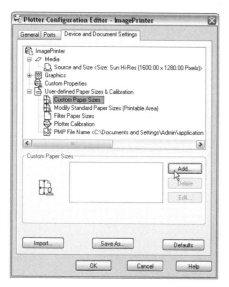

Figure 1.6 Configuring the plot driver

12. In the Custom Paper Size Wizard, choose Start From Scratch and click Next.

13. On the Media Bounds page, type **3000** for Width and **2000** for Height (Figure 1.7). Leave the Units drop-down set to Pixels. Click Next.

14. On the Paper Size Name page, type **ImageSize** in the text box (Figure 1.8).

15. Finally, click Finish to close this wizard. ImageSize appears in the Plotter Configuration Editor now.

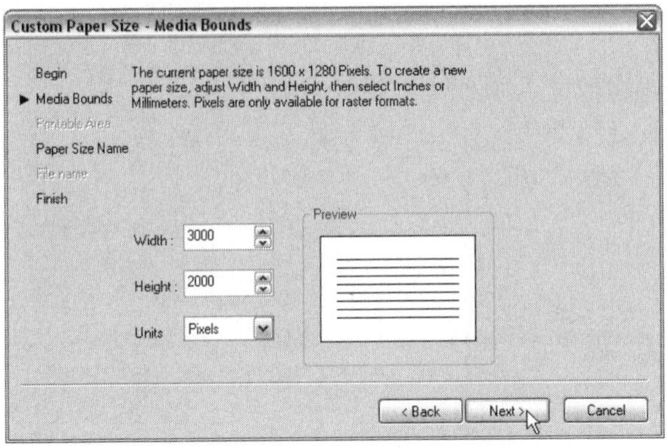

Figure 1.7 Specifying pixel dimensions for the custom paper size

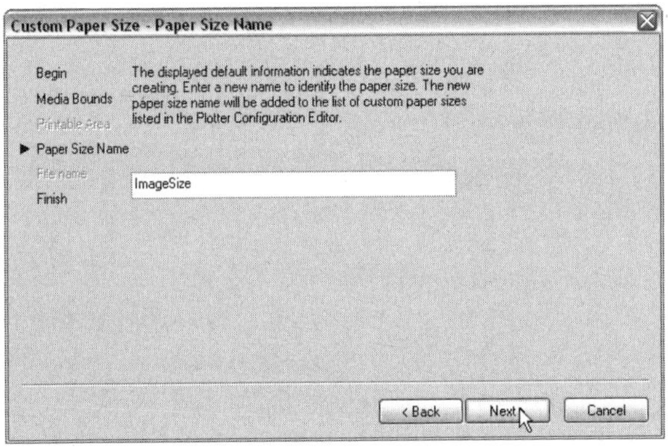

Figure 1.8 Naming the custom paper size

Note: The name *ImageSize* is referenced in the AutoLISP program used later in this chapter. It is important that you use this name exactly.

It is now time to limit the color depth that your ImagePrinter driver uses so you can create images with black and white pixels only. This will make smaller image files and save hard drive space. Follow these steps:

16. Expand the Graphics node in the driver hierarchy and click the Vector Graphics node.

17. In the Color Depth group, click the Monochrome radio button, and then choose 2 Shades Of Gray from the Color Depth drop-down, as shown in Figure 1.9.

18. Click OK to close the Plotter Configuration Editor.

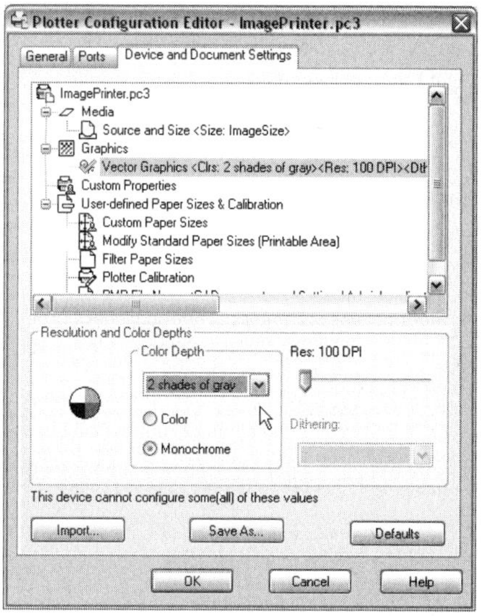

Figure 1.9 Limiting the color depth of the output

19. Finally, click the Finish button in the Add-A-Plotter Wizard to create the `ImagePrinter.pc3` file on your hard drive.

Creating a Plot Style Table for Images

In manual drafting, architects used to press harder on the pencil to make important lines thicker. These days, plot styles control line thickness in AutoCAD. When you convert vector line work, ideally you want the lines showing up as single-pixel-width lines in the image. Thin, unbroken lines provide the most flexibility in Photoshop (as you'll see in Chapter 2). For now, let's focus on how plot styles control line width in AutoCAD output.

> **Note:** I believe it's better to add lineweight intentionally in Photoshop by using the stroke effect, rather than exporting thicker lines directly from AutoCAD because stroked lines in Photoshop feature anti-aliasing, which reduces the jagged appearance of angled lines.

There are two kinds of plot styles available: color-dependent and named. I recommend using color-dependent plot styles in preparing drawings for export to images because of their simplicity, even if you use named plot styles in production work.

> **Note:** Use the CONVERTPSTYLES command in AutoCAD to convert an existing drawing from a named plot style to a color-dependent plot style, or vice versa.

Here's how to create a custom color-dependent plot style to use in creating output with your new ImagePrinter:

1. Type **STYLESMANAGER** and press Enter.

2. Double-click the Add-A-Plot Style Table Wizard.

3. Read the introductory message and then click Next.

4. Make sure the Start From Scratch radio button is selected on the Begin screen and click Next (Figure 1.10).

Add Color-Dependent Plot Style Table - Begin

▶ Begin
Browse File
File Name
Finish

This wizard provides you with the ability to either create a color-dependent plot style table from scratch, or by importing settings from a PCP, PC2, or Release 14 CFG file. The new plot style table can be assigned to any color-dependent drawing.

◉ Start from scratch

Create a new plot style table from scratch.

○ Use a CFG file

Import R14 pen settings that were saved automatically to a CFG file.

○ Use a PCP or PC2 file

Import R14 pen settings that were saved in a PCP or PC2 file.

[< Back] [Next >] [Cancel]

Figure 1.10 Creating a color-dependent plot style table

5. Choose Color Dependent Plot Style Table, and click Next to open the File Name screen.

6. Type the name **Images** in the File Name text box (Figure 1.11).

Add Color-Dependent Plot Style Table - File Name

Begin
Browse File
▶ File Name
Finish

Enter a name for the new plot style table.

File name:

Images

Unlike R14 pen settings, this plot style table can be plotted to any output device.

[< Back] [Next >] [Cancel]

Figure 1.11 Naming the color-dependent plot style

Note: The name *Images* is referenced in the AutoLISP program used later in this chapter. It is important to use this name exactly.

7. Click Next again and then click the Plot Style Table Editor button.
8. Click the Form View tab if it is not already selected.
9. Drag out a selection window in the Plot Styles list box that shows the color numbers (see Figure 1.12). Keep dragging until the list automatically scrolls and all 255 colors are selected.
10. In the Properties group, click the Color drop-down and select the Black option.
11. Click the Lineweight drop-down and select 0.0000 mm (see Figure 1.13). This is the thinnest possible lineweight.

Start here and drag a window all the way to the bottom.

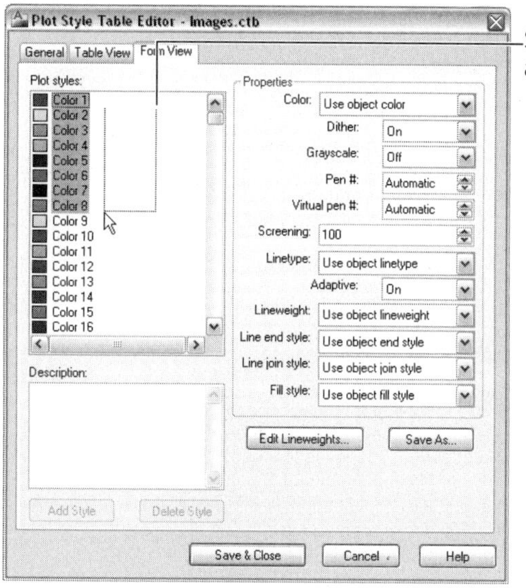

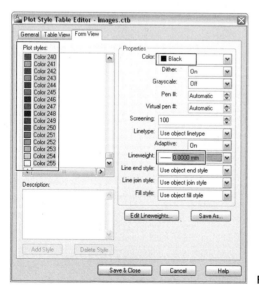

Figure 1.12 The Plot Style Table Editor dialog box

Figure 1.13 Configuring plot style

12. Click the Save & Close button. A file called `Images.ctb` is automatically created in the `Plot Styles` folder on your hard drive.

13. Click Finish to close the Add-A-Plot Style Table Wizard and close the `Plot Styles` folder.

Now you have configured the ImagePrinter as a raster printer driver that you can use to convert vector line work in AutoCAD to the pixels of an image that you'll be able to manipulate with Photoshop.

Making a Test Plot to Determine Scale

Before you use the LISP program to automate the conversion of each AutoCAD layer to a separate image file, you must do one test plot in order to work out the scale of the drawing relative to the image size. Every building has a different physical size, so you'll need to work out the plot scale each time. Let's give it a try:

1. In AutoCAD, open `Home.dwg`, which is the first-floor plan of my home. This file is already "cleaned up" (see the "Cleaning Up Drawings" section earlier in this chapter), so it's ready to be transferred into Photoshop.

Note: If you don't have AutoCAD, you can skip ahead to the next section or Chapter 2. Plotted AutoCAD image files are provided so you can jump right into Photoshop.

2. Press Ctrl+P. Click OK if a warning dialog box appears indicating a missing driver; you'll select the correct driver in a moment.

3. Click the Name drop-down under Printer/Plotter, select `ImagePrinter.pc3`, and click to select the default paper size when prompted.

4. Click the More Options arrow button in the lower-right corner (see Figure 1.14) if the dialog box is not already expanded.

5. Select ImageSize as the Paper Size.

6. Open the Plot Style Table drop-down and select `Images.ctb` (Figure 1.15).

7. Under Plot Area, select Extents from the What To Plot drop-down. Under Plot Offset, select the Center The Plot check box. Under Plot Scale, select Fit To Paper.

At this point, we're ready to plot the entire drawing to an image, but we're not going to do this yet because we still have to work out the scale. Instead, we've simulated the plot with the Fit To Paper option to work out the plot scale. Take a look at the grayed-out numbers in the Plot Scale area, shown in Figure 1.16.

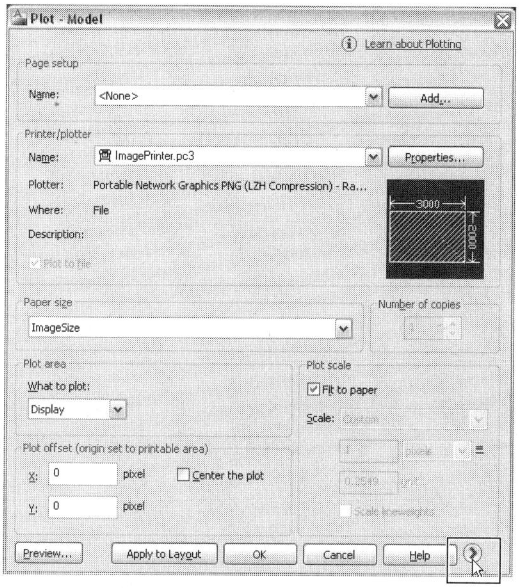

Figure 1.14 Plot dialog box

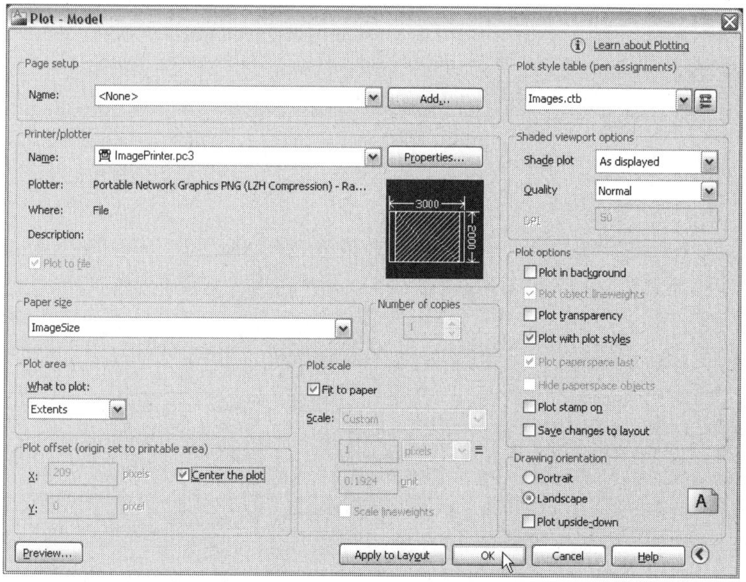

Figure 1.15 Selecting plotter, paper size, and plot style table

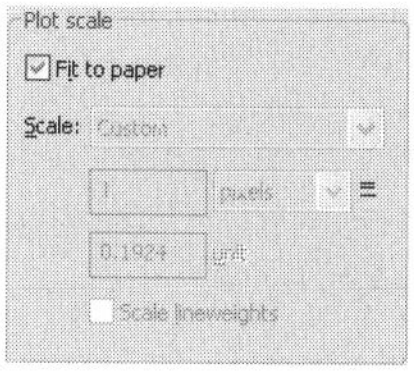

Figure 1.16 Plot Scale area
of the Plot dialog box

With the drawing stretched to the maximum size relative to the image size, 1 pixel in the plot equals 0.1924 units (which are inches in imperial units). We must rationalize this arbitrary measure to the nearest common fraction in order to maintain graphic scale in Photoshop. In other words, rationalizing in this context means changing 0.1924 units to 0.25 units. Continue with these steps:

8. Deselect the Fit To Paper check box in the Plot Scale area of the Plot dialog box.

9. Change the unit value from 0.1924 to **0.25**. Notice the black-and-white preview in the Printer/Plotter area shows the crosshatched plot area fitting within the image size of 3000×2000 pixels.

> **Note:** If the crosshatched area doesn't fit within the image size in the preview, you've gone the wrong way. For example, if you rationalized 0.1924 to 0.125 (⅛), you would have gone the wrong way, numerically speaking. Adjusting 0.1924 to 0.25 (¼) is the correct rationalization in this particular case because the drawing fits within the image size.

At this point, we have found what we are looking for—the numerical relationship between inches and pixels. The rationalized equation is 1 pixel in the image = 0.25 inches in the drawing. If we multiply both sides of the equation by 4, we'll end up with whole numbers.

10. Type **4** on the pixel side of the equation and **1** on the unit side. The black-and-white preview remains unchanged, so the final equation is simply 4 pixels = 1 inch (see Figure 1.17). Press Esc to close the Plot dialog box without plotting.

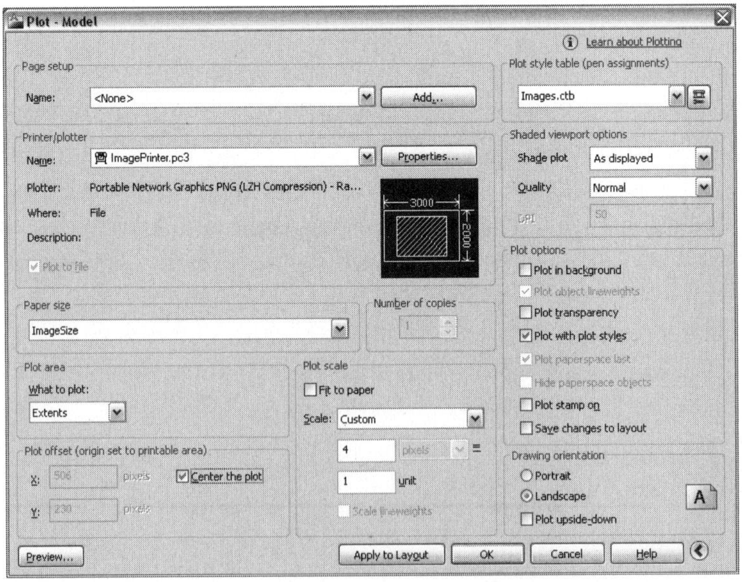

Figure 1.17 Rationalizing plot scale

Make a mental note of the final equation (in this case, 4 pixels = 1 inch) or write it down. We will input this equation into the LISP program next. If you were plotting a drawing depicting something larger than my house, you would likely require a different plot scale to fit the building within the fixed grid of 3000×2000 pixels. Perhaps 8 pixels = 1 inch would rationalize a larger building (⅛″ scale). There can never be a hard-and-fast rule, because every building has a different size; you'll have to work out a rational plot scale every time.

Plotting with the Included LISP Program

Typical CAD drawings contain many layers, and more creative possibilities open up if you can access these as individual image layers in Photoshop. It is possible to transfer the layers from an AutoCAD drawing to Photoshop by plotting each layer one at a time and then integrating the image files in Photoshop. I have written a program (included on the companion DVD) that automates part of this process, saving you many hours of tedium.

The program, called lay2img (Layer to Image), runs in AutoCAD and automates plotting by converting each vector layer into a raster image file. It is written in Autodesk's subset of the ancient list processing language (developed in the 1950s) called AutoLISP. Programming in AutoLISP is beyond the scope of this book, although you will learn how to edit a few simple parameters in the program to suit your needs.

You'll use AutoCAD's built-in Visual LISP integrated development environment to edit the code:

1. Type **VLIDE** and press Enter. This command stands for *Visual LISP integrated development environment.*

2. Within the Visual LISP for AutoCAD window that appears, choose File > Open and select lay2img.lsp from the DVD. Each line is commented for clarity. Read through the program to get a sense of what it does, even if you've never seen LISP code before.

3. Note that the printer driver is specified as ImagePrinter.pc3, the paper size is specified as ImageSize, and the plot style table is Images.ctb. Edit the appropriate lines of text if your drivers, paper sizes, or plot style tables have different names. The program won't work if there are any typographical errors, extra spaces inside the quotes, or misspellings.

4. Change the Plotted pixels = drawing units line to read "4=1". This is the "final equation" we came up with by doing a test plot.

5. Press Ctrl+S to save the LISP file.

6. Click the button shown under the arrow cursor in Figure 1.18 to load the file into memory.

Figure 1.18 lay2img.lsp open for editing in AutoCAD's Visual LISP integrated development environment

7. Switch back to AutoCAD, type **lay2img**, and press Enter to open the Save Image Files Of Each Layer dialog box, which prompts you to choose a path and a prefix name to save the image files of each layer. Make a subfolder called **Output** on your hard drive, type the prefix name **Home**, and click Save.

The automated process begins, and an image is plotted for each layer of the drawing. There is one image file for each layer in the CAD drawing. The filenames are preceded by the name you typed in step 7 (Home), but the layer name from AutoCAD completes the filename after the dash. For example, one of the generated files is called Home-Walls.png; Home is the prefix name you typed, and Walls is the layer name. The program concatenates this descriptive text automatically into each filename.

Working with Revit Architecture 2011 Models

You can enhance Revit plans, elevations, and section drawings in Photoshop, just as you can AutoCAD drawings. However, there is no easy way to automate Revit to output every layer as a separate image file. Therefore, our approach will be to export each drawing as a single image for later enhancement in Photoshop.

In the single-layer approach, we lose the ability to control lineweight in Photoshop, but this isn't the end of the world. You can carry Revit's default treatment of lineweight into Photoshop or force all lines to be as thin as possible prior to transfer. I'll show you both methods because each has its strengths and weaknesses.

Carrying Revit's Default Treatment of Lineweight into Photoshop

Revit has built-in export functionality that supports raster image creation directly from Revit's vector database. Perform the following steps to export an image from Revit:

1. Launch Revit Architecture 2011 and open the Basic sample project.

2. Double-click Level 2 in the View hierarchy panel. Revit automatically generates a 2D floor plan from the 3D building information model stored in its relational database (Figure 1.19).

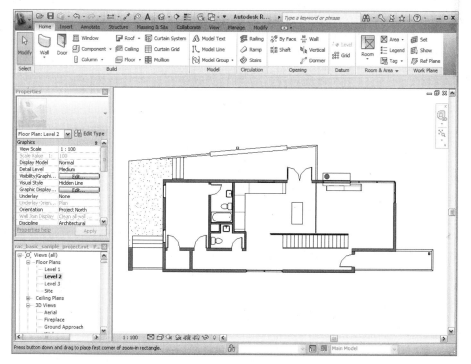

Figure 1.19 Revit sample project Level 2 drawing

3. Choose Revit menu > Export > Images And Animations > Image (Figure 1.20).

4. Click the Change button in the Export Image dialog box and then select a file-name and path.

5. In the Image Size area, select Fit To, type **3000 pixels,** and select Horizontal as the direction.

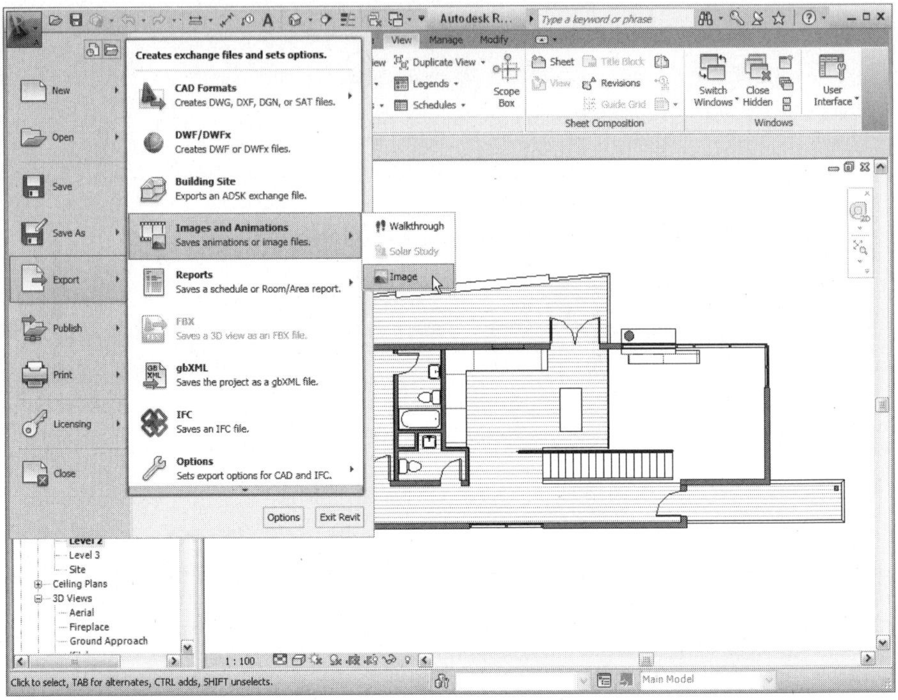

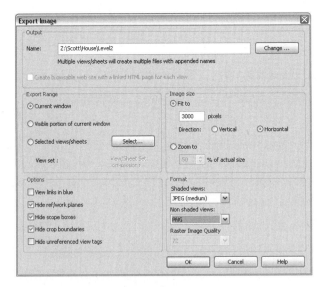

Figure 1.20 Exporting an image from Revit

6. Select Current Window in the Export Range area and set PNG as the format for nonshaded views (Figure 1.21).

Figure 1.21 Export Image settings in Revit

7. Click OK to create the `Level2.png` image file (Figure 1.22).

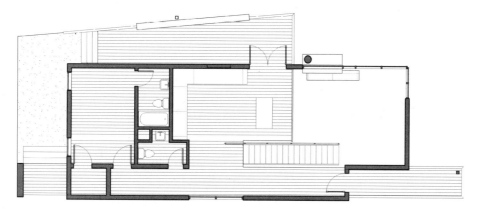

Figure 1.22 Image created through Revit's export feature

Forcing All Lines to Be as Thin as Possible

In Revit Architecture 2011, the export image feature does not respect Revit's Thin Lines mode. Thin Lines mode is useful if you want to forgo lineweights in Revit entirely. If you have a large monitor with a graphics card that supports a high enough resolution, you can take a screen capture to use as the basis for enhancement in Photoshop.

Exactly which resolution setting is good enough depends on many factors, including the physical size of the building you're enhancing, its relationship to the graphic scale you're working in, and the final size you hope to print the enhanced image from Photoshop.

> **Note:** To maximize image quality, set your display resolution to the highest number of pixels before taking a screen capture.

The weakness of the screen-capture transfer method is that it is limited by the number of pixels displayed by your graphics card. However, this is the only way to export single-pixel-width lines from Revit. Here's how it's done:

1. In Revit, close the Properties and View hierarchy panels by clicking their Close buttons to maximize the amount of screen real estate occupied by the drawing itself.

2. Activate Thin Lines mode by clicking its button either on the Quick Access toolbar or on the View ribbon.

3. Select Hidden Line from the rendering menu at the bottom of the screen, if it's not already selected (Figure 1.23).

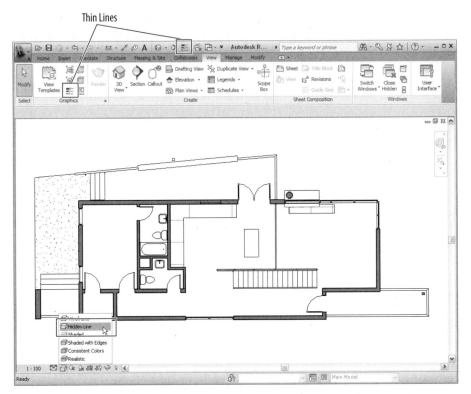

Thin Lines

Figure 1.23 Activating Hidden Line and Thin Lines modes

4. On the Mac, the default keyboard shortcut to save a picture of the screen as a file is Shift+Command+3. The keyboard shortcut for this feature can be changed under the Apple menu > System Preferences > Keyboard And Mouse > Keyboard shortcuts. On Windows, press the Print Screen key to copy everything on the screen to the Clipboard. The Print Screen key is on most extended keyboards having numeric keypads (it might be abbreviated), but you might have to press a key combination to activate this function on a notebook computer.

Note: Screen-capture software is built into most operating systems and is also available from software vendors.

5. Launch Photoshop, and then press Command+N (Mac) or Ctrl+N (Windows). The width and height of the clipboard are automatically entered in the New dialog box.

6. Click OK and then Command+V / Ctrl+V to paste the image from the clipboard into the new document window.

7. Choose Layer > Flatten Image And File > Save. Save the image as `Level2thin.png`. The final image is shown in Figure 1.24.

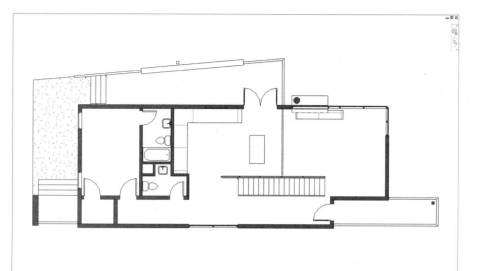

Figure 1.24 Screen-captured image with thin lines

Note: Neither of the methods for exporting images from Revit preserves graphic scale. Use AutoCAD or another CAD program that enables you to map a specific number of pixels to the drawing unit (such as inches or centimeters) if you want your enhanced drawings to print to scale.

Enhancing Drawings in Photoshop

2

Before you can enhance a technical drawing in Photoshop, you need to export either an image of an entire drawing or a series of images (one for each layer) from your CAD or BIM program. If you want to jump right into Photoshop and bypass the steps necessary to create the drawing images, this chapter leads you through this process and also provides sample files to get you started.

Chapter Contents

Importing drawings as smart objects
Setting the resolution to match the graphic scale
Managing and creating patterns
Applying drawing techniques
Applying patterns
Scaling and positioning
Enhancing stairs
Adjusting color
Separating color from pattern
Creating layers from effects
Varying lineweight and dropping shadows to indicate depth

Importing Drawings as Smart Objects

Every time you manipulate pixels, there is a potential for some of the visual information to be irretrievably lost. It's not that Photoshop forgets things in the sense of losing data, but applying filters, adjustments, or transformations can push some of the pixels beyond certain mathematical limits so that the visual information is burned out, under-exposed, pixelated, blurry, and so forth. These deleterious effects are compounded with each pixel manipulation.

Smart objects solve these problems by providing what is known as a *nondestructive workflow*. Smart objects act as containers that store filters, adjustments, and transformations made to the layers inside them. All the smart-object manipulations are then applied all at once to the pixels, thus minimizing deleterious effects. Filters, adjustments, and transformations made to smart objects remain editable and nondestructive, so there is no penalty for changing your mind at a later date. Smart objects are identifiable in the Layers panel with a distinctive thumbnail icon.

In the following example, we'll place the original drawing layers inside a smart object (whether there's only one or many layers) to stay organized and protect the design data.

If you are enhancing a single-layer image (that is, from Revit), do the following to create a smart object:

1. Launch Photoshop, choose File > Open, and select a single-layer drawing image (such as Level2.png or Level2thin.png) created in Chapter 1, "Preparing Drawings in CAD or BIM for Enhancement."

2. Choose Image > Mode > RGB Color to prepare the document for color enhancement.

3. Double-click the Background layer to convert it into a regular layer. Type **CAD Layers** in the New Layer dialog box and click OK.

4. Right-click on the layer name and choose Convert To Smart Object in the context menu.

5. In the Layers panel, change CAD Layers's blend mode to Multiply.

If, on the other hand, you are enhancing a multilayer drawing, do the following:

1. Launch Photoshop and choose File > Scripts > Load Files Into Stack. Click the Browse button in the Load Layers dialog box.

2. Navigate to the Output folder you created in Chapter 1 and select all the PNG files generated by the LISP program, or navigate to the Chapter 1/Samples/Output folder on the DVD if you are jumping in here, and select all the PNG files.

3. Select the Create Smart Object After Loading Layers check box, leave deselected Attempt To Automatically Align Source Images, and click OK (Figure 2.1).

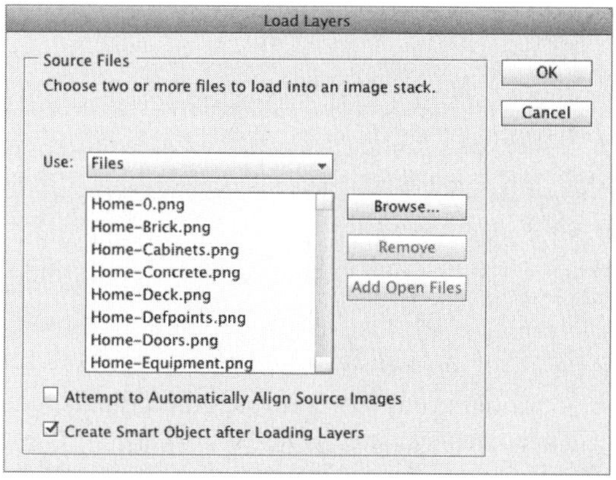

Figure 2.1 Loading files into a smart-object stack

Photoshop goes to work loading all the CAD layers and integrating them into a smart object. After some processing time, you'll have a single document window containing a smart-object layer.

4. In the Layers panel, double-click `Home-0.png` and rename it **CAD Drawing** (Figure 2.2).

Figure 2.2 Creating a smart-object layer

5. Choose Image > Mode > RGB Color to prepare the document for color enhancement. A warning message (shown in Figure 2.3) appears, asking whether you want to rasterize the smart object before mode change. It's important to choose Don't Rasterize, or all the layers you went to the trouble of exporting separately from AutoCAD will be flattened into a single layer.

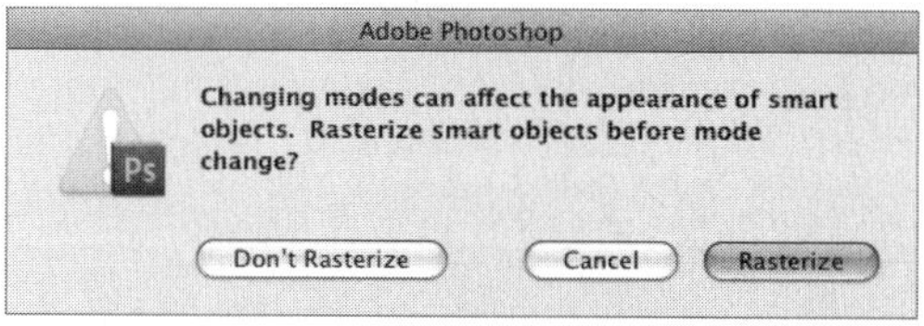

Figure 2.3 Remember to choose Don't Rasterize when prompted.

6. In the Layers panel, change `CAD Layers`'s blend mode to Multiply.

You may notice that the smart object in the multilayer technique doesn't look the same as in the single-layer technique. The reason for this is simple—each layer inside the smart object has both black and white pixels, and the white pixels on each layer obscure everything below in the Layers panel. To correct this situation, we will use the Magic Eraser:

1. Double-click the CAD Layers smart-object layer thumbnail to open it in a new window. Click OK after reading the message shown in Figure 2.4 (consider selecting Don't Show Again after you've read the message). Do not flatten the layers inside the smart object in any case.

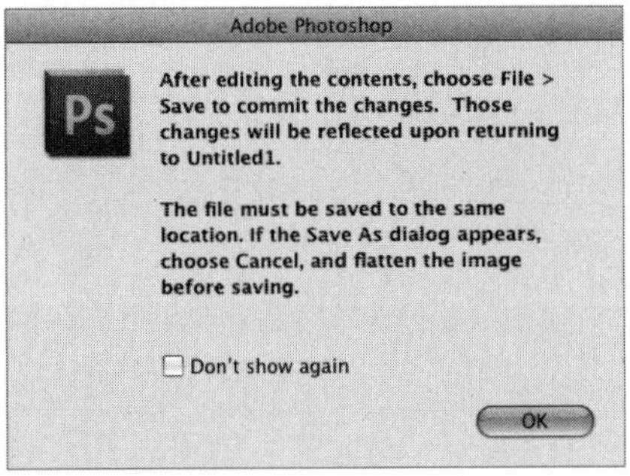

Figure 2.4 Saving smart objects

2. Drag layers Home-0.png and Home-Defpoints.png (Figure 2.5) to the Trash in the lower-right corner of the Layers panel. These layers are all white and are not needed.

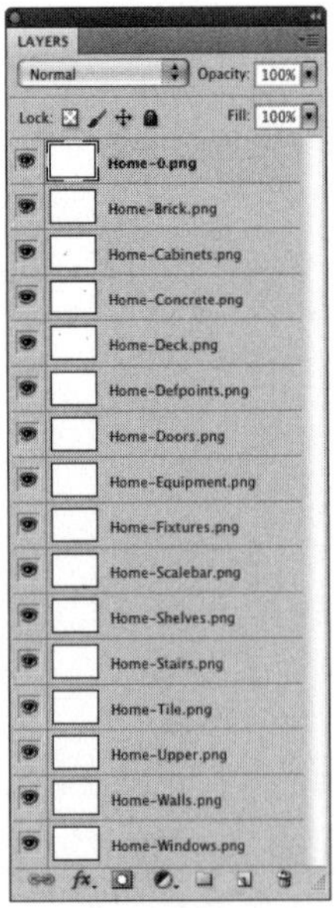

Figure 2.5 Layers within the CAD Drawing smart object

3. Press Shift+E twice to cycle through the eraser tools, or select the Magic Eraser tool expressly from the tool flyout menu after right-clicking or holding down the eraser icon for 1 second.

4. On the options bar, set Tolerance to 0, Opacity to 100%, and leave all other options deselected. We want the Magic Eraser to eliminate white pixels only. Click a white pixel anywhere in the document window.

5. Press Option+[or Alt+[to select the next layer, and click a white pixel anywhere in the document window. Repeat this step until you've removed white pixels from every layer.

6. Choose Layer > New Fill Layer > Solid Color. Type White as the layer name, and click OK. Choose pure white from the Color Picker dialog box that appears and click OK.

7. Drag layer White to the bottom of the Layers panel. Drag layer White's mask to the Trash and click Delete.

8. Press Cmd+W and Return or press Ctrl+W and Enter to close and save the smart-object document.

9. Choose Image > Trim. Select the Top Left Pixel Color option (Figure 2.6) and click OK.

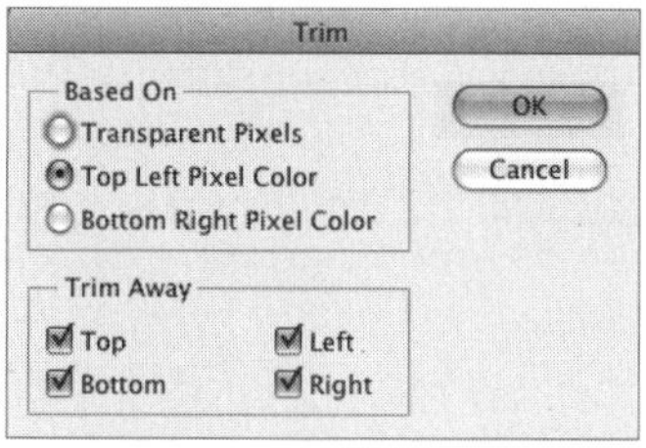

Figure 2.6 Trimming away excess outer pixels

10. Choose Image > Canvas Size. Change the drop-downs to Percent and then set Width and Height to **120**. Leave the anchor set in the middle and click OK (Figure 2.7). An even border of white space appears around the plan.

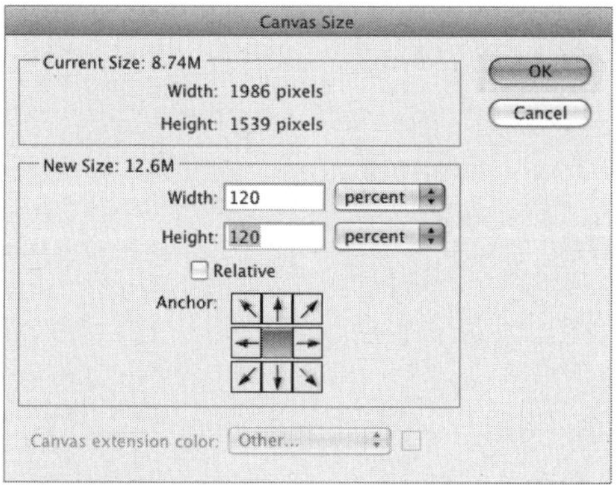

Figure 2.7 Adjusting the canvas size

11. Choose Layer > New Fill Layer > Solid Color. Type Backdrop as the layer name and click OK.

12. Choose a pale yellow (type hex color **#ffffeb**) in the Color Picker dialog box that appears and click OK.

13. Press Cmd+[/ Ctrl+[to move Backdrop below CAD Layers in the Layers panel, as shown in Figure 2.8.

Figure 2.8 Rearranging the layer order

Note: The reason the Backdrop layer color is visible through the CAD Layers smart object is because CAD Layers's blend mode is set to Multiply.

14. Choose File > Save and type **Home.psd** as the filename. The final CAD drawing is shown in Photoshop in Figure 2.9.

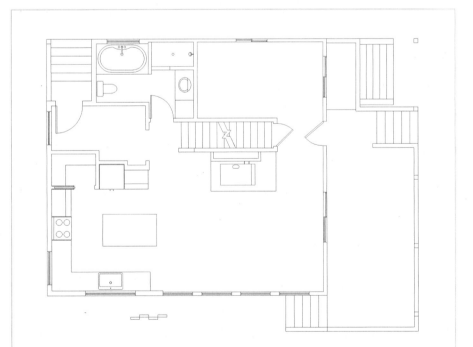

Figure 2.9 CAD drawing prepped for enhancement

CHAPTER 2: ENHANCING DRAWINGS IN PHOTOSHOP ■

Setting the Resolution to Match Graphic Scale

CAD drawings are made in *real-world scale*, meaning they are drawn actual size. Thus, drawing in CAD is easy because you don't have to worry about scale until it comes time to lay out drawings on a sheet of paper. In AutoCAD, you choose a specific *graphic scale* (such as ¼″ = 1′0″) to relate the drawing on paper to real-world measurements. We must combine knowledge of how graphic scale works with how we choose to plot the CAD drawing to pixels in order to maintain graphic scale in Photoshop.

An equally valid way of looking at ¼″ graphic scale is to say 1 inch in CAD = 48 inches (the number of inches in 4 feet) in the real world, which is clearly a 48-fold increase. Recall we plotted the Home drawing so that 4 pixels = 1 inch in the real world. So to maintain ¼″ scale, the resolution we must use in Photoshop is 48 × 4 pixels/inch = 192 pixels/inch.

All this talk of scale can be quite confusing. I drew a scale bar measuring 4 feet in AutoCAD to give you a visual way to verify the proper resolution to use in Photoshop (see Figure 2.9 in the preceding section). Let's see how this works with a practical example:

1. Open Home.psd from the DVD or continue with the file you saved in the previous section.

2. Press Z and zoom into the scale bar at the bottom of the plan drawing. If you are using Photoshop CS5, select Scrubby Zoom on the options bar, position the cursor over what you want to zoom into, and drag to the right to zoom in. If you are using an older version of Photoshop, drag out a window around the area you want to zoom into.

3. Press Cmd+R / Ctrl+R to toggle rulers on.

4. Press Cmd+K / Ctrl+K to open the Preferences dialog box. Select the Units & Rulers page, set Rulers to inches, and click OK.

5. Press V to select the Move tool and drag guides from each ruler to align with the edges of the scale bar, as shown in Figure 2.10. Drag the ruler origin point (upper-left corner of the document window) to the intersection of guides as shown.

6. Choose Image > Image Size. Deselect the Resample Image check box, set the resolution to **192** pixels/inch, and click OK (Figure 2.11).

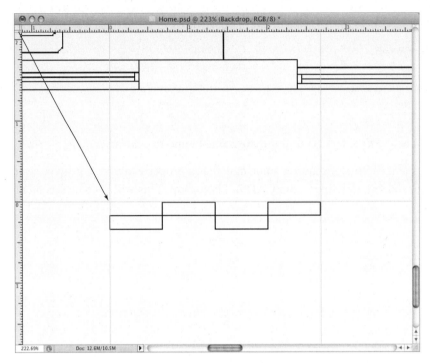

Figure 2.10 Dragging guides from the ruler to align with the scale bar

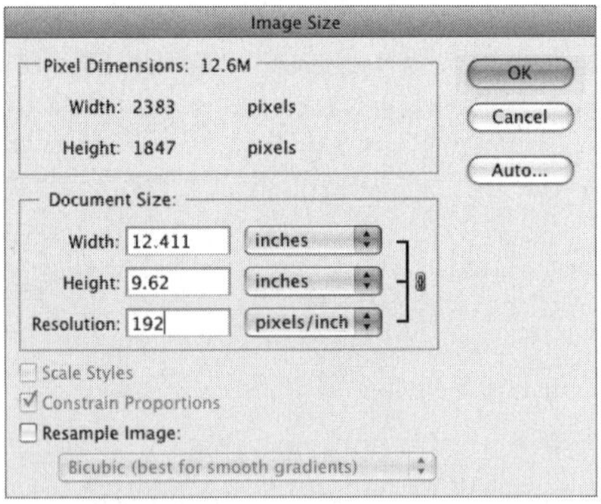

Figure 2.11 Changing resolution without resampling the image

The rulers now indicate that 1 inch = 4 feet on the scale bar. This is the definition of ¼″ scale, so we've seen that the resolution is set correctly.

Note: Doubling the resolution in Photoshop *halves* the graphic scale. If you set resolution to 192 × 2 = 384 pixels/inch, the graphic scale would be ¼″ / 2 = ⅛″.

7. Drag the guides back to their respective rulers to get rid of them. Press Cmd+R / Ctrl+R to toggle rulers off.

8. Double-click CAD Layers's smart-object thumbnail to open it.

9. Turn off layer Home-Scalebar.png.

10. Press Cmd+W and Return / Ctrl+W and Enter to close and save the smart-object document.

11. Choose File > Save As and use the name **Home-to-scale.psd**.

As you can see, it requires some figuring to properly maintain graphic scale when transferring drawings from CAD in Photoshop. This will become second nature to you with some practice.

Managing and Creating Patterns

Patterns are among the primary tools for enhancing CAD drawings. In Photoshop, a *pattern* is an image that is repeated in its application. Patterns are formed from a repetition of smaller image elements called tiles. (A *tile* is a single unit of a pattern.) An image is said to be *tilable* when the edges between tiles are not especially apparent in a pattern (see Figure 2.12).

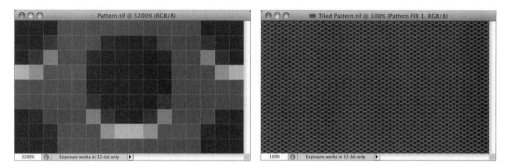

Figure 2.12   Detail of a simple pattern (left) tiled in a larger pattern (right)

To create tiling, real-world material samples are photographed, downloaded, or scanned into the computer. In this section, you will learn how to manage and create tiling patterns directly from sample files.

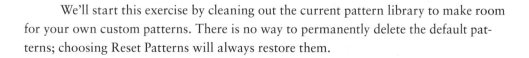

Note: In Chapter 6 you'll also learn ways of creating patterns from scratch.

We'll start this exercise by cleaning out the current pattern library to make room for your own custom patterns. There is no way to permanently delete the default patterns; choosing Reset Patterns will always restore them.

After defining some patterns, we'll organize and save them into a pattern library that can be reused in future projects. We will then apply patterns to specific parts of the drawing in the next section.

To clean out the current pattern library, follow these steps:

1. Choose Edit > Preset Manager. Select Patterns from the Preset Type drop-down. Click the arrow button and choose Reset Patterns from the context menu (Figure 2.13).

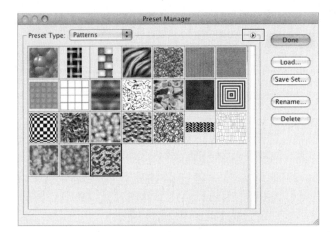

Figure 2.13 Deleting patterns from the default pattern library

2. Select one of the patterns and then click the Delete button. Repeat this step until all the default patterns are gone. The default pattern library is only temporarily empty. Click Done/OK to close the Preset Manager.

3. To visualize the pattern samples provided on this book's DVD, open the Mini Bridge panel within Photoshop CS5 by clicking its panel button or by choosing Window > Extensions > Mini Bridge. If you're using an older version of Photoshop, choose File > Browse to launch the stand-alone Bridge application.

4. Navigate to the Textures folder on the DVD. A dozen pattern files have been provided for the Home project (Figure 2.14).

5. Double-click Wood.jpg in Bridge or Mini Bridge to open it in Photoshop. Choose Edit > Define Pattern. The filename is highlighted in the Pattern Name dialog box.

6. Delete the dot and the file extension so the pattern name is a word (Wood) rather than a filename and then click OK (see Figure 2.15). Press Cmd+W / Ctrl+W to close the texture without saving. Repeat this step until all the sample textures have been defined as patterns.

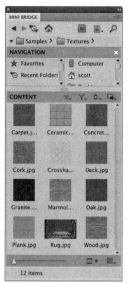

Figure 2.14 Using Mini Bridge to browse for textures

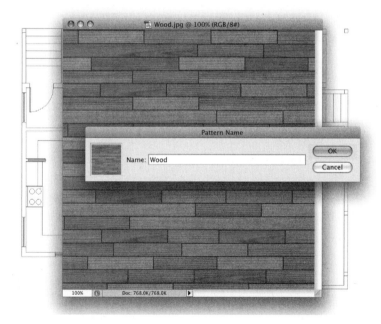

Figure 2.15 Defining a texture image as a pattern

Note: The act of defining a pattern causes it to be appended to the current pattern library.

7. Choose Edit > Preset Manager. Select Patterns from the Preset Type drop-down. Shift+click all the patterns in the current library. Click the Save Set button and then type **Home.pat**. Click OK/Save and Done.

8. Quit Photoshop and relaunch. Now Home will appear as one of the pattern libraries in the context menu.

 Note: You can share pattern libraries with others in your office by copying .pat files. Photoshop saves patterns in `~/Library/Application Support/Adobe/Adobe Photoshop CS5/Presets/Patterns` on the Mac and `C:\Program Files\Adobe\Adobe Photoshop CS5\Presets\Patterns` in Windows.

Applying Drawing Techniques

Photoshop has a few simple drawing tools, including the Line and Rectangle tools. Chances are you'll need to draw a few simple shapes in order to separate spaces that are to receive different textures, or to separate areas that are to receive directional textures, such as wood grain that needs to be oriented vertically or horizontally.

Our example plan doesn't have a floor transitions layer indicating where different materials are to appear. We therefore need to create a new layer and draw a few lines in Photoshop to indicate these material transitions. Here are the steps:

1. Press Cmd+Shift+N / Ctrl+Shift+N. Type **Transitions** in the New Layer dialog box and click OK. Drag this layer between Backdrop and CAD Layers (Figure 2.16).

Figure 2.16 Creating the new Transitions layer between Backdrop and CAD Layers

2. Press D to set the default colors with black in the foreground.

3. Press U to select the drawing tools. On the options bar, select the Line tool. Click the third button from the left, which is Fill Pixels mode. Set Weight to 1 px and deselect Anti-alias. Start dragging from the start point, hold down Shift, and release at the end point, as shown in Figure 2.17.

 Note: Fill Pixels mode is the only mode supporting aliased lines. Aliased lines work best as transitions because they can be drawn at the minimum 1-pixel width.

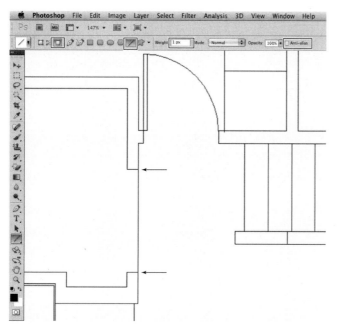

Figure 2.17 Drawing a vertical transition line

4. Draw six additional transition lines (there is a total of seven lines) at the locations shown in Figure 2.18. Zoom in for accuracy while drawing.

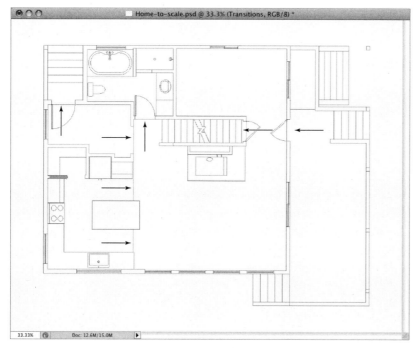

Figure 2.18 Locations of floor transition lines

5. There is one area that needs to be separated into two parts because it is to receive directional textures. Zoom into the lower-left corner counter in the kitchen and draw a line at a 45-degree angle, as shown in Figure 2.19. Holding down Shift constrains lines horizontally, vertically, or in 45-degree increments.

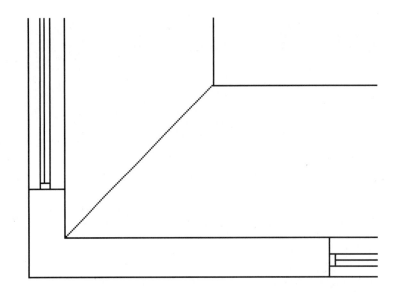

Figure 2.19 Drawing a directional-texture separator line at 45 degrees

Applying Patterns

There are three methods used in applying patterns in Photoshop:

- Painting with the Pattern Stamp tool
- Adding a pattern fill layer
- Adding a pattern overlay layer effect

Note: Pattern stamping can be useful in creating artistic effects in places where pattern application is tied to brush strokes. Obviously, it's hard to fill precisely drawn CAD plans with a brush, so pattern stamping is best used along the outer edges of a composition, where there are no hard edges.

The pattern fill layers aren't as flexible as pattern overlays because that's all pattern fill layers are: fill. When you apply a pattern overlay as a layer effect, you have simultaneous access to all the other layer effects in the Layer Style dialog, box such as Drop Shadow, Outer Glow, Color Overlay, Gradient Overlay, and so forth, so I prefer using pattern overlays. We'll use pattern overlays most frequently in enhancing drawings, which is essentially the equivalent of the childhood activity of painting inside the lines. Let's give it a try:

1. Target the Transitions layer, press Cmd+Shift+N / Ctrl+Shift+N, type **Mudroom** in the New Layer dialog box, and click OK.

2. Press Shift+G until the Paint Bucket tool is active in the toolbox. On the options bar, set Tolerance to 0, deselect Anti-alias, and select Contiguous and All Layers. Click inside the mudroom, and paint will flood most of the space. The door swing cuts off part of the floor area, so click again inside the door swing to fill the remaining floor area with black paint (see Figure 2.20).

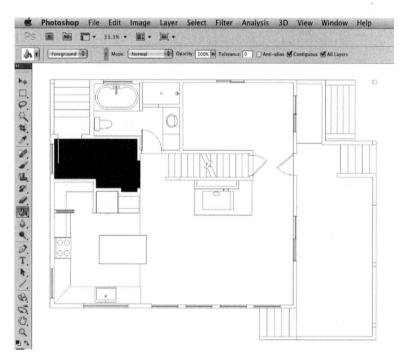

Figure 2.20 Flooding a space with paint

> **Note:** It does not matter what color paint you pour with the Paint Bucket tool when creating layer effects. Layer effects operate on pixels of any hue, saturation, or brightness.

3. Click the fx icon at the bottom of the Layers panel to open the list of layer style effects. Choose Pattern Overlay from the list, and the Layer Style dialog box appears. Drag the Layer Style dialog box out of the way so you can see how the pattern overlay looks on the plan (see Figure 2.21).

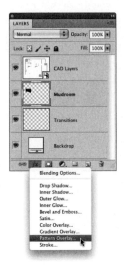

Figure 2.21 Adding a pattern overlay effect

4. Click to open the Pattern Picker, and then click the small triangle button and select Home (the pattern library you created earlier) from the context menu (Figure 2.22). Select the Marmoleum pattern, and click OK to close the Layer Style dialog box.

5. Press Cmd+Shift+N / Ctrl+Shift+N, type **Kitchen** in the New Layer dialog box, and click OK.

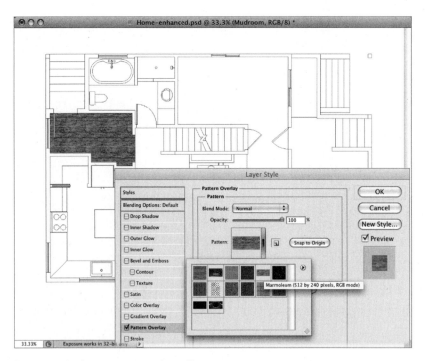

Figure 2.22 Overlaying a pattern as a layer effect

6. Press G to select the Paint Bucket tool and then click inside the kitchen space—paint floods outside of the intended area (Figure 2.23). I created this situation to illustrate what often happens with CAD drawings. There is a very small gap in the line work that paint floods through. Press Cmd+Z / Ctrl+Z to undo. We will fix the drawing inside the CAD Layers smart object.

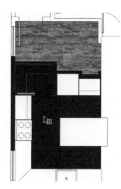

Figure 2.23 Paint flooding beyond the proper border

7. Double-click the CAD Layers thumbnail to open the smart object in another window.

8. Zoom into the pantry pocket door just off the kitchen. Paint floods in, between the door and the pocket, and fills wall cavities. Target the Home-Walls.png layer. Press U to select the drawing tools and draw a short, vertical line closing off the pocket from the exterior walls.

9. Paint also floods through a single-pixel gap in the shelving. Target layer Home-Shelves.png and then press Shift+B to select the Pencil tool. Click once to add the missing pixel that completes the shelving boundary (Figure 2.24).

10. Press Cmd+W and Return / Ctrl+W and Enter to close and save the smart object.

11. Target the Kitchen layer and press G to select the Paint Bucket tool. Click inside the kitchen to flood it with paint.

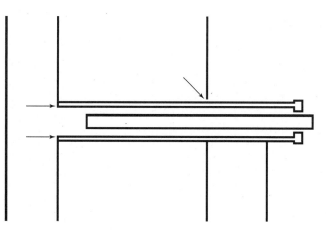

Figure 2.24 Filling gaps in the line work discovered when pouring paint

12. Assign a pattern overlay effect to the Kitchen layer and select the Marmoleum pattern you used in the mudroom. This floor covering will ultimately have a different color than in the mudroom, and you'll learn how to change it in the "Adjusting Color" section later in this chapter.

 Note: Hold down the Option/Alt key and then drag a layer effect to another layer to copy the effect. Dragging a layer effect without the modifier key moves the effect between layers.

13. Use the Paint Bucket and Pattern Overlay effect to pattern the remaining spaces with the textures in the following list. Create a new layer for each space as you've done before (see Figure 2.25).

Space	Texture
Living	Wood
Bathroom	Marmoleum
Walls	Crosshatch
Deck	Deck
Porch	Deck
Woodstove Pad	CeramicTile
Shower	CeramicTile

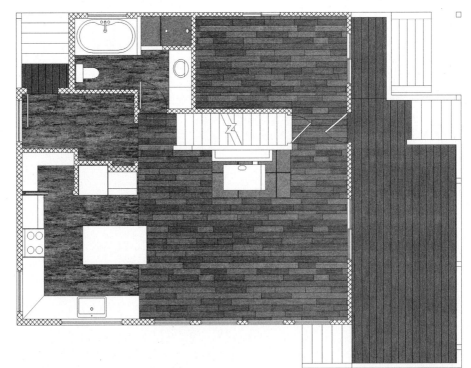

Figure 2.25 Texturing spaces with pattern overlays

Scaling and Positioning

After you have created pattern overlays, it's easy to change the patterns' scales and move them relative to the rest of the drawing. To do this, follow these steps:

1. Zoom into the bathroom. Double-click the Shower layer's Pattern Overlay effect (see Figure 2.26). Drag the Layer Style dialog box out of the way so you can see what's happening in the document window in real time.

Figure 2.26 Accessing existing layer effects in the Layers panel

2. Drag the Scale slider to the left. Click inside the scale amount text box and use the up- and down-arrow keys on the keyboard to nudge values 1 percent at a time. Set Scale at 8% (Figure 2.27).

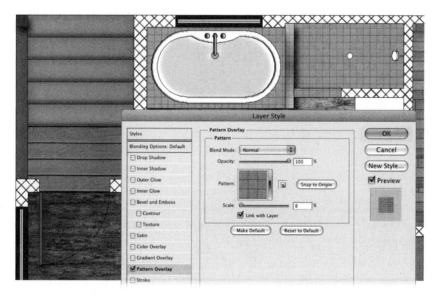

Figure 2.27 Scaling and repositioning a pattern

Note: Patterns appear their sharpest at 25%, 50%, 100%, 200%, 400%, and 800% scale.

3. Position your cursor outside the Layer Style dialog box (but leave it open) and over the document window. Drag to move the pattern until the shower drain is centered on a grout-line intersection. Click OK to close the Layer Style dialog box.

4. To stay organized, Shift+click all layers between CAD Layers and Transitions. Press Cmd+G / Ctrl+G to group them inside a folder. Rename this folder **Floors** (see Figure 2.28).

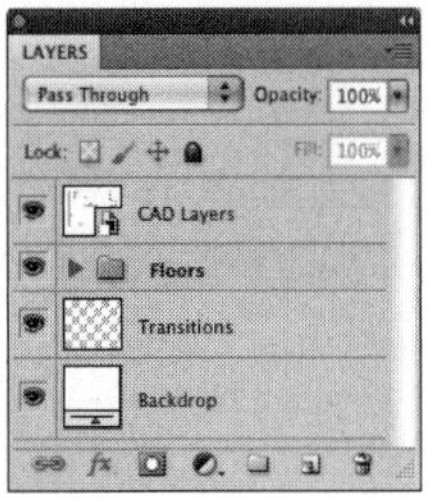

Figure 2.28 Grouping layers to stay organized

Enhancing Stairs

Stairs are generally composed of small, bounded treads that you need to fill one at a time. Using a layer style is a quick way of assigning the same effects to each stair tread. Here's how to do it:

1. Press Cmd+Shift+N / Ctrl+Shift+N, type S1 in the New Layer dialog box, and click OK.

2. Press G to select the Paint Bucket and then click inside the first stair tread.

3. Assign a pattern overlay effect to layer S1. Select the Carpet pattern from the picker and set its scale at 25%.

4. Adding an Inner Shadow effect is a good way to indicate depth on stair treads. To do this, select Inner Shadow within the Layer Style dialog box and click the words *Inner Shadow* to load its page of settings. Set Angle to 0, Distance to 3 px, Choke to 0%, and Size to 5 px (Figure 2.29). Click OK.

Note: Unlike drop shadows, inner shadow effects stay within their fill boundaries.

5. Click the New Style button in the Layer Style dialog box. Type **Carpeted Stairs** in the New Style dialog box, select Include Layer Effects, and click OK (Figure 2.30).

6. Create a new layer called S2 and then fill the next tread with the Paint Bucket tool.

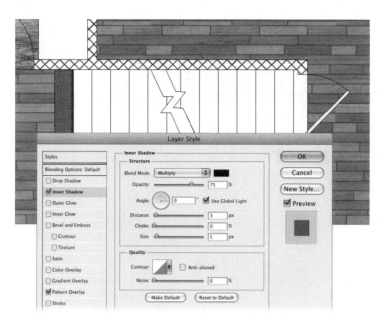

Figure 2.29 Adding an inner shadow to a stair tread to indicate depth

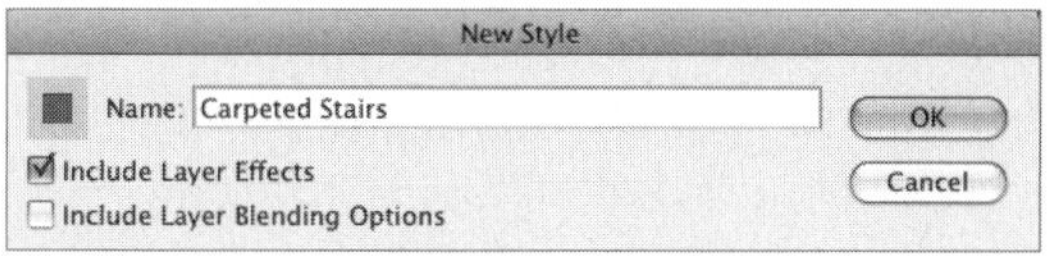

Figure 2.30 Saving a new style

7. Open the Styles panel, and click the Carpeted Stairs style to immediately assign the Pattern Overlay and Inner Shadow effects (see Figure 2.31). Repeat this for every stair tread until you reach the break line in this flight.

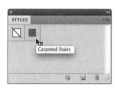

Figure 2.31 Assigning the saved style to each stair layer

8. Shift+click all *S* layers and press Cmd+G / Ctrl+G to group them inside a folder. Rename this folder `Interior Stairs Up`.

9. Repeat this process for the interior flight going down into the basement. Group the new layers as `Interior Stairs Dn` (Figure 2.32). We will change this flight's carpet color in the next section.

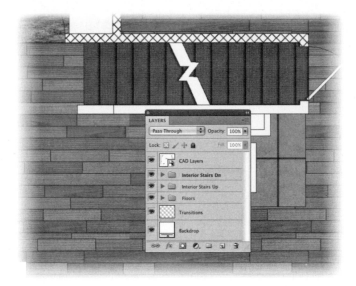

Figure 2.32   Two flights styled

Adjusting Color

Color is an essential component of every pattern. You can adjust the color of patterns without having to redefine the patterns themselves. This gives your pattern library a lot more mileage because the same patterns can be reused over and over again with different hues, saturations, or lightness and darkness. There are two methods for adjusting color, depending on whether you're working on a single or multiple layers. You can use either an adjustment layer or a layer effect to adjust color.

Adjusting Color with an Adjustment Layer

Let's say we want to differentiate the two flights of interior stairs by using different-colored carpets. In the previous section, you put each individual step on its own layer and placed the layers from each flight into their own layer-group folders. Adjusting color on multiple layers is done with an adjustment layer, as shown here:

1. Expand the Interior Stairs Up group in the Layers panel and target the S7 layer at the top of the contained list of layers.

2. Open the Adjustments panel and click the Hue/Saturation icon. Drag the Hue slider to −43 to adjust the carpet color (Figure 2.33).

3. The adjustment layer affects all the layers below it in the Layers panel, including those layers that are not part of the Interior Stairs Up group. In order to contain the adjustment within the group, you must change the blend mode of the group itself. To do this, target the Interior Stairs Up group and change its layer blend mode from Pass Through to Normal (see Figure 2.34).

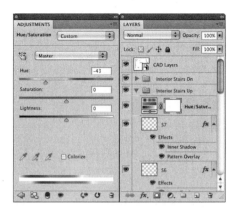

Figure 2.33 Adjusting the color of a group of layers

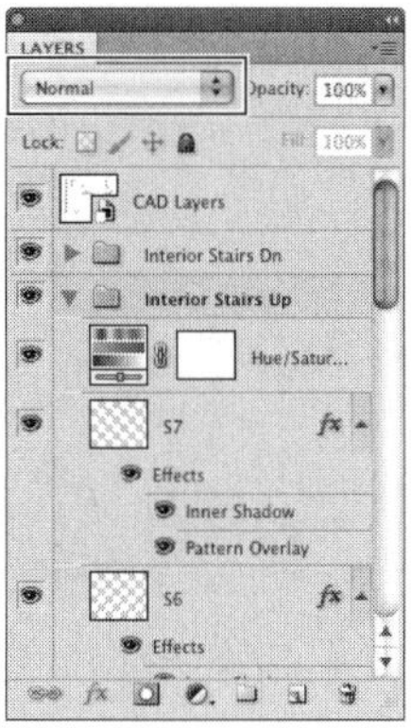

Figure 2.34 Changing the group blend mode to Normal

4. Close the `Interior Stairs Up` group.

Adjusting Color with a Layer Effect

Let's say we want to colorize the ceramic-tile pattern on the `Woodstove Pad` layer. Rather than using the technique for multiple layers involving a group and an adjustment layer, it's more efficient to use the color overlay effect in combination with the pattern overlay that's already assigned. To do this, follow these steps:

1. Expand the `Floors` group and target the `Woodstove Pad` layer. Double-click on the Pattern Overlay effect in the Layers panel to open the Layer Style dialog box. While you're here, set the pattern scale to 30% and drag the tile pattern so there's a whole tile in the lower-right corner.

2. Select the Color Overlay option and click the words *Color Overlay* to open its page in the Layer Style dialog box. Click the color swatch to open the Color Picker, type the hexadecimal code **beb392** in the # text box, and click OK.

3. The color obscures the pattern because the Color Overlay effect is above Pattern Overlay within the Layer Style dialog box.

Note: Think of the effects within the Layer Style dialog box as being in a kind of stack, akin to layers in the Layers panel. In Normal blend mode, an effect obscures all the effects below it in the stack (this is how layers work). However, you can't reorder effects as you could if they were actually independent layers. Instead, merge effects through strategic use of blend modes.

4. Change the blend mode of the Color Overlay effect to Color. Now only the color is blended with the texture coming from the ceramic-tile pattern overlay. Click OK to close the Layer Style dialog box.

Every situation with combined effects is different. I always drag the Layer Style dialog box out of the way (or onto a secondary monitor) so I can see the result of an effect blend in the document window. Try Soft Light, Overlay, Color, Multiply, or Screen blend modes to see which gives you what you're looking for. You can also tone down a particular effect by adjusting its opacity slider.

Separating Color from Pattern

In searching for real-world textures, you might browse manufacturer websites and come across thumbnail images that represent particular materials. If you define these as patterns in Photoshop, sometimes undesirable color noise will appear, especially if you scale the pattern up to a larger size. It's useful to be able to separate pattern detail from color so you can adjust the color independently.

In our example, the hardwood floor texture has greens and magentas that detract from the natural finish we are trying to represent. Let's fix it by separating color from pattern:

1. Target the Living layer in the Floors group. Double-click the Pattern Overlay effect in the Layers panel. Change the blend mode to Luminosity in order to focus on detail at the exclusion of color (see Figure 2.35).

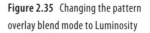

Figure 2.35 Changing the pattern overlay blend mode to Luminosity

2. Click the words *Color Overlay* in the Layer Style dialog box to both activate this effect and load its page. Change the blend mode to Soft Light.

3. Click the color swatch to open the Color Picker. Type the hex code **e4a94b** in the # text box and click OK. The hardwood floor appears in natural tones only, no green or magenta.

Creating Layers from Effects

Sometimes you'll have a directional texture that runs horizontally in a pattern, but you need it to run vertically (or vice versa) where you want to apply it. Unfortunately, there is no way to rotate a pattern overlay within the Layer Style dialog box. However, you can rotate patterns by first converting effects to layers, as we do here using the chapter's example:

1. Target the Porch layer, which has the Deck pattern assigned with boards running vertically.

2. Right-click this layer's Pattern Overlay effect and choose Create Layers from the context menu. A new layer called Porch's Pattern Fill is generated automatically. It's clipped by the Porch layer, which contains the original black pixels from the Paint Bucket tool.

3. Target the Porch's Pattern Fill layer and press Cmd+T / Ctrl+T to transform it. Type **90** in the Rotate text box in the options bar. Drag the texture to align the seams between boards with the porch, and then click the Commit button. The pattern is rotated properly (see Figure 2.36).

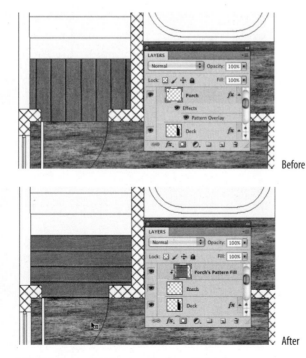

Before

After

Figure 2.36 Rotating a pattern by converting layer effects to layers

Varying Lineweight and Dropping Shadows to Indicate Depth

Stroke and Drop Shadow layer effects are best applied at the end of an enhancement project because both of these effects add pixels "outside the lines." Pixels added in this way would interfere with adjacent areas unless layer order is taken into consideration. Your example should therefore look like Figure 2.37 before you start adjusting shadows.

Figure 2.37 Patterned drawing prior to depth enhancements

When you are ready to add lineweight or shadows, you'll need to begin by dragging layers whose effects extend beyond their boundaries to the top of the layer stack so these pixels won't be obscured by pixels on neighboring layers. To do this, follow these steps:

Note: Before you thicken any lines or drop any shadows, spend some time practicing what you've learned so far and enhance the rest of the drawing as you see fit. Use different patterns, adjust colors, orient textures, and so on until all the spaces between the CAD Layers lines are enhanced. Feel free to go back and change any of the enhancements you've made up to this point.

Note: Gradient overlays can add interest to otherwise flat color or pattern overlays.

1. Double-click the CAD Layers thumbnail to open the smart object in a separate document window. Target the Home-Walls.png layer and add a Stroke layer effect. Set Size at 3 px and set Position to Center. Click OK to close the Layer Style dialog box, shown in Figure 2.38.

Note: The stroke effect applies anti-aliasing to the edges of the thickened lines to make the lines appear smoother. Anti-aliasing is especially helpful in softening lines that are neither horizontal nor vertical.

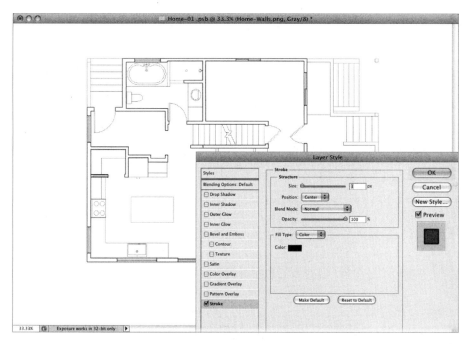

Figure 2.38 Adding a stroke effect to the CAD drawing layer

2. Press Cmd+W and Return / Ctrl+W and Enter to close the document and save it.

3. Drag the Walls layer underneath CAD Layers in the Layers panel so that the drop shadow effect you're about to apply is visible.

4. Double-click the word *Effects* nested under the Walls layer to open the Layer Style dialog box. Click the check box for Drop Shadow. Deselect the Global Light option, set Angle to 132 degrees, Distance to 11 px, Spread to 14%, and

Size to 10 px (see Figure 2.39). Click OK. Click OK again to close the Layer Style dialog box.

Figure 2.39 Specifying parameters for a drop shadow effect

5. Some of the drop shadows aren't realistic or desirable; for example, you wouldn't see the shadow on top of the refrigerator and adjacent upper cabinet. To omit these unnecessary shadows from the image, right-click the word *Effects* under the Walls layer and choose Create Layers from the context menu that appears.

6. Click OK to close the warning dialog box, shown in Figure 2.40, stating that some of the effects cannot be reproduced with layers; we lose some abilities but gain others when converting effects to layers.

Figure 2.40 A warning appears when converting effects to layers.

7. Target Walls' Drop Shadow layer and click the Add Layer Mask button at the bottom of the Layers panel. Choose the Brush tool from the toolbox and paint away the shadows you don't want to be visible.

8. Add additional drop shadow effects to any layer where you want to indicate depth. I added drop shadows to the kitchen island, tub surround, doors, brick

wall behind the woodstove, and so on. Feel free to experiment and enhance the drawing however you like. Figure 2.41 shows how my plan ended up.

Figure 2.41 Final drawing enhanced with Photoshop

Congratulations on completing this lengthy tutorial. Now you know how to enhance CAD and BIM drawings with Photoshop. Your speed in getting the job done will definitely improve with practice. I recommend enhancing your own project from start to finish to really own the skills you've learned in this chapter. The completed project is provided on the DVD as Home-enhanced.psd for your examination.

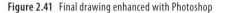

Stretching the Photographic Truth

Your integrity as a professional is what your clients trust. If your images stretch the photographic truth to paint a positive impression, that's your artistic license. However, if your intent is outright deception, you will bear the consequences for painting a false impression. Because determining where the line lies is beyond the scope of this book, this chapter instead offers accepted techniques to shift your work's visual focus. How much you stretch depends on what is acceptable for your client and job, yet most likely your professional work "stretching" will cover the following topics:

Chapter Contents

Removing unwanted objects

Replacing the sky

Adjusting color

Altering content

Expanding dynamic range

Removing Unwanted Objects

Power lines, construction equipment, cars, and people often divert attention away from the subject of architectural images. Fortunately, it's easier than ever to remove unwanted objects from your photos. CS5 has new content-aware tools that can automatically fill in and heal pixels surrounding affected areas. If you are using an older version of Photoshop, you can still remove unwanted objects; it just takes a bit more effort to do a convincing job. Let's now try some old-school methods before trying the new content-aware spot-healing feature in CS5. In the following section, we will remove people by using a variety of retouching tools to focus attention on the architecture.

1. Open `Removing objects.jpg` on the DVD (Figure 3.1).

Figure 3.1 Original image

2. It's arguable whether showing a few people in an architectural image is a bad thing (a crowd could be more distracting), but for the sake of this tutorial, let us assume you want to remove the five people on the sidewalk. Zoom in for a closer view of the people and then press Shift+J until you have selected the Patch tool, which has been available in Photoshop since version 7.

3. Using the Patch tool, carefully drag a lasso around the people and their shadows, coming back to the point where you started before releasing the mouse (see Figure 3.2). This is the area you want to remove.

Figure 3.2 Drawing a lasso around the area you want to remove with the Patch tool

4. Put the cursor inside the selection and then drag to the right a short distance. As you drag, you'll see the content you drag over appear within the selection. When you release the mouse, the pixels within the selection are "patched," meaning the texture, lighting, and shading are matched as closely as possible (Figure 3.3). Press Command+D / Ctrl+D to deselect.

Figure 3.3 Patching an unwanted area

5. Like most patch jobs, it's not perfect. We will follow up the patch operation with the Clone Stamp tool to take care of smaller details. Oldest of old-school, the

Clone Stamp tool has been around since Photoshop version 1. Press S for Clone Stamp.

6. Hold down the Opt/Alt key, click a point that you'd like to sample, and release the key. Ideally, the sampled point will contain "good pixels," adjacent and very similar in content to the blemished area.

7. The Clone Stamp tool uses the Brush Engine. Adjust the brush size to match the scale of the area you want to retouch by pressing the square bracket keys. Press Shift+[four times to select the softest possible brush. Deselect the Aligned option to paint starting from the initial sampling point, no matter how many times you stop and resume painting. Paint over any problem areas such as the man's head that is higher than the wall, or any especially bright or dark regions produced by the Patch tool.

Note: Keep adjusting the brush size while clone stamping to ensure that you are cloning only the pixels needed to cover any blemished areas.

8. Let's now get rid of the construction crane and contrails in the sky by using an amazing new feature called content-aware spot healing. Press Shift+J twice and verify that you have the Spot Healing Brush tool selected in the toolbox. Select Content-Aware on the options bar and adjust the brush size to be slightly larger than the area you'd like to retouch. Paint over the crane and contrails and watch them disappear as if by magic (Figure 3.4).

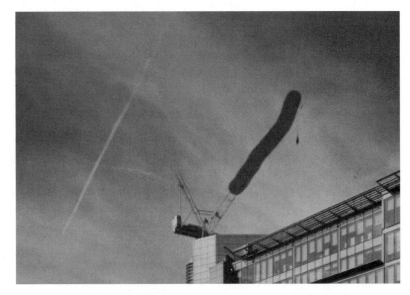

Figure 3.4 Removing objects as if by magic with the content-aware Spot Healing Brush

9. Content-aware spot healing generally does a fine job, but there may be areas at the interface of dissimilar materials that need additional retouching. Press S and clone stamp out the base of the crane where it meets the building (Figure 3.5).

Pixels in this area need retouching with the Clone Stamp tool.

Figure 3.5 Some areas require clone stamping.

10. Save the image as Removing objects.psd.

> **Note:** Another way to access the content-aware algorithm is to make a selection and press Shift+F5. Select Content-Aware in the Fill dialog box that appears, and click OK to fill the selection based on the surrounding content.

Removing "objects" from images is always somewhat of a challenge because Photoshop doesn't understand where one object begins and another ends as the human mind does—it's all a sea of undifferentiated pixels to Photoshop. Every image presents different retouching challenges when it comes to removing objects.

The new content-aware algorithm is remarkably easy to use and generates amazing results in most situations. However, older tools such as Clone Stamp, Patch, and the Healing Brush are still necessary for accurate retouching. Figure 3.6 shows the final retouched image with people, contrails, and construction crane removed.

Figure 3.6 Retouched image with specific objects removed

Replacing the Sky

Whether you are conscious of it or not, weather undeniably influences mood. Cloudy days may bring a bit of the blues. Shooting architectural exteriors when it's pouring down rain is generally a bad idea, unless you are seeking that specific dramatic effect. However, we don't always have the luxury of waiting for a perfect sunny day to photograph buildings.

Photoshop can grant one of humanity's deepest desires and give you control over the weather (at least in appearance). With this amazing power, you can subtly influence how someone feels about a building simply by replacing the sky. Let's see how it's done:

1. Open `Replacing the sky.jpg` from the `Chapter 3 Samples` folder on the DVD (Figure 3.7).

2. Press W to select the Quick Selection tool. Adjust the brush size to 30 px by using the square bracket keys. Press Shift+] four times to increase the brush to maximum hardness and select Auto-Enhance on the options bar. Make a brushstroke in the sky and watch while the selection grows automatically as Photoshop analyzes the pixels you're painting over for similarity.

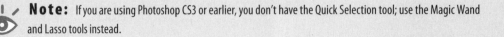

Note: If you are using Photoshop CS3 or earlier, you don't have the Quick Selection tool; use the Magic Wand and Lasso tools instead.

Figure 3.7 An image that would benefit from sky replacement

3. Click once in the opaque white sky under the palm tree leaves to add this area to the selection. Hold down the Opt/Alt key and paint over any areas of the selection that include the building (Figure 3.8). You don't have to be too accurate because the next step will take care of fixing fine details, such as the sky visible through the palm fronds.

Figure 3.8 Making a rough selection with the Quick Selection tool

4. Click the Refine Edge button on the options bar to open the Refine Edge dialog box. Open the View drop-down and select On Black. Under Edge Detection, select Smart Radius and set the Radius slider to 1 px.

5. The Refine Radius tool along the left edge of the dialog box should be selected by default; press E if it is not. Paint over the palm tree fronds as shown in Figure 3.9 to have Photoshop automatically determine where the edges are—only the sky is added to the selection. Under the Output section, select Decontaminate Colors, set Output To to New Layer With Layer Mask, and click OK (Figure 3.10).

Paint over the palm fronds to have Photoshop find the edges.

Figure 3.9 Painting over the area to be refined

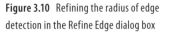

Figure 3.10 Refining the radius of edge detection in the Refine Edge dialog box

6. A new layer called `Background copy` appears with a layer mask representing the output of the Refine Edge tool. Rename this layer `Sky masked` and target the mask; a thin border appears surrounding the layer mask thumbnail when you click on it. Press Cmd+I / Ctrl+I to invert the mask and thereby hide the sky (Figure 3.11).

Figure 3.11 The output of the Refine Edge tool can be a layer mask.

Once the sky is masked, you can place another layer underneath to simulate the type of sky you're looking for. Of course, this could be a photo of a beautiful sky, or a sky that's generated procedurally. We'll take the latter approach in this tutorial by creating a gradient fill layer and customizing the gradient to simulate a clear, sunny sky.

7. Choose Layer > New Fill Layer > Gradient. Type **Sky** in the New Layer dialog box and then click OK. Choose the Black, White gradient from the picker (Figure 3.12) and click OK. Drag `Sky` below the `Sky masked` layer so the gradient shows up.

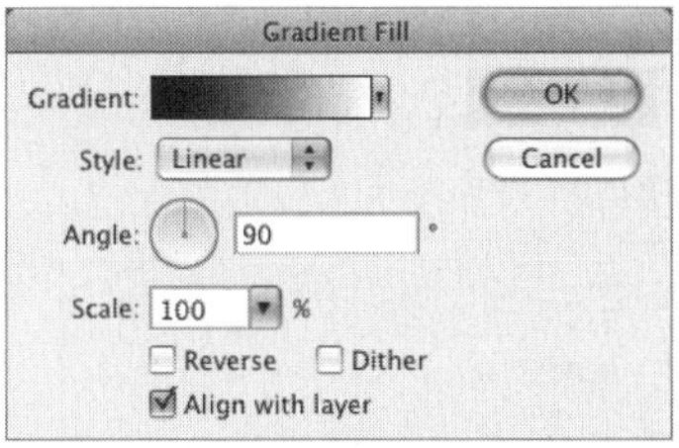

Figure 3.12 Selecting the Black, White gradient as a starting point for your custom gradient

8. Double-click the `Sky` layer thumbnail and click the gradient swatch in the Gradient Fill dialog box to open the Gradient Editor. Select the bottom-left color stop marker and double-click the color swatch on the marker to set the lower sky color in the Select Color dialog box. Pick a pale, light-blue hue such as #dff5ff. Select the bottom-right marker and double-click the color swatch to set the upper sky color. Pick a deeper sky-blue hue such as # a7bcff.

9. Type **Sky** in the Name field within the Gradient Editor and click the New button to add it to your gradient presets (Figure 3.13). Click the Save button within the Gradient Editor and save `My Gradients.grd` so you'll be able to use these gradients again. Click OK and OK again to close both open dialog boxes.

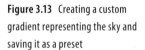

Figure 3.13 Creating a custom gradient representing the sky and saving it as a preset

10. Save the image as `Replacing the Sky.psd`.

Note: Toggle the `Sky` layer off and on to see before and after versions of what you've learned in this section. It helps to compare images repeatedly to see how replacing an overcast sky can change the mood of a photo.

The eye focuses more on the architecture with a clear blue sky (Figure 3.14) rather than with bright opaque clouds (back in Figure 3.7). However, bright saturated colors of cars, motorcycles, and signage distract some attention away from the intended architectural subject. We'll address these issues in the next section.

Figure 3.14 Sky replaced with gradient

Adjusting Color

Photoshop has a plethora of tools for adjusting color. In this section, you'll learn how to emphasize a particular space or building with color, to explore color options using different materials, and to fix color problems in photos.

Desaturating Color

Saturation refers to how much color is present, as opposed to which hue is used, or how bright or dark the color is. Taking away color is called *desaturation*. Taken to the limit, fully desaturated images are best known as black-and-white photos. Toning down color (without eliminating it) can have two very different effects: It can reduce that garish feeling you sometimes get when the colors are just too much, or it can be used for dramatic effect to emphasize a particular object, space, or building.

In the following section, we will desaturate some of the garish colors in the sample image that divert attention away from the building. In particular, the motorcycles, cars, and signs appear oversaturated in the bright California sunshine.

1. Continue with the same file you were working on in the last section, or open `Replacing the sky.psd` from the DVD.

2. Target the `Sky masked` layer in the Layers panel. Open the Adjustments panel, press D to select the default colors, and click the Black & White button. Press Cmd+Delete / Ctrl+Backspace to fill the Black & White layer's mask with black.

3. Press B to select the Brush tool. Select a small, soft brush and paint white pixels on the mask where you'd like to desaturate color. Vary the Flow percentage on the options bar to control how much color is removed. Paint over the motorcycle and cars at 25% flow to tone them down without turning them gray. Paint over the pink sign and frame at 100% flow to remove this hue entirely (Figure 3.15).

Figure 3.15 Painting on the mask partially desaturates the selected areas

4. Save the image as `Removing color.psd`.

Another approach is to use color to draw attention to something. You've seen this approach in advertising; the colorful object in a gray world is the one we all pay attention to. Let's try it out:

1. Open Desaturating color.jpg from the DVD.

2. Press P to select the Pen tool. Single-click points around the borders of the shop, as shown in Figure 3.16. Click the last point on top of the first one to close the path.

PHOTO COURTESY OF ISTOCKPHOTO, © MLENNY, IMAGE # 1000006

Figure 3.16 Removing color for dramatic effect

3. Press Shift+A once or twice to select the Direct Selection tool. Tighten up the path around your intended border by moving any of the points you laid down with the Pen tool. First click to select a point and then nudge it with the arrow keys, 1 pixel at a time.

4. Press U to select the drawing tools and select the Rectangle tool on the options bar. Click the second mode button, which is named Paths, and the last Boolean button, which is called Exclude, to overlap path areas (Figure 3.17). Enlarge the document window slightly by dragging its resize handle so you can see some of the surrounding canvas. Drag out a rectangle that is slightly larger than the image.

Figure 3.17 Selecting drawing options

5. Click the Black & White button in the Adjustments panel to create the adjustment layer and automatically assign the path you've drawn as its vector mask (Figure 3.18).

Figure 3.18 Converting the drawn path to a vector layer mask

6. The highlighted store is in color, and everything else is in grayscale. The effect is quite dramatic, perhaps too much so. Lower the opacity of the Black & White 1 layer to 80% to saturate the environment slightly with color and soften the effect.

7. This particular image needs to be straightened because the camera was tilted slightly when the photo was taken. Press Shift+I and repeat to select the Ruler tool. Drag out a line along a vertical seam in the glass at the corner of the retail space. If you're using CS5, click the Straighten button on the options bar. If you're using an older version, choose Image > Image Rotation > Arbitrary, and click OK.

Note: Deselect the vector mask thumbnail to hide the path onscreen. Viewing vector paths onscreen can be distracting unless you need to adjust the path itself.

Shifting Color

Sometimes the best way to select a particular material finish is to see it in the context of the rest of the building. Photoshop can help you explore color options by shifting selected pixels' hues—giving you instant visual feedback needed to make finish decisions.

Let us assume you want to explore different glazing options in the sample file. Because glazing is composed of straight edges, the vector Pen tool can be used to create an accurate selection. For organic shapes, the raster Quick Select and Refine Edge tools would be preferable. The following steps detail how to do this:

1. Open the Removing objects.psd file you saved earlier or open the version on the DVD.

2. Press P to select the Pen tool. Then click Paths mode and the Add To Path Area button on the options bar (Figure 3.19). Click points around each expanse of glass until you close each path by clicking where you started (see Figure 3.20). Cover each of the individual windows in the stair tower separately.

Figure 3.19 Adding to a path

Figure 3.20 Drawing paths around groups of windows

3. Click the Hue/Saturation button in the Adjustments panel. The paths you drew in step 2 automatically appear as a vector mask on this adjustment layer (Figure 3.21).

Figure 3.21 Drawn paths appear as a vector mask on the adjustment layer.

4. Drag the Hue, Saturation, and Lightness sliders to see real-time changes in the document window. I settled on green glazing using Hue –36, Saturation –18, and Lightness –21 (Figure 3.22).

Figure 3.22 Shifting color with a
Hue/Saturation adjustment layer

5.   Overall the image is very blue. Let's reduce the blue saturation with a Selective
Color adjustment. Click the left-facing arrow at the bottom of the Adjustments
panel to return to the adjustments list. Click the Selective Color button (the
last icon in the display) to add it as an adjustment layer. Choose Blues from the
Colors drop-down, and drag the Black slider all the way left to remove the darkest blues from the image (Figure 3.23).

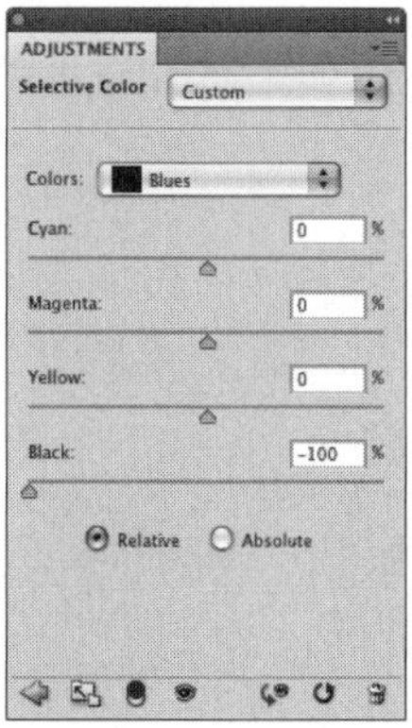

Figure 3.23 Shifting specific colors with
the Selective Color adjustment

Note: Try adding a Gradient Map adjustment layer for non–photo-realistic artistic effects.

6.   Save the image as `Shifting color.psd`. This file is provided on the DVD for comparison with your own work.

Correcting Color

Occasionally you'll need to correct images whose color looks off. Images can be color-shifted by combinations of cameras, lenses, and lighting conditions, but sometimes we need to "correct" images so they match our perception of how we think they should look. Whatever the problem, you'll learn how to color-correct like a pro by using Curves. In order to do this, you'll need to identify black, white, and gray points, which correspond to the darkest, lightest, and most neutral pixels in the image. The following steps show you how to do this:

1. Open the file `Correcting color.jpg` from the DVD (Figure 3.24).

Figure 3.24 Original image requiring color correction

2. We'll now use the Threshold adjustment to identify the darkest and lightest pixels in the image. Open the Adjustments panel and click the Threshold button (Figure 3.25).

3. Drag the slider under the histogram all the way to the left. The document window shows black pixels representing the darkest shadows in the image.

4. Press Shift+I to cycle through the tools until you select the Color Sampler tool, or choose it directly from the flyout menu in the toolbox. On the options bar, set Sample Size to Point Sample and click within the black pixels displayed by the Threshold adjustment layer. A marker with subscript 1 is left behind. This is your black point.

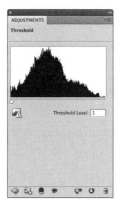

Figure 3.25 Using the Threshold adjustment to identify black and white points

5. Drag the threshold slider all the way to the right. As you move the slider, the majority of pixels change from white to black. Drag the slider to threshold level 246 and you'll see the lightest areas of the image identified by small patches of white. Click inside one of these white areas; a marker with subscript 2 is left behind, identifying the white point (Figure 3.26).

Figure 3.26 Marking white and black points with the Color Sampler tool over the Threshold adjustment layer

6. Delete the Threshold adjustment layer by dragging its thumbnail to the Trash at the bottom of the Layers panel.

7. Click the Curves button in the Adjustments panel. Choose the Set Black Point tool along the left edge of the Adjustments panel and click inside color marker 1 (Figure 3.27).

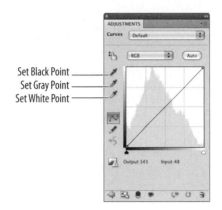

Set Black Point
Set Gray Point
Set White Point

Figure 3.27 Setting black, white, and gray points

8. Choose the Set White Point tool and click inside color marker 2.

9. Press I to select the Color Sampler tool. Click a point on something as close to neutral gray as you can find in the image (this creates color marker 3). Unlike choosing the black and white points, choosing the gray point is more subjective. The pier just to the right of marker 1 is a good gray point in this image (Figure 3.28).

Figure 3.28 Setting the gray point

10. Choose the Set Gray Point tool along the left edge of the Adjustments panel and click inside color marker 3. The color channels are automatically adjusted. If you don't like the effect, try clicking a different gray point. The color channels are independently adjusted according to the gray point, as you can see from the curves. In this image, the blue channel's midtones were reduced while the red channels were increased, making the image appear to be more color-balanced (Figure 3.29).

11. The image appears to be color-balanced but oversaturated. Apply a Vibrance adjustment layer and drag its Vibrance slider to –30 to remove some of the color.

12. Save the image as `Correcting color.psd`. This file is provided on the DVD for comparison with your own work.

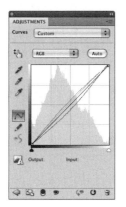

Figure 3.29 Curves resulting from setting black, white, and gray points

Note: Try replacing the sky in this image to elevate the mood.

Altering Content

In some instances, stretching the photographic truth is appropriate. Stretching the landscape surrounding a pastoral building or straightening a crooked tree seem to be acceptable uses of Photoshop's amazing new tools. In these cases, try altering content with content-aware scale or Puppet Warp. Content-aware scale debuted in CS4, and Puppet Warp is new in CS5.

Content-Aware Scale

When you stretch images in Free Transform mode, they become distorted and unbelievable. As the name suggests, content-aware scale takes what you're stretching into account and tries to protect it from distortion while the rest of the image gets scaled. For the case of a building, you will need to help this amazing algorithm out by creating an alpha channel indicating what you want to protect, as shown here:

1. Open Altering content.jpg from the DVD (Figure 3.30). This file is in portrait orientation, and we'll scale it to landscape orientation without distorting the building.

PHOTO COURTESY OF ISTOCKPHOTO, © FONTMONSTER, IMAGE #5167238

Figure 3.30 Original image in portrait orientation

2. Although you don't have to crop the image in order to use content-aware scale, this particular image has too much sky and not enough building (it's too small relative to the rest of the image). Press C for the Crop tool. Type **600 px** in both the Width and Height boxes in the options bar. Drag out a square filling the image and drag it down to the bottom of the image so the sky will be cropped (Figure 3.31). Click the Commit button on the options bar.

3. Press W for the Quick Select tool. Adjust the brush size to 15 pixels with the square bracket keys, and paint over the building to make a selection. Click Refine Edge on the options bar, select Smart Radius, and set Radius at 4 px. Click OK.

4. Open the Channels panel and click the Save Selection As Channel button along its lower edge to create the Alpha 1 channel.

5. Open the Layers panel, double-click the Background layer, and click OK to convert it to a regular layer.

Figure 3.31 Cropping away excess sky

6. Choose Image > Canvas Size, change the unit drop-downs to pixels, type **800** in the Width box, and click OK (Figure 3.32).

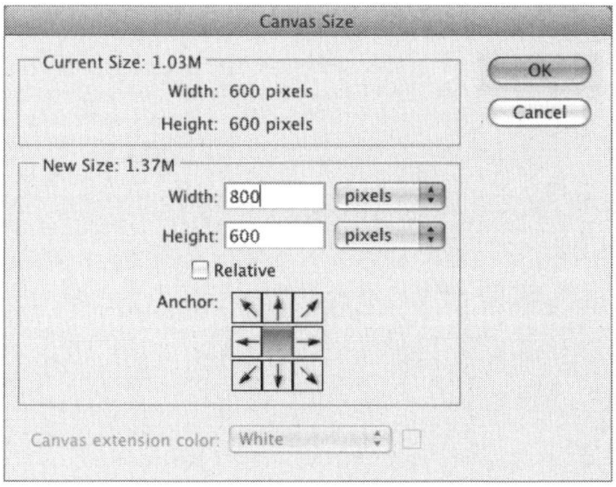

Figure 3.32 Adjusting the canvas size to accommodate landscape orientation

7. Choose Edit > Content-Aware Scale. Choose Alpha 1 from the Protect drop-down, type **800px** in the Width box (Figure 3.33), and click the Commit button.

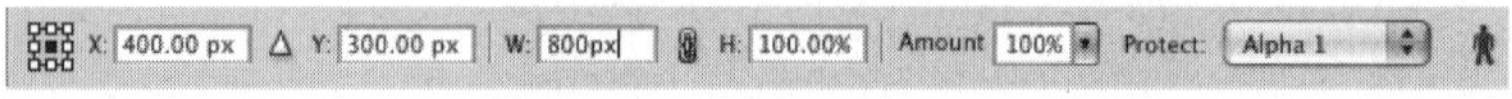

| X: 400.00 px | △ Y: 300.00 px | W: 800px | 🔗 | H: 100.00% | Amount 100% ▾ | Protect: Alpha 1 ⬍ | 🧍 |

Figure 3.33 Content-aware scale options

8. Save the image as `Altering content.psd`. This file is provided on the DVD for comparison with your own work.

The result (see Figure 3.34) is a more-appropriate image of the clubhouse in landscape orientation. The building remained undistorted while the surrounding trees got stretched to accommodate the new layout.

Figure 3.34 Scaled image in landscape orientation

The Puppet Master

Photoshop CS5 comes with an amazing new transformation tool called Puppet Warp. It's much better than the old Warp refinement on the Transform tool, and it blows the doors off the Liquify filter too. However, this feature has limited usefulness in regards to architecture. If you ever need to straighten a leaning tree or repair the leaning tower of Pisa, we've got you covered.

1. Open `Puppet warp.jpg` from the `Chapter 3 Samples` folder on the DVD (Figure 3.35).

Figure 3.35 Original bent tree

2. Choose Select > Color Range, click the Add To Sample button (an eyedropper with a plus subscript), and click a point in the upper-left corner of the preview window within the Color Range dialog box. Drag down within the sky to select the entire range of blues that make up the sky gradient. Drag the Fuzziness slider to 40 and click OK (Figure 3.36).

3. Press Cmd+Shift+I / Ctrl+Shift+I to invert the selection. Now everything but the sky is selected.

4. Press L to select the Lasso tool. Click the Subtract From Selection button on the options bar (Figure 3.37) and drag a lasso around the grass and trees in the distance. Now only the tree and man are selected.

Figure 3.36 Selecting the entire sky gradient with Color Range

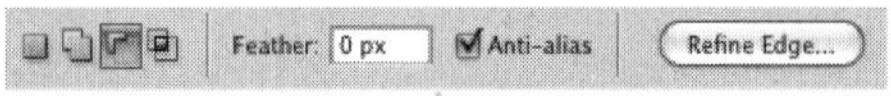

Feather: 0 px ☑ Anti-alias Refine Edge...

Figure 3.37 Subtract From Selection option

5. Press Cmd+J / Ctrl+J to jump the selected pixels to a new layer.

6. Choose Edit > Puppet Warp and click the points shown on the left of Figure 3.38. Placing points close together protects adjoining areas from moving, while spacing points out provides you with handles for transformation. Drag the top two points to the left to straighten the tree, as shown on the right of Figure 3.38. Click the Commit button on the options bar.

7. The original bent tree still appears on the Background layer. Target the Background layer, press M to select the Marquee tool, and drag out a tall, thin rectangular selection, as shown on the left of Figure 3.39. Press Cmd+T / Ctrl+T to enter Free Transform mode. Drag the middle-right handle of the transform box all the way to the right edge of the image and press Return/Enter to obscure the original tree with sky.

8. Press J to select the Spot Healing Brush tool, and select the Content-Aware radio button on the options bar if it's not already selected. Paint over any edges that appear in the sky from covering up the original tree in the previous step. Figure 3.40 shows what the tree looks like in the end.

Placing pins

Dragging a pin warps the tree.

Figure 3.38 Placing pins to anchor the mesh and then moving selected pins to straighten the tree

Figure 3.39 Obscuring the original tree with the copied sky

Figure 3.40 Tree straightened by Puppet Warp

9. Save the image as `Puppet warp.psd`. This file is provided on the DVD for comparison with your own work.

Expanding Dynamic Range

Dynamic range is the spread of light intensity values in an image, all the way from pure white to pure black. Most digital devices are able to capture and display their brightest whites about a thousand times more brightly than their blackest blacks. This sounds like quite a range, but light is an exponential phenomenon, and our eyes handle much larger dynamic ranges. For instance, sunlight in the tropics is over a billion times brighter than faint starlight you might see in the countryside.

Professional photographers often bracket important shots—taking several exposures at different shutter speeds to ensure they have enough light data to create a high dynamic range (HDR) image in Photoshop. HDR images seem "hyper-real" because they are closer to the dynamic range our eyes perceive. HDR images are therefore closer to the ineffable *photographic truth* than "regular" images can ever be.

Although it has been possible to create HDR images in Photoshop since CS2, Photoshop CS5 has a revamped HDR interface called HDR Pro that gives more artistic options than ever before. In addition, there is a new adjustment in CS5 called HDR Toning that fakes "the HDR look" in a single image. Let's take a look at both new features.

HDR Pro

In order to use HDR Pro, you must shoot multiple bracketed images. It is preferable to bracket by changing shutter speed rather than f-stop because changing the lens aperture affects the depth of field (area in sharp focus). However, not all consumer cameras have the capability to manually set shutter speed; you might need a higher-end "pro-sumer" or pro digital camera in order to bracket shots. New cameras are starting to offer autobracketing as an option in their continuous shooting or burst modes. Figure 3.41 shows nine bracketed shots we'll be using in this tutorial.

IMAGES COURTESY OF RICHARD TRUEMAN

Figure 3.41 Nine shots of the same subject, bracketed by shutter speed , and shot with a tripod

1. Choose File > Automate > Merge To HDR Pro and select Folder from the Use drop-down. Click the Browse button and navigate to the Chapter 3/HDR folder on the DVD. Select all nine images and click OK to begin processing (Figure 3.42).

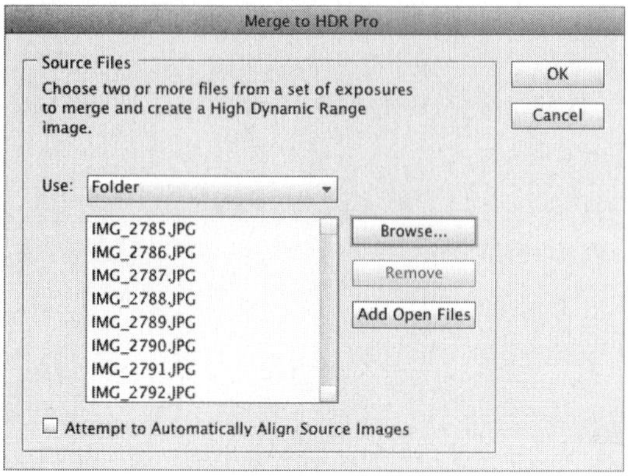

Figure 3.42 Merging images to HDR Pro

Note: Select the the Attempt To Automatically Align Source Images option in the initial Merge To HDR Pro dialog box if the shots you bracketed were handheld. It is not necessary to do this additional processing if you used a tripod.

2. After some time, the larger Merge To HDR Pro dialog box appears with a series of thumbnails running across the bottom; these are the bracketed shots with each exposure value (EV) shown below its thumbnail. Choose Photorealistic from the Preset drop-down. The result is shown in Figure 3.43.

Note: Notice that the image in the main part of the Merge To HDR Pro dialog box shows both the interior and the world outside the windows properly exposed—this is the wonder of HDR imagery (Figure 3.43). No one exposure could have captured all of this detail.

Note: Select Remove Ghosts in the Merge To HDR Pro dialog box if anything moved during the time you shot the bracketed images (such as wind moving tree branches). Photoshop will intelligently remove these unwelcome artifacts.

3. The image is still a bit dark overall, so drag the Exposure slider to 1.00. This brightens the room but burns out the highlights in the clouds. To compensate, drag the Highlight slider to –80 and click OK. After some more time for processing, Photoshop returns a single 16-bit HDR image to the document window. The final result is shown in Figure 3.44.

4. Save the image as HDR Pro Result.psd. This file is provided on the DVD for comparison with your own work.

Figure 3.43 Merge To HDR Pro interface

Figure 3.44 After using HDR Pro, we can see detail inside the room and outside the window.

HDR Toning

HDR Toning simulates the way true HDR images often look, but without increasing the dynamic range. It's a trick, plain and simple. You're not going to recover any blown-out or underexposed pixels using HDR Toning as you can with HDR Pro. However, HDR Toning is very effective in generating hyper-real and even surreal looks that are popular these days in advertising and in movies.

The following steps explore HDR Toning:

1. Open the file `Removing objects.psd` that you saved earlier or open the version on the DVD.

2. Choose Image > Adjustments > HDR Toning and click Yes in reponse to the warning that appears (Figure 3.45).

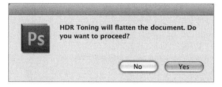

Figure 3.45 HDR Toning flattens layers.

Note: HDR Toning should be done in a copy of a layered Photoshop file because it must flatten the document. Perhaps in a future version of Photoshop, Adobe will allow HDR Toning to be assigned to a smart object so its parameters could be edited after their initial application.

3. Choose Photorealistic from the Preset drop down. Drag the HDR Toning dialog box out of the way of the document window so you can preview the result. Try each of the presets (Figure 3.46) to see how they look and then return to Photorealistic after you're finished exploring.

> ✓ Default
>
> Flat
> Monochromatic artistic
> Monochromatic high contrast
> Monochromatic low contrast
> Monochromatic
> More Saturated
> Photorealistic high contrast
> Photorealistic low contrast
> Photorealistic
> Saturated
> Surrealistic high contrast
> Surrealistic low contrast
> Surrealistic
>
> Custom

Figure 3.46 HDR Toning preset options

4. Drag the Detail slider to 100% for increased sharpening. Drag Vibrance to –25% to remove some of the color saturation. Expand the Toning Curve And Histogram section of the dialog box and increase contrast by adding the points as shown in Figure 3.47. Click OK when you're satisfied.

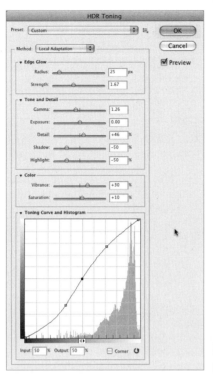

Figure 3.47 Tweaking HDR Toning parameters to create hyper-real imagery

5. Save the image as HDR Toning.psd (see Figure 3.48).

Figure 3.48 Result of HDR Toning (compare with original image in Figure 3.1)

In this chapter, you've learned a variety of techniques to stretch the photographic truth and create something more impressive than was originally captured by a camera's light sensors. From removing unwanted objects to replacing the sky, adjusting color, altering content, and expanding dynamic range, the creative possibilities for enhancing photos is unlimited.

Crafting Interactive Panoramas

Humans see more information than what is directly in front of their eyes. Your peripheral vision registers what's around you, and when you turn your head, you build a mental picture of a space. Unlike still images, interactive panoramas stimulate this natural process and are therefore a compelling way to showcase your projects.

This chapter covers all of Photoshop's native options for adding interactivity so you can create your own interactive panoramas. You will also explore several third-party solutions to craft interactive panoramas by using a variety of web technologies, including Java, Flash, and QuickTime VR.

4

Chapter Contents

Tips for Shooting Panoramic Images

Photoshop can stitch together multiple photos into a seamless panoramic image. These, of course, can be printed, turned into a video, or exported to become an interactive web experience. Yet whatever you do with your panoramic product, it's important to remember the many factors you need to consider before shooting the source images that make up any panorama. The following is a list to keep in mind.

How Panoramic Images Evolved in Photoshop

Photoshop has had the capability to merge multiple photos into seamless panoramas since CS2. In CS3, Photoshop became much better at aligning and blending the seams between images, and in CS5 options were introduced to remove geometric distortion and/or vignetting inherent in some wide-angle lenses. All of these features mean it's easy to create beautiful panoramas of arbitrary resolution in Photoshop. The latest *content-aware* technology in CS5 enables you to also clean up any hairline seams or regions of missing pixels along the edges of the photos. This means it's now easy to create larger panoramas without cropping, yet Photoshop still has limited options for building interactivity into these panoramas.

Overlapping Images Ideally, images should overlap by about 40 percent for Photoshop to properly merge them. However, photos with a minimum of about 20 percent overlap can still be merged, although the blending between adjacent photos might not be optimized.

Note: Be forewarned that Photoshop might not be able to merge images with more than 70 percent overlap.

Planning Shot Quantity Images are typically shot in rows, composing an entire 360-degree ring, or in multiple rings at different altitudes in order to capture more of the sky. The number of pictures required depends on the focal length of your camera lens.

Zooming In for Higher Resolution When creating a panorama, you would need to take only three images if using an 8 mm hemispherical fish-eye lens, because each image has close to a 180-degree field of view (the third image is required for overlap). On the other hand, hundreds of images would be required to capture a full 360-degree panorama if using a 300 mm telephoto lens. Zooming in and capturing more photos and subsequently stitching them together is the way to build incredible resolution that far exceeds any camera sensor's ability to capture megapixels.

Note: Motorized robotic camera mounts are available for creating extremely large panoramas measured in gigapixels. See http://gigapansystems.com for more information.

Understanding Focal Length vs. Field of View Camera focal length is more or less inversely proportional to field of view. Figure 4.1 shows a wide-angle lens having a large field of view.

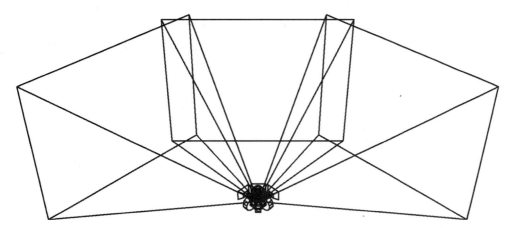

Figure 4.1 This wide-angle lens has a large field of view.

Fewer images are required to capture a panorama with a wide-angle lens as compared with a telephoto lens (see Figure 4.2).

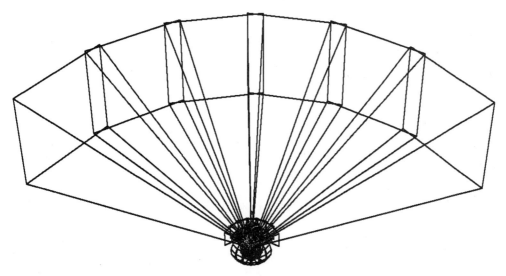

Figure 4.2 A telephoto lens requires more pictures to cover the same space.

Holding the Camera vs. Using a Tripod Should you hold the camera or use a tripod? Photoshop is incredibly forgiving in the panorama-stitching process because the advanced Auto-Align and Auto-Blend algorithms it employs make stitching a mostly automatic process. However, if you are shooting a full 360-degree panorama by holding the camera, you are unlikely to overlap photos consistently and may even miss whole areas, making the panorama unusable.

The upside of using a telephoto lens is you can capture many more pixels in the same space as compared with a wide-angle lens. More pixels mean higher resolution, which translates into higher print quality, or a greater ability to zoom in and perceive detail in an interactive panorama. I recommend using a tripod if you have one, and holding the camera only for partial panoramas (fewer than 360 degrees). A degree ring is a welcome addition to any tripod because it helps you take pictures with consistent overlap (see Figure 4.3).

— Degree ring

Figure 4.3 Use a tripod for the best results.

Using the LivePreview Mode The best way to figure out the number of degrees you need to rotate the camera between each shot is to activate the LivePreview mode on your camera (turning on its LCD) or to look through the viewfinder. Compare the position of a fixed object in adjacent shots. See how many degrees you can turn the camera while leaving about 40 percent overlap between shots.

Keeping Focal Length Consistent It's critical not to change the focal length while you're shooting panoramic photos, or Photoshop won't be able to stitch the images together. If you are using a zoom lens with an adjustable focal length, I recommend resorting to one of the greatest of all human inventions: duct tape. That's right, duct tape the zoom ring to the camera body, so the focal length doesn't change during panorama capture.

Keeping the Camera Fixed in One Position Another rule is to keep the camera fixed in one position during panorama capture. If you are holding the camera, try to rotate the camera about an invisible axis running vertically through the camera body. If you're using a tripod, make sure it has a firm footing before shooting, and try to get the vertical shaft plumb so that the tripod head is level. I've made the mistake of leveling the head without considering whether the shaft is plumb. The first few shots were fine, but the camera wasn't level when the head was rotated more than 90 degrees.

Using a Bracket If you have a bracket that enables you to mount your camera in portrait orientation, consider shooting your panoramas this way (see Figure 4.4). You'll capture a tall swath and may not have to shoot multiple rings to create a spherical panorama. On the other hand, you'll have to take more photos going around the circle as compared with photos taken in landscape orientation.

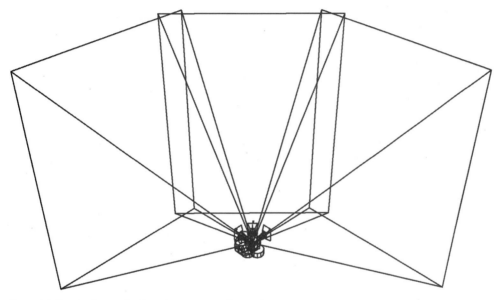

Figure 4.4 Shooting in portrait orientation captures a taller swath.

Avoiding Automatic Camera Settings Photoshop will have problems blending images in a panorama if you let your camera automatically determine exposure values. Therefore, it's essential to manually set white balance, aperture, ISO (light sensitivity) values, and shutter speed.

Choosing an Aperture Setting for the Size of the Iris When setting exposure manually, you'll have to choose an aperture setting for the size of the iris (see Figure 4.5). If you leave the iris wide open, you'll likely have problems with reduced depth of field. This can be used for dramatic effect in single photos so that only a narrow region is in sharp focus, but in panoramas you generally want everything to be in focus, so you might be tempted to go to the other extreme and tighten the aperture down all the way. However, the smallest aperture can introduce diffraction problems, causing everything to appear in soft focus. Therefore, I recommend selecting an aperture setting one or two stops from the smallest available on your lens. Note that the smallest aperture has the highest f-stop number.

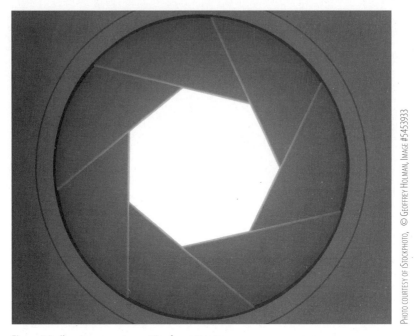

Figure 4.5 Choosing an aperture setting for a panorama

Using a High ISO Value Select a high ISO value because modern digital single lens reflex (DSLR) cameras typically have very low noise and can handle a high value. Those of us who remember film photography are usually blown away by the high ISO values available in modern cameras. The higher the ISO, the faster shutter speed you can use. All things being equal, it's preferable to use a faster shutter speed to minimize blur that can happen from vibration due to wind or cars driving past when working with a tripod, or due to camera shake when working handheld. These become even more of a problem when using a large focal length. Because of the potential for noise, I wouldn't select the maximum ISO available, but a setting high in the camera's range.

Selecting Shutter Speed Point the camera at the brightest region in your panorama (but not right at the sun, of course). Use this frame to select the shutter speed. You don't want the highlights to be blown out, and you can recover detail from blacks later in Photoshop if necessary. Given your chosen aperture and ISO settings, select the shutter speed that properly exposes the image.

Balancing Autofocus with Manual The final consideration is focus. If you leave Autofocus on, the camera might refuse to shoot in areas of low contrast such as the sky. If you turn Autofocus off, and manually set focus at infinity, you might not capture detail in closer objects, especially while zoomed in. A hybrid approach is to shoot the first ring along the horizon with Autofocus on, and shoot the second elevated ring (capturing mostly the sky) with manual focus set at infinity.

Merging Photos into Panoramas

In order to create a panoramic image from a series of stills, you must merge the individual shots into a composite whole. Photoshop's Photomerge feature loads all merged shots as a series of layers in one document, and then repositions and distorts the layers so they align. Since Photoshop CS3, Photomerge also automatically blends the seams between the layers by creating layer masks to more accurately blend between adjacent shots. Before you begin, however, it's important to understand the images you'll be using in this section and how they were created.

Shooting Photos for Your Panoramic Image

You can either shoot your own panorama photos or use the sample photos provided on the DVD. For the sample photos, I used a tripod with a degree ring and mounted the camera in landscape orientation. I determined by looking through the viewfinder that I needed to rotate the camera 60 degrees between shots while using a 24 mm lens. I shot a ring of six photos with the camera level and then tilted the camera up and shot another ring of six photos. After previewing the photos on the camera's LCD screen, I noticed that one of the treetops was cropped, so I took another photo (09higher.JPG) to capture the missing pixels, bringing the shot count to thirteen. Figure 4.6 shows the results.

Figure 4.6 A collection of shots that will be used to create a panorama

The photos were stored in raw format on the camera SD card. Although Photoshop can merge raw files, it would take an inordinate amount of time because of their massive size. If you were creating a panorama for print, you might want to merge raw files for the highest resolution, but our goals in this chapter's tutorials are to create interactive panoramas for the Web. With this goal in mind, I greatly reduced the amount of data that will be handed to Photomerge through the use of Image Processor.

In other words, I chose File > Scripts > Image Processor, selected the folder of raw images, selected Save As JPEG and Resize To Fit, typed **1200** for width and **800 for** height, and clicked Run (Figure 4.7). The samples provided on the DVD are these JPEGs.

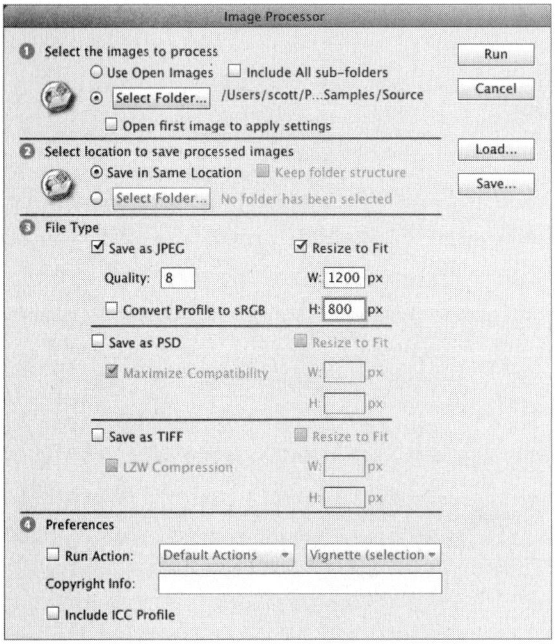

Figure 4.7 Use Image Processor to convert raw files to JPEG

Note: You can optionally access Image Processor from Adobe Bridge by choosing Tools > Photoshop > Image Processor.

Using Photomerge

Photomerge is the name of the feature in Photoshop that stitches individual shots together into (mostly) seamless panoramas. Photomerge can do quite a lot of processing on source photos to blend them into a panorama. It can reposition, rotate, remove lens distortion and vignetting, load files into a stack, create layer masks to blend layers together, map the resulting image onto the inside of a cylinder or sphere, or alternately try to keep lines of perspective straight.

You don't have to have Photomerge to perform all of the preceding tasks, however. For example, Figure 4.8 shows the result of the Collage option, which merely repositions and rotates the source images to align areas of similarity. Although this isn't very practical, it does show you that Photomerge is doing a lot more than aligning pixels when creating a typical panorama. We'll be creating two panoramas with the source files on the DVD: a cylindrical panorama using the photos from the first ring, and a spherical panorama using all 13 shots.

Figure 4.8 Photomerge Collage option

Note: Choose Auto layout if using a fish-eye lens, and Photomerge will correct for spherical distortion associated with such a lens. Choose Perspective layout only if you are doing a partial panorama centered on a building.

Cylindrical Panoramas

Cylindrical panoramas typically require fewer source images than spherical panoramas. Both geometries describe the inner surfaces of mathematical objects that images are mapped onto. Cylindrical panoramas enable the viewer to pan left and right as though they were turning a gigantic cylinder while standing in its center. Cylindrical panoramas are more appropriate in scenes that do not have a lot of detail in the vertical dimension, such as the distant view of a city's skyline. The following steps show how to create a cylindrical panorama:

1. Choose File > Automate > Photomerge.

2. Select Files from the Use drop-down, click the Browse button, and navigate to the Source folder on the DVD.

3. Select the photos you plan to merge. Hold down the Shift button and then click each image in the selection, up to six images. If using the images I've provided, select 01.JPG through 06.JPG.

4. Select the Blend Images Together and Geometric Distortion Correction check boxes (Figure 4.9). Vignette Removal is not needed here because the aperture was stopped down sufficiently to avoid noticeable vignetting (darkening around the outer edges of the image due to optical issues associated with a large iris).

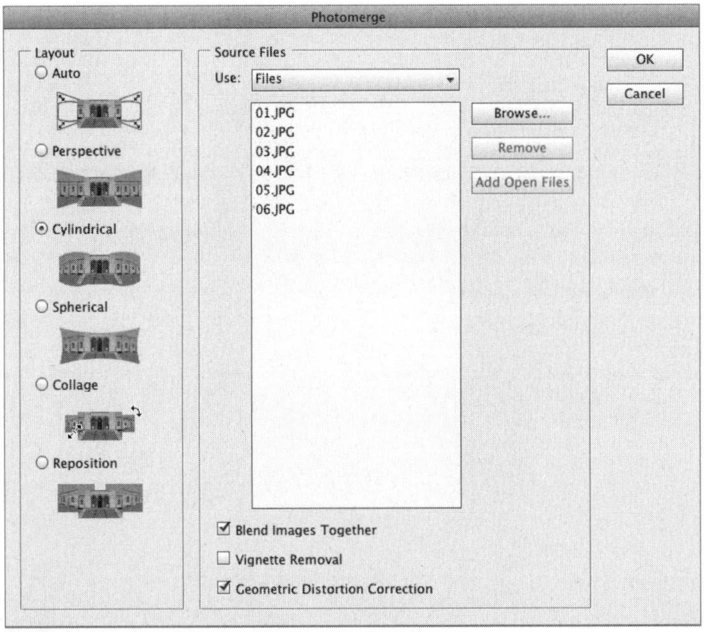

Figure 4.9 Photomerge dialog box

5. Under the Layout section of the dialog box, select Cylindrical and click OK. Photoshop will go to work creating the panorama, and you'll see images flicker on the screen for a minute or two. Figure 4.10 shows the result.

Note: You can paint directly on the layer masks that were automatically generated to customize the blend between images if you feel that Photoshop didn't get it right. Shift+click layer masks to toggle them off and on to see what they are doing.

Figure 4.10 Cylindrical panorama

6. Save the file as `Cylindrical Panorama.psd`.

Photoshop has done an excellent job blending the seams between individual images. However, this panorama still has some issues that require cleanup; we will get to them in due course.

Spherical Panoramas

The most immersive of all projection methods, spherical panoramas put the viewer in the center of a giant sphere with photographic imagery mapped onto its inner surface. Spherical panoramas allow up-and-down in addition to left-and-right rotation.

Spherical projection is most appropriate to exterior scenes that have tall objects nearby, such as the street-level view of an urban canyon filled with high-rise buildings, or the 200′ trees surrounding my house. Spherical panoramas are also appropriate in interior spaces where too much ceiling and floor would be cropped if using cylindrical projection. To create a spherical panorama, follow these steps:

1. Choose File > Automate > Photomerge.

2. Select Files from the Use drop-down, click the Browse button, and navigate to the Source folder on the DVD.

3. Select the images you plan to use. If using my images, select 01.JPG, hold down Shift, and click 12.JPG to select all 13 images.

4. Select the Blend Images Together and Geometric Distortion Correction options. Choose Spherical layout and click OK. Figure 4.11 shows the result.

Figure 4.11 Spherical panorama

5. Save the file as Spherical Panorama.psd.

Don't be alarmed at the way spherical projection looks in 2D. The wavy ground line seems unnatural but gets straightened out when the pixels are stretched to fill the inside surface of a sphere. There are holes at the top and bottom of the image where pixels were not captured. We will fill these holes in the next section.

Cleaning Up Panoramas

You'll notice that neither cylindrical nor spherical panoramas completely fill their document windows; there is a ragged transparent border around the pixels. The missing pixels typically occur at the zenith (straight up) and nadir (straight down). These transparent areas can either be cropped away or filled with pixels by using a variety of techniques. In the case of the spherical panorama, the hole in the sky must be filled or this flaw would unnecessarily distract from the immersive illusion we are trying to create. We'll start by retouching the zenith and nadir, and then blend the seams that still exist between the extreme left and right edges of the panoramas.

Zenith and Nadir Retouching

If you're using Photoshop CS5, the new content-aware features make zenith and nadir retouching much easier. If you're using an older version, there are still plenty of retouching tools to get the job done. The following steps show how to fill the holes at the top and bottom of the cylindrical panorama:

1. Open Cylindrical Panorama.psd from the work you did before or use the sample file from the DVD.

2. Choose Layer > Flatten Image, and transparent areas are filled with white.

3. Press Shift+W once or twice to select the Magic Wand tool. Set the options as shown in Figure 4.12, namely New Selection, zero Tolerance, Contiguous, and Sample All Layers. Click a white pixel along the ragged outer edge to select the whole region comprising both zenith and nadir areas.

![Magic Wand options toolbar: Tolerance: 0, Anti-alias unchecked, Contiguous checked, Sample All Layers checked, Refine Edge...]

Figure 4.12 Magic Wand options

4. Choose Edit > Fill and verify that Content-Aware is selected in the Use drop-down (Figure 4.13). Click OK, and after a short delay for processing, the trees and grass are filled in as if by magic.

Note: If you are using a version of Photoshop prior to CS5 or CS5 Extended, use the Clone Stamp tool to painstakingly brush similar pixels into white areas.

Figure 4.13 Content-aware fill

5. Press Cmd+D / Ctrl+D to deselect all pixels. Figure 4.14 shows the result. The upper and lower edges of the image look very good.

Figure 4.14 Zenith and nadir filled

6. Save the image as `Cylindrical Panorama.jpg` and select High as the quality level.

Making Seamless 360-Degree Panoramas

Photoshop generally does a good job of blending the seams between adjacent images. However, the seam between the extreme left and right edges is not blended at all. This becomes a problem if you want to add interactivity to a 360-degree panoramic image, because this final seam would be visible. Fortunately, there is a method to blend this last seam that I call the Switcheroo. However, before you get to that, you'll have to cut up the panorama in order to blend the last remaining seam and then retouch both zenith and nadir.

Cutting Your Cylindrical Panorama and Blending the Seam

To cut the image into two equal parts and then place them in independent layers, follow these steps:

1. Open `Cylindrical Panorama.jpg` from the work you did before or use the sample file from the DVD.

2. Press Cmd+A / Ctrl+A to select all pixels.

3. Choose Select > Transform Selection. Click the tiny middle-left anchor on the options bar to set the transform center along the left edge. Verify that width and height are unlinked (click the Link button if necessary), and then type **50.00%** for width and click the Commit button (Figure 4.15). Now you have the left half of the image precisely selected.

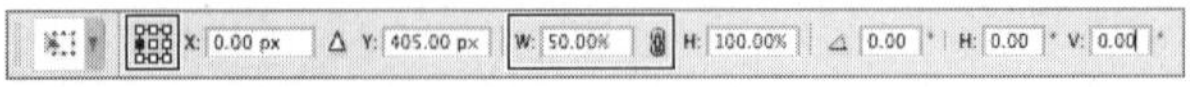

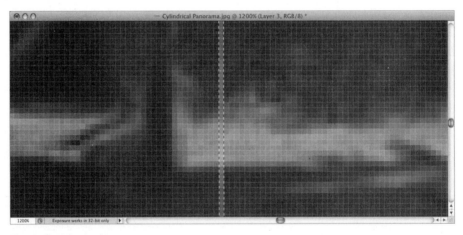

Figure 4.15 Setting selection transformation options

4. Choose Layer > New > Layer Via Copy. The selection disappears, and the left half of the image is pasted on Layer 1.

5. Cmd+click / Ctrl+click Layer 1's thumbnail to select all the pixels on this layer.

6. Press Shift+Cmd+I / Shift+Ctrl+I to invert the selection, thus selecting the right half of the image.

7. Target the Background layer and choose Layer > New > Layer Via Copy. The selection disappears, and the right half of the image is pasted on Layer 2.

8. Toggle the Background layer off and notice the thin seam that appears in the middle of the document window. Zoom way in until you can see the individual pixels of the seam (Figure 4.16).

9. Choose the Single Column Marquee tool. Click and drag in the document window until the column is perfectly aligned with the seam.

10. Toggle the Background layer on, target the Background layer, and press Cmd+J / Ctrl+J to copy the selection to a new layer, called Layer 3. Rename Layer 3 to **Seam 1.**

Figure 4.16 Selecting the seam

11. Cmd+click / Ctrl+click Seam 1's layer thumbnail to load its pixels as a selection.

12. Target Layer 2 and press the Delete key on the Mac or the Backspace key on a PC to remove the seam from this layer. Choose Select > Deselect.

13. While holding Cmd/Ctrl, click both Layer 1 and Seam 1 and then press Cmd+E / Ctrl+E to merge them.

14. Double-click the Background layer to convert it into a regular layer and click OK. Now you can get rid of it by dragging the Background layer into the Trash at the bottom of the Layers panel.

   You have successfully cut the image into two equal parts and placed them on independent layers. Now for the Switcheroo.

15. Press V to select the Move tool.

16. Hold down Shift and drag the Layer 2 image all the way to the left edge of the document window.

17. Target Layer 1, hold down Shift, and drag the image to the right edge of the document window. The layers will snap into position when you get close to the edge of the document window. Figure 4.17 shows the result.

Figure 4.17 Switching the left and right sides of the image

18. The seam between Layer 1 and Layer 2 is too noticeable. There is a fair bit of overlap but not close enough to 40 percent for Photoshop to align automatically. Zoom in and press V to move the layer closer to align it manually with Layer 2.

19. Turn the opacity of Layer 1 down to 50% so you can see partially through it.

20. Nudge Layer 1 to the left and up slightly by using the arrow keys when you get close. Use the light coming through the tree branches to help you align the layers. Restore the opacity of Layer 1 to 100%.

21. Shift+select Layer 1 and Layer 2 and choose Edit > Auto-Blend Layers.

22. Select Panorama and select Seamless Tones And Colors in the Auto-Blend Layers dialog box (Figure 4.18).

23. Click OK, and masks are added to both layers, making the blend between the layers much better.

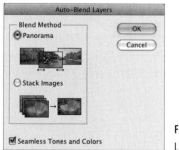

Figure 4.18 Auto-Blend Layers dialog box

24. Choose Image > Trim. Choose the Bottom Right Pixel Color radio button and click OK (Figure 4.19). The extra space left over after aligning the last seam is trimmed away.

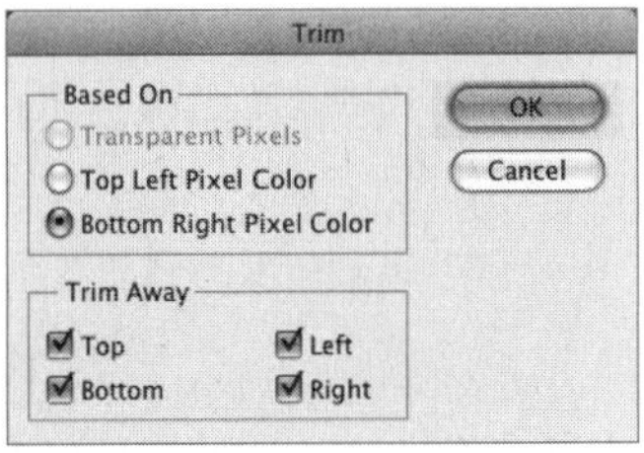

Figure 4.19 Trim dialog box

25. Choose Layer > Flatten Image. Press W to select the Magic Wand tool and then click within the thin strip of white that exists along the lower-right edge.

26. Press Shift+F5 and click OK to use the content-aware algorithm to fill in the missing pixels. Choose Select > Deselect.

27. Save as `Retouched Seamless Cylindrical Panorama.jpg` with High quality (see Figure 4.20).

Figure 4.20 Seamless cylindrical panorama

Cutting Your Spherical Panorama and Blending the Seam

The spherical panorama's final seam is blended in much the same way by dividing the image into two equal layers and then swapping their positions to expose the last seam. After we blend this seam, we'll retouch the missing zenith and nadir areas:

1. Open `Spherical Panorama.psd` from the work you did before or use the sample file from the DVD.

2. Press Cmd+E / Ctrl+E to merge all the layers (which by default are selected) into a single layer. Rename this layer **Base**.

3. Press Cmd+A / Ctrl+A to select all. Choose Select > Transform Selection. Click the tiny middle-left anchor on the options bar to set the transform center along the left edge, type **50.00%** for width, and click the Commit button.

4. Press Cmd+J / Ctrl+J to copy the selection to `Layer 1`.

5. Target the Base layer. Press Cmd+A / Ctrl+A to select all. Choose Select > Transform Selection. Click the tiny middle-right anchor on the options bar to set the transform center along the right edge, type 50% for width (Figure 4.21), and click the Commit button.

Figure 4.21 Transforming the selection by 50% in width

6. Press Cmd+J / Ctrl+J to copy the selection to Layer 2.

7. Toggle the Base layer off and notice the thin seam that appears in the middle of the document window. Zoom way in until you can see the individual pixels of the seam. Choose the Single Column Marquee tool. Click and drag in the document window until the column is perfectly aligned with the seam (Figure 4.22).

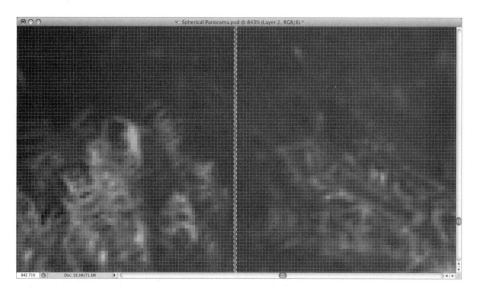

Figure 4.22 Selecting the single-pixel-wide seam

8. Toggle the Base layer on, target Base, and press Cmd+J / Ctrl+J to copy the selection to a new layer, called Layer 3. Rename Layer 3 to **Seam**. (There is no Seam 2, so Seam 1 should just be Seam).

9. While holding Cmd/Ctrl, click Seam's layer thumbnail to load its pixels as a selection. Target Layer 2 and press the Delete key on the Mac or the Backspace key on the PC to remove the seam from this layer. Choose Select > Deselect.

10. Drag the Base layer into the Trash at the bottom of the Layers panel.

You have again cut an image into two equal parts and placed them on independent layers—now for the Switcheroo.

11. Press V to select the Move tool. Shift+drag Layer 2 all the way to the left edge of the document window. Target Layer 1 and drag it to the right edge of the document window.

12. Use the left- and right-arrow keys to nudge Layer 1 pixel by pixel until it aligns with Layer 2 (Figure 4.23).

Figure 4.23 After the Switcheroo

13. Shift+click Layer 2 and choose Edit > Auto Blend Layers. Click OK in the Auto Blend Layers dialog box.

14. Choose Image > Trim, select the Transparent Pixels radio button, and click OK. The seam between Layer 1 and Layer 2 disappears.

15. Save the image as Seamless Spherical Panorama.jpg with High quality (Figure 4.24).

Next on the agenda is to retouch the hole in the sky that is visible at the zenith of the spherical panorama and to clone in more grass at the nadir.

16. Choose Layer > Flatten Image, press W to select the Magic Wand, and click a white pixel inside the hole in the sky.

Figure 4.24 Seamless spherical panorama needing zenith and nadir retouching

17. Press Shift+F5 and click OK in the Fill dialog box. The hole is filled with blue sky that matches the color and luminance values fairly well. Choose Select > Deselect.

18. Click in the large white area, hold down Shift, and click in the smaller noncontiguous adjacent white area to select the entire nadir of the spherical panorama. Press Shift+F5 and click OK to use the content-aware algorithm to fill in the missing pixels. This time the result is flawed, almost comically so (Figure 4.25). The content-aware algorithm fails when the area to fill is too large.

Figure 4.25 Flawed content-aware fill in too large an area

19. Choose Select > Deselect, press S to select the Clone Stamp tool, and press the square bracket keys to adjust the brush size if necessary.

20. Hold down the Option/Alt key and click a point within the grass that you'd like to clone.

21. Release the key and then paint to stamp these pixels in a new location. Continue reselecting new clone points as you paint to keep sampling areas of grass. Fill in the entire nadir with grass by using the Clone Stamp tool (see Figure 4.26).

Figure 4.26 Retouched seamless spherical panorama

22. Save the image as `Retouched Seamless Spherical Panorama.jpg` and select High as the quality level.

3D Painting

If you're using Photoshop CS4 Extended or CS5 Extended, you can preview the way the spherical panorama will look mapped to the inside of a sphere. In addition, you can optionally perform zenith and nadir retouching directly on the sphere with 3D painting tools. In the following steps, you'll map the spherical panorama inside a sphere and paint on it in 3D:

1. Open `Seamless Spherical Panorama.jpg` from the work you did before or use the sample file from the DVD.

2. Choose 3D > New Shape From Layer > Spherical Panorama. After waiting a while for processing, you'll see a zoomed-in detail of one part of the panorama. Notice in the Layers panel that you now have a vector 3D layer with a nested texture map containing the raster panorama image.

3. You can resize vector layers without loss of image quality. Choose Image > Image Size. Select the Resample Image option, deselect Constrain Proportions, and type **800** for Width and **600** for Height (Figure 4.27). Click OK. Double-click the Zoom tool to quickly switch to 100% magnification.

4. Press N to select the 3D camera toolset. Choose the Zoom The Camera tool and drag upward in the document window to zoom out. Keep doing this until the Standard Field Of View is close to 11 mm on the options bar (Figure 4.28).

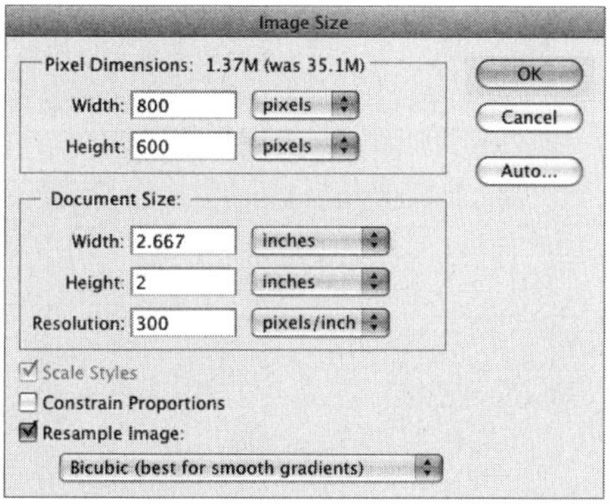

Figure 4.27 Adjusting the image size after 3D layer creation

Figure 4.28 3D Camera toolset

5. Using a combination of the Orbit and Roll The 3D Camera tools (on the options bar), reorient the camera so you are looking at the house. As you do this, you'll get a sense of how the 3D panorama works interactively within Photoshop.

6. Navigate to the zenith and retouch the hole in the sky by using the Spot Healing Brush or Clone Stamp tool. Navigate to the nadir and clone stamp in the grass. The nice thing about painting in 3D is that what you see is what you get. The downside is that painting is slowed by the overhead of translating the 3D mapping coordinates to pixel locations in the 2D texture map.

> **Note:** You can employ 2D retouching techniques on a texture mapped onto a 3D object by double-clicking the nested map in the Layers panel, and thus opening it in a separate document window.

7. Save the image as 3D Panorama.psd.

Adding Interactivity to Panoramas

This section offers several methods for adding interactivity to panoramas so that viewers of your imagery can gain a better understanding of the space in love which your design exists. In the previous section, you mapped a spherical panorama onto the inside of a 3D sphere and saw how you could rotate it in real time. In this section, you'll record this interaction in a video. Then you'll export the panorama to Zoomify, which gives a degree of user interaction, although it is not a true panorama technology. In addition, you'll create truly interactive panoramas by using Java, QuickTime VR, and Flash.

Animating and Rendering 3D Panoramic Videos

By using the animation capabilities in Photoshop CS4 Extended or CS5 Extended, you can export a video that shows the virtual camera panning and zooming within the 3D sphere. Although this method isn't really interactive (because the video follows a predetermined flight path), it gives viewers a spatial sense through camera motion. It's also notable because we are creating video without using a video camera. These steps show how to export a video from a 3D panorama:

1. Open 3D Panorama.psd from the work you did before or use the sample file from the DVD.

2. Choose Window > Animation.

3. Expand the Background layer track by clicking its disclosure triangle.

4. Click the time-vary stopwatch in the 3D Camera Position track to create an initial keyframe at time zero.

5. Drag the Current Time Indicator (CTI) to the extreme-right edge of the timeline (Figure 4.29).

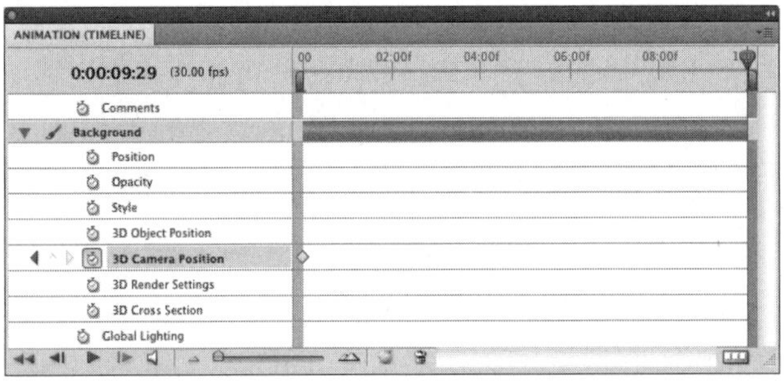

Figure 4.29 Creating the initial keyframe in the Animation panel

6. Press N to select the 3D Camera tools. Using a combination of the Orbit and Roll tools (on the options bar), reorient the camera so you are looking at a different part of the panorama. Try to keep the horizon line level. Pressing the spacebar toggles playback onscreen.

> **Note:** Adding intermediate keyframes helps control camera roll and orientation. To add a keyframe, simply move the CTI and then transform the camera by using the 3D toolset.

7. Choose File > Export > Render To Video. Specify an output path and codec options, and click Export.

8. Play your rendered video or open the 3D Panorama.mov sample file provided on the DVD (Figure 4.30).

Figure 4.30 3D Panorama movie

9. Save the file as `Animated 3D Panorama.psd`.

Exporting to Zoomify

Zoomify is an interesting technology that slices a large image into many smaller tiles and then reassembles the tiles in an interactive web control that loads tiles as needed. Zoomify is similar to Google Maps in how it works, and best of all there is a Zoomify exporter within Photoshop that you can use without "royalties, usage fees, traffic tracking requirements, or other strings."

> **Note:** Zoomify offers several commercial versions of its product with additional functionality at its website, www.Zoomify.com.

To use Zoomify, follow these steps:

1. Open `Retouched Seamless Cylindrical Panorama.jpg` from the work you did before or use the sample file from the DVD.

2. Choose File > Export > Zoomify.

3. In the Zoomify Export dialog box, select Zoomify Viewer (Black Background) from the Template drop-down. Choose an output folder on your hard drive by clicking the Folder button. Type **Cylindrical-Panorama** as the base name, set Quality to High, and set Width and Height to 640 and 480 repectively.

4. Select the Open In Web Browser check box and click OK (Figure 4.31).

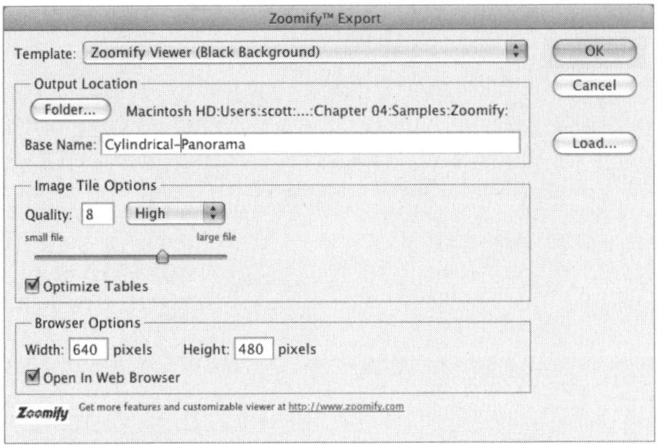

Figure 4.31 Zoomify Export options

5. Use the navigation controls at the bottom of the Zoomify control to navigate the panoramic image. As you navigate, observe how the tiles appear blurry at first and then get sharper (Figure 4.32).

Figure 4.32 Using the Zoomify control in a browser

Creating Java Panoramas with PTViewer

PTViewer is a free Java applet (available at www.fsoft.it/panorama/ptviewer.htm) that displays panoramic images. Java was released in 1995 and developed by Sun Microsystems (now a subsidiary of Oracle Corporation). Java applets will run in any web browser that has a Java Virtual Machine (JVM) installed. According to a June 2010 survey (which you can see at www.adobe.com/products/player_census/flashplayer/), Java reaches 76 percent of Internet viewers.

To run the Java applet, you must first have a JVM. (You can get one at www.java.com). Then three files placed in the same folder are all that's required to display the interactive panorama: the panorama image, the HTML file, and the Java archive file containing the applet code. You can play the applet locally or remotely on the Web. The following steps show how to create a Java panorama with PTViewer:

1. Open Retouched Seamless Cylindrical Panorama.jpg from the work you did before or use the sample file from the DVD.

2. Choose Image > Image Size. Select the Constrain Proportions check box and select Bicubic Sharper (Best For Reduction) as the resizing algorithm. Type **480** as the Height and click OK (Figure 4.33).

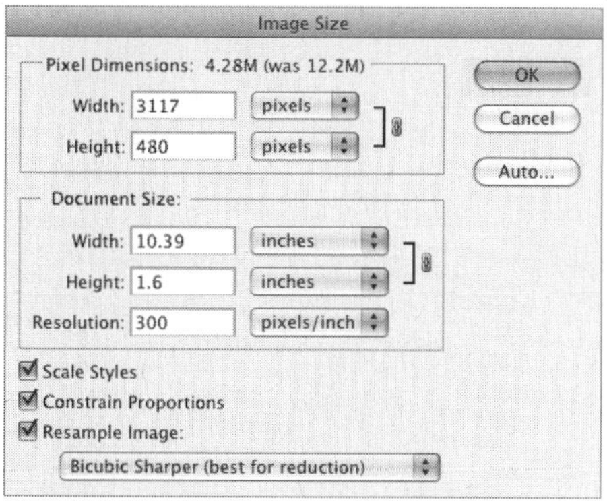

Figure 4.33 Downsampling a large panorama

3. Copy the PTViewer folder from the DVD to your hard drive. Choose File > Save As, navigate to the PTViewer folder, and use the abbreviation RSCP.jpg rather than the full description *Retouched Seamless Cylindrical Panorama*, because spaces in the filename will not work on a web server.

4. Open java-pano.html in a simple text editor that does not apply formatting, such as Notepad on the PC or TextWrangler on the Mac. Edit the file value from panorama.jpg to RSCP.jpg and save java-pano.html (Figure 4.34).

```
<html>
<head>
<meta http-equiv="Content-Type" content="text/html">
<meta http-equiv="Content-Language" content="en-us">
<title>Java Panorama</title>
<style type="text/css">
<!--
body {
    background-color: #666666;
}
-->
</style></head>
<body>
<div align="center">
    <br />
    <applet code="ptviewer.class" archive="ptviewer.jar" width=800 height=400>
        <param name="file" value="RSCP.jpg">
        <param name="cursor" value="MOVE">
        <param name="pan" value=30>
        <param name="showToolbar" value="false">
        <param name="imgLoadFeedback" value="true">
        <param name="auto" value=0.1>
        <param name="autoTime" value=100>
    </applet>
</div>
</body>
</html>
```

Figure 4.34 Editing HTML code that controls the Java applet

5. Double-click `java-pano.html` to load the page locally in your default web browser (Figure 4.35). Watch as the panorama starts to automatically rotate, with speed and initial location set by other parameters in the HTML file. Drag in the panorama to pan left and right. There is a limited ability to pan up and down, controlled by the relationship between the aspect ratio set for the applet (currently 800×400) and the aspect ratio of the panorama (3117×480).

Figure 4.35 The Java panorama in a browser

Generating QuickTime VR and Flash Panoramas with Pano2VR

There are several third-party solutions for generating QuickTime VR and Flash interactive panoramas. My favorite is Pano2VR by Garden Gnome Software (available at `http://gardengnomesoftware.com/pano2vr.php`), which works on Mac, PC, and Linux and generates both QuickTime VR and Flash interactive panoramas. You can use a free trial version to follow along with this tutorial. I'm using the Mac version here, but the other versions are similar.

According to the same June 2010 survey noted earlier, QuickTime reaches 58 percent of Internet viewers, and Flash reaches 99 percent. The figures are a little misleading because QuickTime reaches 100 percent of Mac users, and there are serious security issues surrounding Flash. You should consult your webmaster to select the appropriate web technology to deploy panoramas.

The following steps show how to generate QuickTime VR and Flash panoramas with Pano2VR:

1. Launch Pano2VR and click the Select Input button. In the Input dialog box (Figure 4.36), select Equirectangular as the type and click the Open button for the panorama. Locate and select `Retouched Seamless Spherical Panorama.jpg` either from your own work or the DVD. Click OK to close the Input dialog box.

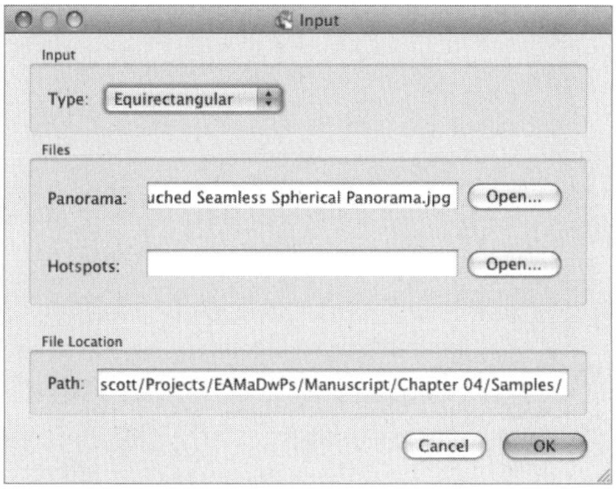

Figure 4.36 Input option in Pano2VR

2. In the main Pano2VR interface, select Transformation from the New Output Format drop-down and click the adjacent Add button.

3. In the Transformation/Thumbnail Output dialog box that appears, select Equirectangular from the Type drop-down and deselect the Use Default View check box in the Preview area.

4. Drag the Tilt and Roll sliders until the horizon flattens out in the preview image. I used 42.2 for Tilt and −33.7 for Roll (Figure 4.37). Type **5235** as the Width value (the original size of the input), select PNG as the output format, and click OK. Choose Yes when prompted whether you want to create the output file now.

5. Click the Select Input button again. In the Input dialog box, select Equirectangular as the type and click the Open button for the panorama. Locate and select the file you just transformed: `Retouched Seamless Spherical Panorama_out.png`. Click OK to close the Input dialog box.

6. Click the Modify button in the Viewing Parameters area of the main dialog box to open Panorama Viewing Parameters dialog box. Set the FoV (field of view) to 50 degrees. Drag the preview in the Panorama Viewing Parameters dialog box toward the house to set the initial view (see Figure 4.38). Click OK and then Yes.

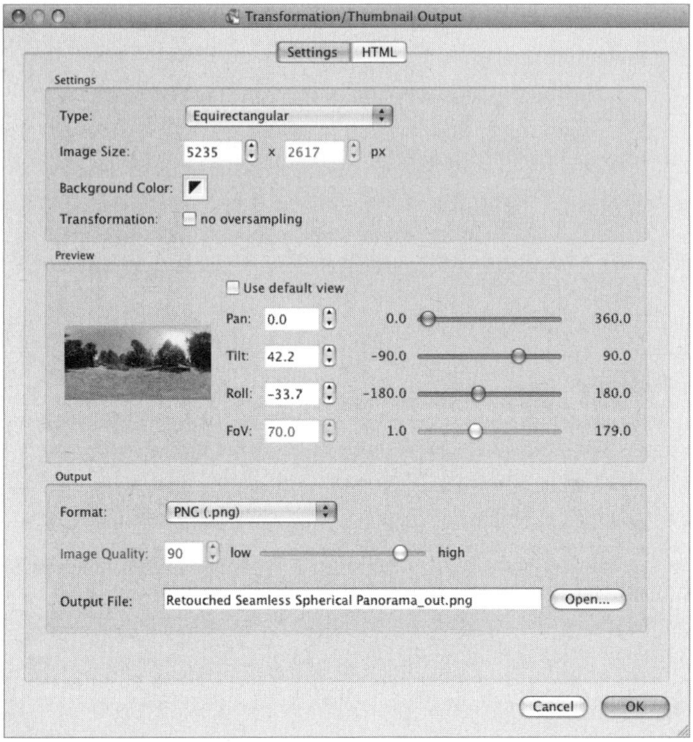

Figure 4.37 Transformation options

Figure 4.38 Panorama Viewing Parameters

7. Click the red minus button for the Transformation output to remove it from the queue. Select QuickTime from the New Output Format drop-down and click the Add button (Figure 4.39).

Figure 4.39 The Pano2VR main interface

8. In the QuickTimeVR Output dialog box, set Cube Face Size to 1600 (above-optimal values are sharper), select Enable Auto Rotation, and set QTVR/Panorama.mov as the output filename and relative path (Figure 4.40).

9. Click the HTML tab at the top of the dialog box. Select the Enable HTML File check box and select normal.ggt from the Template drop-down. Use QTVR/Panorama.html as the output file (Figure 4.41). Click OK and Yes.

10. Double-click the Panorama.html file to view the embedded QuickTime VR panorama.

11. Flash panoramas are exported in the same way as QuickTime VR panoramas. I'll leave it up to you to export a Flash panorama of this project on your own. Double-click Panorama.html inside the Flash folder on the DVD to view the final result (Figure 4.42).

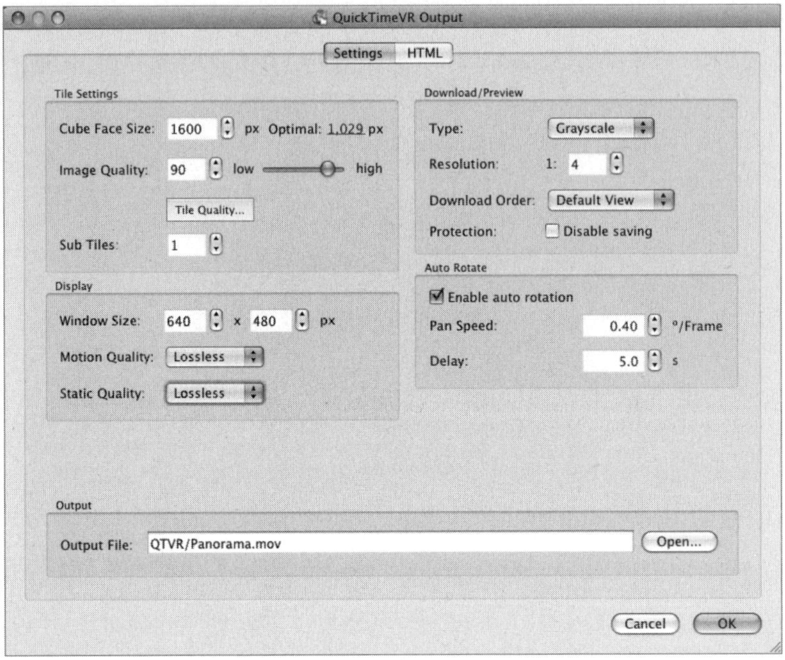

Figure 4.40 QuickTime VR settings

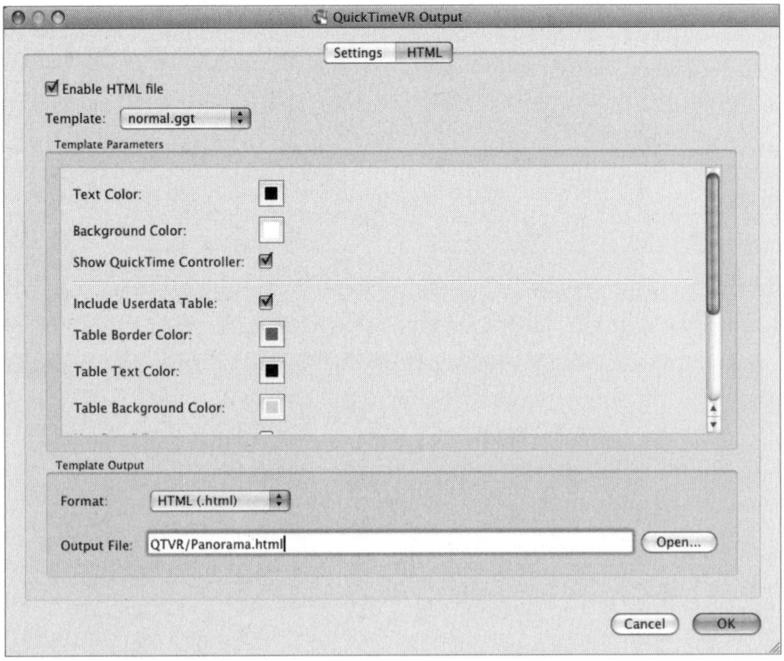

Figure 4.41 HTML settings

Figure 4.42 Flash panorama with skin (controls at bottom of screen)

In this chapter, you've learned everything you need to know to create interactive panoramas. From all the considerations required to shoot panoramic images, to merging photos into panoramas, to cleaning up and retouching zenith and nadir areas, to a wide variety of ways for adding interactivity, you have new skills to showcase your projects in compelling ways.

Exploring Multiple-Exposure Tricks

Why shoot multiple exposures of the same subject? There are many tricks available when you shoot a series of images taken from the same vantage point. Such tricks include eliminating moving objects such as pedestrians and cars, reducing noise, creating artistic effects, rendering time-lapse video, and expanding dynamic range. None of these so-called tricks are possible in traditional photography because the results must be computed in Photoshop.

Loading and Manipulating Stacks of Images

In Photoshop, an *image stack* is a collection of images arranged as layers within a single document. An image stack can be composed of layers alone, or the layers can be placed within a smart-object container. There is a script, which has been part of Photoshop since CS3, called Load Files Into Stack that automates this process of creating image stacks from files. You can find this under File > Scripts > Load Files Into Stack.

 Note: Image stacks in Photoshop have different functionality than stacks in Bridge. What makes this especially confusing is you can load files into a Photoshop image stack from Bridge by selecting a number of images and choosing Tools > Photoshop > Load Files Into Photoshop Layers.

It's important that you shoot photos from the same location when planning to load them into an image stack in Photoshop. If you shoot photos in different locations, there is really no reason to load them into a stack unless you're making a slideshow. You can either hold the camera or use a tripod when shooting images destined to be in a stack. If you hold the camera, Photoshop can apply its Auto-Align algorithm to match the photos, because variation will always occur as you breathe (and therefore move the camera) between shots. To prepare an image stack, follow these steps:

1. Launch Photoshop and choose File > Scripts > Load Files Into Stack. Choose Folder from the Use drop-down menu and navigate to the Images folder on the DVD.

2. After the filenames appear in the list, select both Attempt To Automatically Align Source Images (because the sample images were created from a handheld camera) and Create Smart Object After Loading Layers (Figure 5.1). Click OK, and Photoshop goes to work opening and loading images as multiple layers in a single document window.

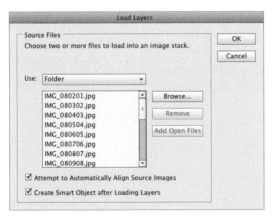

Figure 5.1 Loading files into a stack

3. The last image in the file list appears as the smart-object layer name. Rename this layer Image Stack. Notice that the thumbnail has an icon indicating this layer is a smart object (Figure 5.2).

Figure 5.2
Smart-object layer

4. Observe that the document window has a ragged border surrounding the images in the stack—you can just make out the corners of different images surrounded by transparency. The ragged border is the result of the Auto-Align algorithm repositioning images so they line up. Press C to select the Crop tool and Caps Lock to use the precise cursor. Drag out a window inside all the ragged edges (Figure 5.3). Click the Commit button on the options bar to crop. Toggle Caps Lock back off.

Figure 5.3 Cropping the image stack

5. The shadows appear to be too dark. Choose Image > Adjustments > Shadows/ Highlights. Select the Show More Options check box and then in the Shadows area drag the Amount slider to 68%, Tonal Width to 15%, and Radius to 15 px. Click OK to close the Shadows/Highlights dialog box (Figure 5.4).

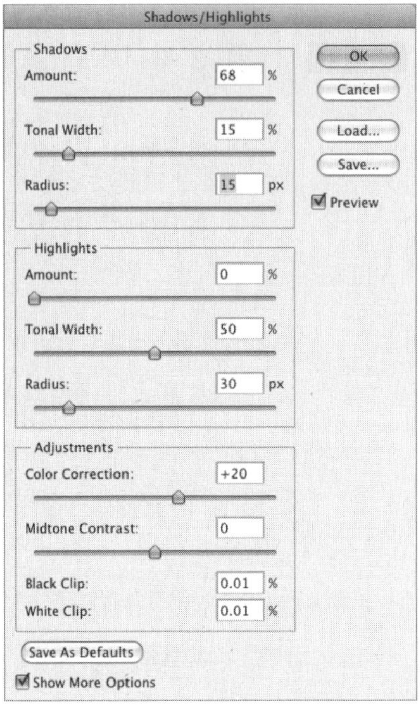

Figure 5.4 Shadows/Highlights adjustment

6. Choose Filter > Sharpen > Smart Sharpen. Set the Amount at 60%, set the Radius at 1.0 px, and choose Lens Blur from the Remove drop-down (Figure 5.5). Click OK to apply the sharpening.

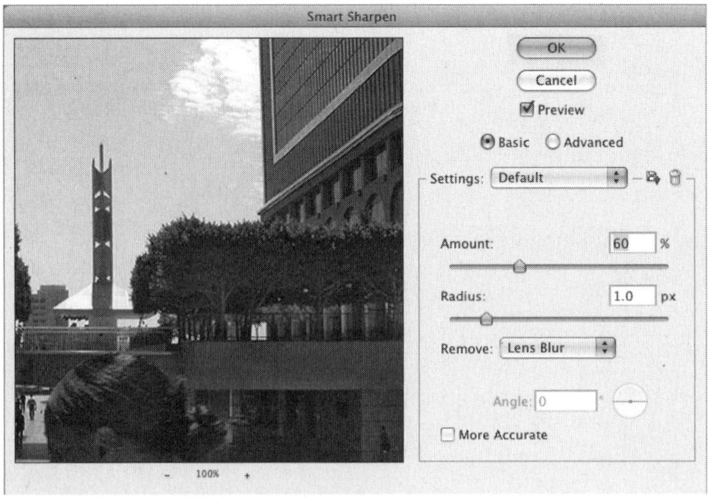

Figure 5.5 Smart sharpening the smart object

7. The Shadows/Highlights adjustment and Smart Sharpen filter remain editable because they were applied to the smart object. These changes are nondestructive, leaving you the creative freedom to change your mind and make alterations at some future point without degrading the image quality. Double-click each of the "filters" nested below the phrase *Smart Filters* that appears in the Layers panel (Figure 5.6). Make any adjustments you deem necessary, and click OK to close each respective dialog box.

Figure 5.6 Smart filters and adjustments remain editable into the future.

8. Save the image stack as Smart object image stack.psd.

Altering Images with Stack Modes

Photoshop has a collection of algorithms for analyzing image stacks and returning widely varying results. These go by the unassuming name *stack modes* and are nested three levels deep in the Layer menu. Because they're difficult to find, you might never discover them if you didn't learn about them here. Stack modes take a long time to appear after being chosen because they must process all the pixels in the image stack. Here's how to use them:

1. Open Smart object image stack.psd from the work you did before or use the sample file from the DVD.

2. Choose Layer > Smart Objects > Stack Mode > Median (Figure 5.7). As the cascade of menus suggests, stack modes can be assigned only to smart objects.

After a short wait, Photoshop displays the result of Median stack mode. As you can see, all the people are gone (see Figure 5.8). Median returns pixels that appear more than half the time in the image stack, so moving objects are effectively eliminated. Median will work on moving cars or walking pedestrians equally well, but it will not remove parked cars or seated persons.

Median also automatically removes noise, because noise is actually random variation that typically appears in darker areas. Variation is what is eliminated when taking the median pixel values into account. Therefore, Median stack mode is an excellent tool for getting "clean" architectural shots even in busy public spaces.

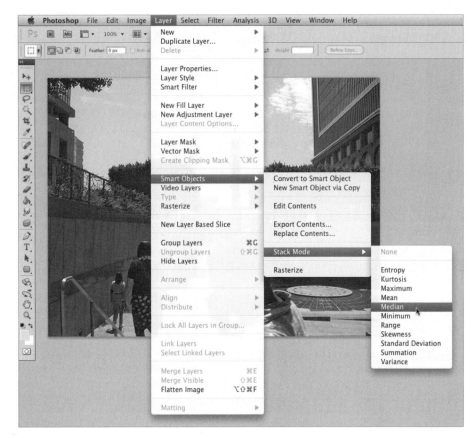

Figure 5.7 Assigning stack modes

Figure 5.8 Median stack mode eliminates moving objects.

3. Try each one of the stack modes in turn to see its effects. Maximum creates specular ghosts of moving objects such as people or cars—great for flow studies. Many of the other stack modes (see Figure 5.9) produce interesting artistic effects.

Maximum

Mean

Minimum

Range

Skewness

Standard Deviation

Figure 5.9 A variety of effects produced by stack modes

4. Save the image stack as `Median stack mode.psd`.

Stack modes are nondestructive effects. You can turn off stack mode processing at any time by choosing Layer > Smart Objects > Stack Mode > None.

Cloning within Image Stacks

Since Photoshop CS3, there has been a Clone Source panel that enables you to store up to five sources for Clone Stamp operations. It's a little-known fact that a clone source can be located inside a smart object. Putting this knowledge together, you can target one particular image within a smart-object layer stack and use it to paint details back in to the stack mode result.

Imagine that you've eliminated all moving objects from an image by using Median stack mode, so all the people are gone. What if you now want one or two people back in the picture? It's possible to pull them back by using image-stack cloning. Here's how to do it:

1. Open Median stack mode.psd from the work you did before or use the sample file from the DVD.

2. Double-click the smart-object layer thumbnail. The nested PSB document opens in its own document window.

3. Turn off layers one by one, starting at the top. Look for a layer that contains figures you'd like to clone back into the space. Turn off the first six layers, leaving IMG_080807.jpg and all the other layers below it on (Figure 5.10). Target layer IMG_080807.jpg. This layer has many figures.

Figure 5.10 Turning off layers inside the smart object to reveal figures you want to clone

Note: You can toggle multiple layers on or off by clicking one of the layer's eye icons in the Layers panel and then dragging upward or downward in the panel. This is much faster than turning layers on or off individually.

4. Press S to select the Clone Stamp tool. Choose Window > Clone Source and observe that there are five buttons across the top of the Clone Source panel; each of these can hold a separate clone source.

5. Hold down the Option/Alt key and click on one of the figures standing on the landing in the foreground. As you do this, notice that the name of the PSB document and the layer you targeted are listed in the Clone Source panel (see Figure 5.11).

Figure 5.11 The Clone Source panel showing the layer inside the PSB file targeted as a clone source

6. Choose Window > Median stack mode.psd to bring the original document window to the front.

7. Press Cmd+Shift+N / Ctrl+Shift+N to create a new layer. Type **Stamped** in the New Layer dialog box and click OK.

8. Select Show Overlay in the Clone Source panel so you can see the figure at your brush tip. Proceed to paint the two figures back onto the landing, as shown in Figure 5.12.

Figure 5.12 Painting back in two figures

9.   Press Cmd+W / Ctrl+W to close the PSB file; click Don't Save when prompted.

10.   Save the main document as Image stack cloned.psd.

Rendering Time-Lapse Video from Stills

You can use any Extended version of Photoshop (CS3 or later) to create a time-lapse video from a series of still images shot in the same location. A tripod is required for all time-lapse photography because it's imperative that the camera not move during the entire shooting period.

You'll also need a couple of pieces of specialty hardware for quality time-lapse photography, including an intervalometer and a neutral-density filter. As its name suggests, an intervalometer lets you set the interval between shots from a second to several hours.

A neutral-density filter (ND filter) is like a pair of sunglasses for your camera. It's called *neutral* because the filter is gray and does not shift color as it reduces the intensity of all wavelengths of light equally. So why would you need to limit the amount of light reaching the sensor?

The best time-lapse videos show motion as a blur. Think of car taillights streaking along a road. When moving objects are shot in sharp focus, they seem to appear and disappear in staccato fashion when the time-lapse video is played back.

In photography, the way to create motion blur is to use long exposure times (which equate to slow shutter speeds). At night you might get away without using an ND filter because the low levels of illumination allow light to accumulate on the sensor without overexposure. However, during daylight you'll need an ND filter because keeping the shutter open for a long time to create motion blur would overexpose the image.

By using an ND filter, you reduce the amount of light reaching the sensor and can therefore afford to have a longer exposure. I recommend setting exposure control to manual in your camera and selecting a small aperture—but not the smallest available on your lens—to avoid diffraction issues and problems with soft focus. Then mount an ND filter and select a slow shutter speed such as 1 second so you'll be sure to have motion blur.

Note: Set white balance to manual and use manual focus as well for the best time-lapse results.

The following steps show you how to render a time-lapse video from stills:

1.   Choose File > Browse in Bridge.

2.   Navigate to the Time lapse folder on the DVD. Observe the 157 images in the folder showing people hurriedly moving around a busy train station

(Figure 5.13). Each frame shows blurry people moving because of slow shutter speeds and thus long exposure times.

Figure 5.13 Thumbnails in Bridge

3. Switch back to Photoshop and choose File > Open. In the Open dialog box, select Frame001.jpg in the Time lapse folder, select the Image Sequence check box, and click Open (Figure 5.14). As long as the files are named sequentially, Photoshop will convert the entire sequence to a video layer.

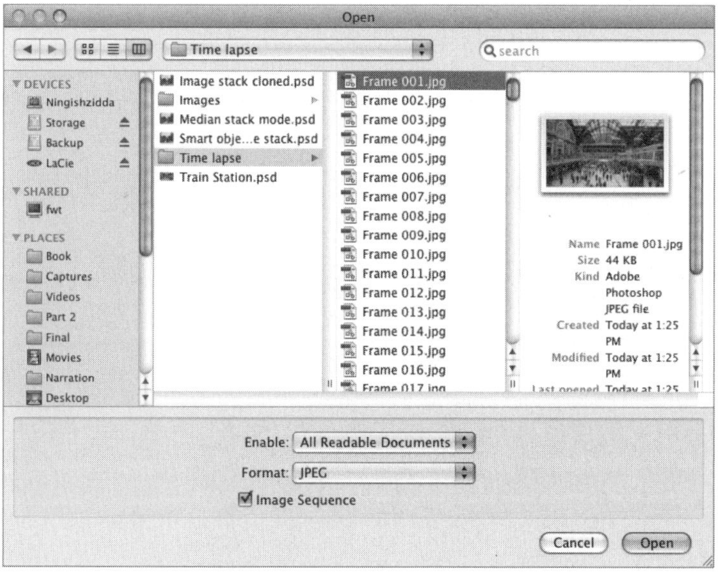

Figure 5.14 Opening an image sequence

4. Choose 30 frames per second (fps) in the Frame Rate dialog box that appears (Figure 5.15). You could double the duration of the video by selecting 15 fps as a custom frame rate. Rates below 15 fps look jerky because they fall below the flicker fusion threshold of the persistence of vision that makes movies seem continuous.

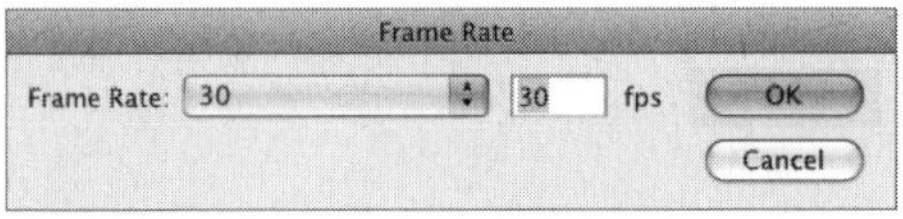

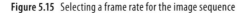

Figure 5.15 Selecting a frame rate for the image sequence

5. Choose Window > Animation and click the Play button along the lower edge of the panel. Voilà; instant time-lapse video!

 Note: Playback in RAM can be jerky, no matter what frame rate you choose. When you export to video, playback will be smoother.

6. Choose File > Export > Render Video, and select a folder on your hard drive to save the video file. Type **Time lapse** in the Name field (Figure 5.16). Choose your preferred export options and click Render. I chose QuickTime Movie (click the Settings button and select the H.264 codec for reasonable quality with small file size).

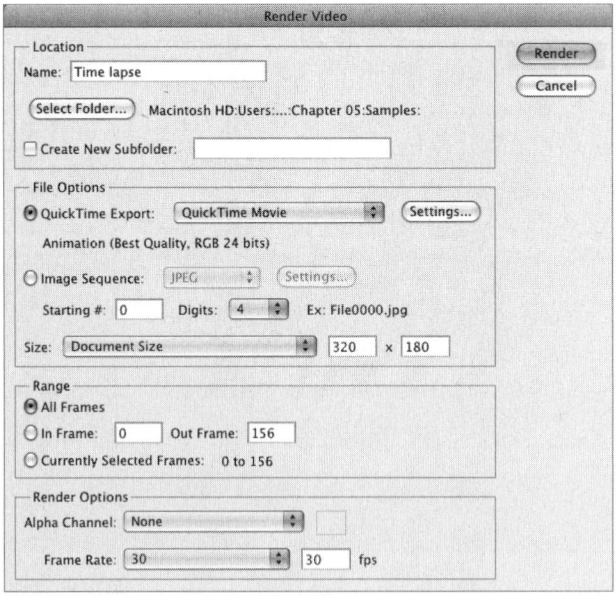

Figure 5.16 Render video options

7. Double-click Time lapse.mov on your hard drive or the DVD. Click the Play arrow and enjoy your first time-lapse video (Figure 5.17).

Figure 5.17 Time-lapse video in the QuickTime player

Processing Video with Stack Modes

Just as you learned earlier in this chapter how to eliminate moving objects, reduce noise, and create artistic effects by using stack modes and a series of still images as input, you can do the same thing with short video clips. The secret of this trick is to convert the frames of the video layer into a series of separate layers. Once you have multiple layers, you can place them within a smart object and apply stack modes to the container. Here's an example of how to do this:

1. Open Video.mov from the DVD (Figure 5.18).

Figure 5.18 A short video clip opened in Photoshop

2. Choose Window > Animation if the Animation panel is not already open. Open the Animation panel menu (upper right) and choose Flatten Frames Into Layers (Figure 5.19).

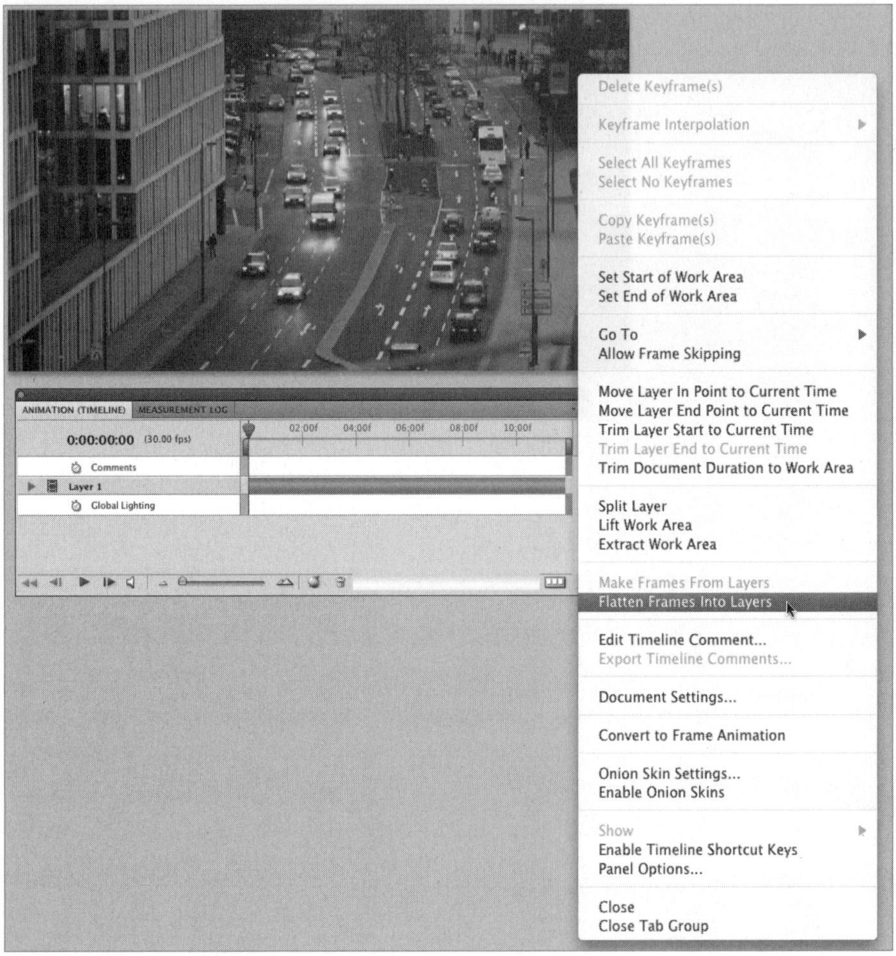

Figure 5.19 Converting video frames to layers

3.   You don't need the video layer any longer. To get rid of it, just drag Layer 1 into
the Trash at the bottom of the Layers panel (Figure 5.20).

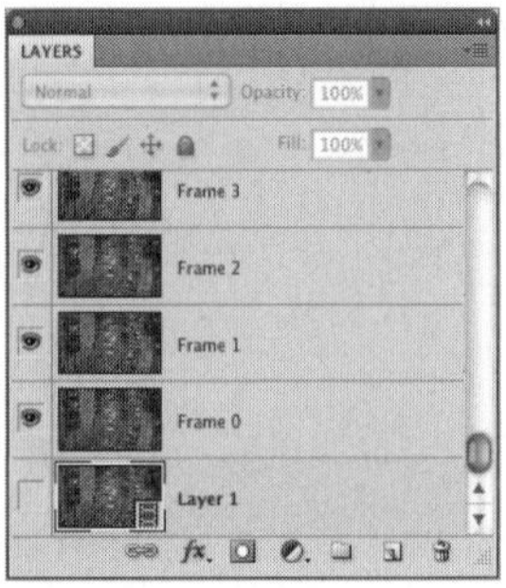

Figure 5.20 Trash the video layer
after you've harvested its frames.

4. With layer Frame 0 selected, scroll to the top of the layers list and while holding down Shift, click layer Frame 354. All the layers are now selected.

5. Right-click and choose Convert To Smart Object. Rename the one remaining layer Smart Object. Choose Layer > Smart Objects > Stack Mode > Range. The car lights streak across the road, producing an attractive artistic effect (Figure 5.21). Median stack mode would remove all the moving cars.

Figure 5.21 Range stack mode produces an artistic effect on video frames converted into a smart object.

6. To avoid stack mode processing each time you open this file, create a stamped version of the effect. To do this, press Cmd+Shift+N / Ctrl+Shift+N to create a new layer, type **Range** in the New Layer dialog box, and click OK.

7. Press Cmd+Shift+Option+E / Ctrl+Shift+Alt+E to stamp all visible layers into layer Range.

8. Target layer Smart Object and choose Layer > Smart Objects > Stack Mode > None.

9. Save the image stack as Video processed by stack mode.psd.

Using Poor Man's HDR

The last multiple-exposure trick you'll learn in this chapter is a method to increase dynamic range that works in any version of Photoshop—well, at least since layers were introduced in Photoshop 3. This trick doesn't create a true 32-bit high dynamic range (HDR) image; instead it expands dynamic range through creative 8-bit masking.

Dynamic range refers to the difference in light intensity between the darkest blacks and whitest whites in an image. Individual photos are able to record a small dynamic range as compared to what the human eye is capable of perceiving. Bright sunlight is on the order of a billion times brighter than faint starlight, and we can perceive them both with our eyes. On a bright day, photographers need to bracket multiple exposures in order to capture detail in bright and dark areas. In this section, you'll learn how to put them together and create a composite image that shows detail in bright and dark areas.

You can bracket shots by using any camera that offers manual shutter speed control. Some point-and-shoots, pro-sumer (professional consumer), and pro cameras offer manual control. It is preferable to bracket by varying shutter speed rather than by varying aperture to avoid problems with depth of field, vignetting, and soft focus that can come with changing iris size. This technique requires exactly two bracketed images taken from the same vantage point, as shown here:

1. Open both `Highlight-detail.jpg` and `Shadow-detail.jpg` from the `Poor Man's HDR` folder on the DVD (Figure 5.22).

Figure 5.22 Two exposures bracketed by shutter speed

  Note: Do not try to "develop" the bracketed images in Adobe Camera Raw; neither image contains detail in both highlights and shadows.

2. Choose Window > Arrange > Float All In Windows (document windows, not the operating system).

3. Target the document window of `Highlight-detail.jpg`. Drag its layer thumbnail into the `Shadow-detail.jpg` document window. The `Shadow-detail.jpg` document now contains two layers.

4. Close the `Highlight-detail.jpg` document window without saving. "Choose Window > Arrange > Float All In Windows. Target the document window of `Highlight-detail.jpg`. Drag the layer thumbnail into `Shadow-detail.jpg`. The `Shadow-detail.jpg` image now contains two layers. Close the `Highlight-detail.jpg` document without saving.

5. Rename `Layer 1` to **Dark**. Double-click the `Background` layer to convert it into a regular layer, type **Light** in the New Layer dialog box, and click OK. Figure 5.23 shows the Layers panel.

Figure 5.23 Bracketed shots assembled in one document as layers

Note: If you hold the camera when bracketing shots, select both layers and choose Edit > Auto-Align Layers. The images in this tutorial were shot using a tripod, so this step is unnecessary.

6. Target the `Dark` layer and click the Add Layer Mask button along the lower edge of the Layers panel.

7. Target the `Light` layer, select all by pressing Cmd+A / Ctrl+A, and copy the light image to the Clipboard by pressing Cmd+C / Ctrl+C.

8. Option+click / Alt+click the `Dark` layer mask thumbnail. The document window goes completely white, showing you the content of the mask, which is currently empty.

9. Press Cmd+V / Ctrl+V to paste the contents of the Clipboard to the mask; Photoshop automatically converts the `Light` color image into a grayscale mask on the `Dark` layer (see Figure 5.24). Areas that are darker in the mask hide the `Dark` layer and thereby reveal the `Light` layer underneath. Press Cmd+D / Ctrl+D to deselect all.

10. To see what this mask is doing, Option+click / Alt+click the `Dark` layer mask thumbnail. The result isn't perfect, but it is a good start; you can see detail in the interior and detail outside the windows, but the color is off (Figure 5.25).

Figure 5.24 The Light layer pasted as a mask on the Dark layer

Figure 5.25 Result of the initial mask

11. The mask is way too sharp. Option+click / Alt+click the mask again and choose Filter > Blur > Gaussian Blur. Give the mask an extreme blur so you lose all detail. A radius of about 10 pixels should do it (Figure 5.26). Click OK.

Figure 5.26 Blurring the mask to improve the blend

12. Option+click / Alt+click the mask thumbnail again to show the result, which should look much better now.

13. We can improve the mask even more with Levels. Verify that the Dark layer mask is still targeted in the Layers panel and press Cmd+L / Ctrl+L. The amount that you drag the sliders depends on the images you're working with. You can see what's happening to the image as you adjust the mask in real time, so drag the Levels dialog box out of the way if necessary. Experiment with the sliders in the Levels dialog box and then drag the Shadow input slider to 50 and the Midtone slider to 0.66 (Figure 5.27). Click OK to close the Levels dialog box.

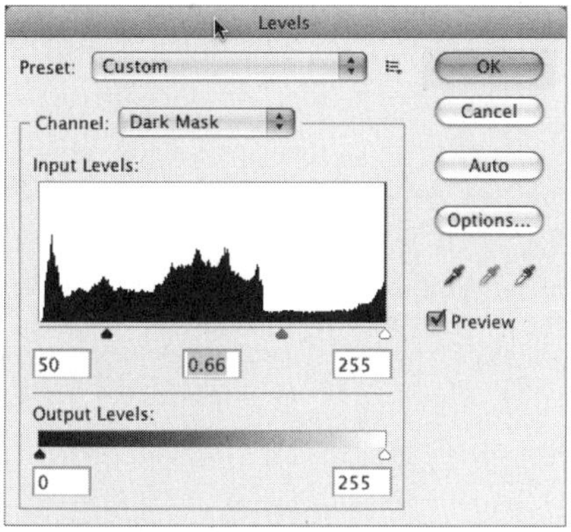

Figure 5.27 Adjusting levels on the mask

14. Through creative masking, we have successfully merged the highlights from the Dark layer into the shadow detail present in the Light layer. The resulting image (Figure 5.28) has an increased dynamic range compared to the original bracketed images—and now we can see into the interior and out the windows at the same time. Choose File > Save As and type **Poor Mans HDR.psd** as the filename. This file is provided on the DVD for comparison with your own work.

Figure 5.28 Final Poor Man's HDR image

In this chapter, you have learned many tricks for working with multiple exposures, from loading and manipulating stacks of images to processing image stacks, cloning image stacks, rendering time-lapse video from stills, processing video with stack modes, and my poor man's HDR technique. So the next time you go out shooting, consider taking multiple exposures of each subject to take advantage of some of the amazing techniques in this chapter.

Creating Texture Maps

Texture maps are raster images that are stretched to fit bounded areas within drawings or the geometrical surfaces of models to make them appear more realistic. Without texture maps, models appear flat and lifeless. In Chapter 2, "Enhancing Drawings in Photoshop," you learned a bit about texture maps by converting preexisting textures into patterns and using them to enhance a floorplan drawing. You will now explore how to create texture maps so you can then learn the tricks for adjusting how they are assigned to 3D models in Photoshop in Chapter 7, "Compositing Imagery from 3D Applications."

Chapter Contents

Creating textures from scratch

Making seamless textures from photos

Harvesting textures from photos

Extracting entourage from photos

Creating Textures from Scratch

As mentioned in this chapter's introduction, texture maps help bring models to life, as shown in Figure 6.1. A few of Photoshop's filters can create the textures needed to do this without requiring photographic input because they are generated procedurally (for example, Noise, Clouds, and Difference Clouds). On the other hand, most filters require pixel variation to start with, or they don't return anything interesting. You can get both types of filters to play together by connecting the output of a noise-generating filter to the input of another filter. Following a noise-generating filter with a sequence of smart filters can create a wide range of visual effects.

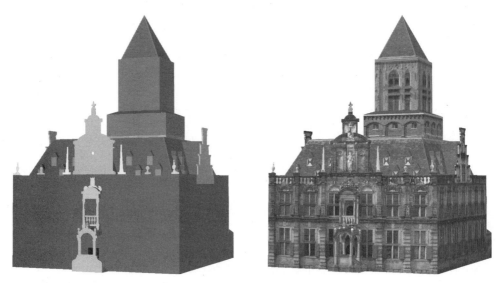

Figure 6.1 3D model without texture maps (left) and with texture maps (right)

Each filter has parameters that control how its mathematical algorithms interact with pixels to produce visual effects. Considering the fact that you can apply dozens of filters in any sequence you choose, there is an unlimited number of textures you can create from scratch.

I owe the idea for the technique of creating textures from scratch to a fellow columnist at *Photoshop User* magazine, Deke McClelland. Anyone can apply filters haphazardly, but it takes smarts to apply them in a way that offers flexibility and room for experimentation. Let's see how this is done:

1. Choose File > New. In the New dialog box, type **Texture Generator** as the Name, and type 800 pixels for both Width and Height. Select a Resolution of **72** pixels/inch, and select RGB 8-bit color. Choose Transparent from the Background Contents drop-down and click OK (Figure 6.2).

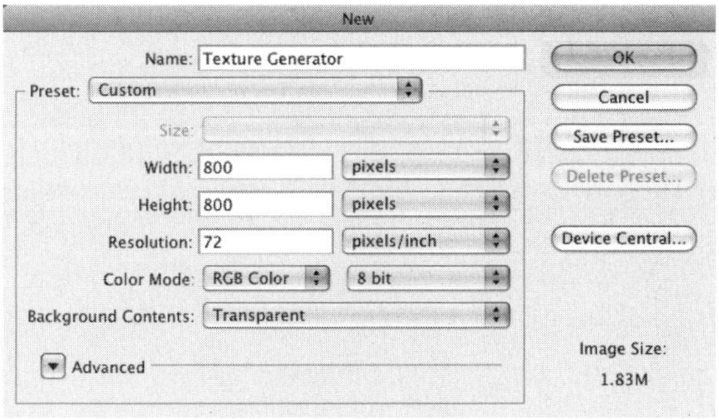

Figure 6.2 Creating a blank document from scratch

2. Choose Edit > Fill or press Shift+F5. In the Fill dialog box, select 50% Gray from the Use drop-down and click OK. The document window is filled with medium gray in preparation for the application of Noise.

3. Rename Layer 1 to Base. Right-click just to the right of the layer name and choose Convert To Smart Object from the contextual menu. Smart objects allow you to apply filters nondestructively so you can edit the results (or toggle them on or off) anytime without damaging image quality.

4. Choose Filter > Noise > Add Noise. Drag the Amount slider to 50%, choose Gaussian distribution, select Monochromatic, and click OK (Figure 6.3).

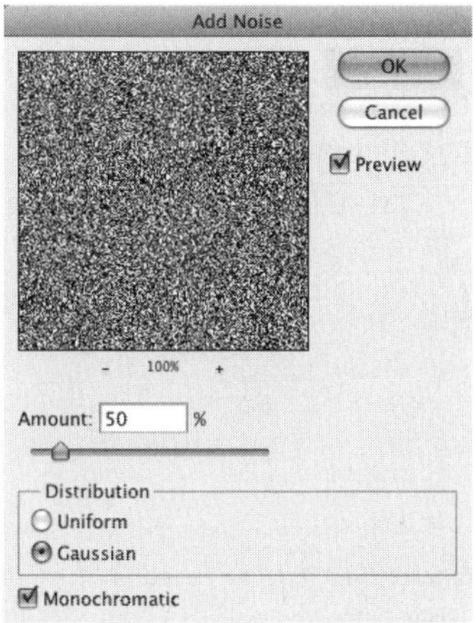

Figure 6.3 Adding noise

5. Choose Filter > Blur > Gaussian Blur. Drag the Radius slider to 2 pixels and click OK (Figure 6.4).

CREATING TEXTURES FROM SCRATCH

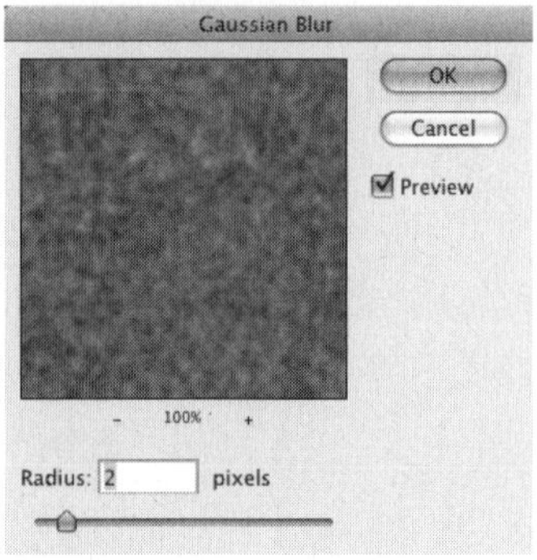

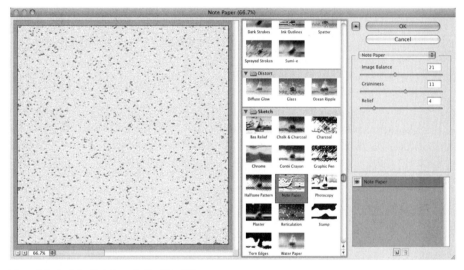

Figure 6.4 Applying Gaussian Blur

6. Choose Filter > Filter Gallery. Expand the various categories and click different filters to preview the results. Click Note Paper in the Sketch category and set Image Balance to 21, Graininess to 11, and Relief to 4. Click OK (Figure 6.5).

Figure 6.5 Applying Note Paper in the Filter Gallery

7. The image has a nice texture but is in grayscale. Choose Layer > New Adjustment Layer > Hue/Saturation. In the Adjustments panel, select Colorize and drag the Hue slider to 53, drag Saturation to 33, and leave Lightness at 0. Figure 6.6 shows the resulting stucco-like texture, which you've synthesized entirely from scratch.

Figure 6.6 Stucco-like texture created from scratch

8. Minor adjustments are all that's needed to produce entirely different textures. To do this, target the Base layer and choose Filter > Render > Clouds. In the Layers panel, drag Clouds immediately above Add Noise. Toggle Add Noise off by clicking its eye icon. The Clouds filter generates fractal noise and can form the basis of many textures.

9. Double-click Filter Gallery to reopen the large dialog box. Open the Distort category and click Diffuse Glow. Set Graininess to 6, Glow Amount to 10, and Clear Amount to 15.

10. The Filter Gallery interface is designed for quick experimentation. The filters are evaluated in order from bottom to top, just as layers are evaluated in the Layers panel. You can drag and drop filters within the filter list to change their order. Click the New button at the bottom of the filter list and then click the

Glass filter. Set Distortion to 5 and Smoothness to 3, and select Blocks from the Texture drop-down. Drag Scaling all the way to the right for a value of 200% (Figure 6.7). Click OK.

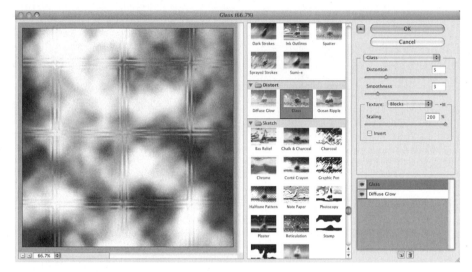

Figure 6.7 Stacking filters in the Filter Gallery

11. To reduce clutter, right-click the Smart Filter mask thumbnail in the Layers panel and choose Delete Mask. Drag the Hue/Saturation layer mask to the Trash icon at the bottom of the Layers panel. I like to delete masks I'm not using, for clarity, but this isn't strictly necessary. Figure 6.8 shows the cleaned-up Layers panel.

Figure 6.8 Cleaning up unused masks in the Layers panel

12. Target the Hue/Saturation 1 layer and drag the Hue slider to 234 for blue. Figure 6.9 shows the final glass-block texture.

Figure 6.9 Glass-block texture generated procedurally

13. Save the texture as `TextureGenerator.psd`.

The number of textures you can create from scratch is limited only by your imagination. Experiment on your own with Emboss, Bas Relief, Angled Strokes, and Rough Pastels in the Filter Gallery to create water, carpet, plaster, and painted surface textures.

Making Seamless Textures from Photos

Textures are often *tiled* (repeated) across 3D surfaces they are mapped to. Images are typically tiled at a small scale to avoid problems with pixelation—where you see individual pixels.

Tiling presents its own set of challenges. Tiled texture maps that retain the look of continuous surfaces must blend together so that their edges appear seamless, or at least nearly so. Otherwise, textures will look literally like ceramic tiles with obvious repetitive features highlighting each discrete tile.

To avoid this, there are a couple of tools for highlighting texture map edges so you can retouch them:

- The Offset filter

- The Tiled Painting feature available in the Extended version of Photoshop

We'll use them both in this tutorial.

In the preceding section, you learned how to generate textures from scratch by manipulating various filters and adjustments. You can also use a digital camera to capture textures you see in your daily life. For example, I was roasting sesame seeds on the stove the other day and realized the seeds formed a nice texture, so I snapped a picture with my point-and-shoot. We'll use that picture as the basis of this tutorial because it highlights many of the typical problems that arise when attempting to make textures seamless. The following steps show how to make a photo a seamless texture:

1. Open Sesame.jpg (Figure 6.10) from the DVD.

Figure 6.10 Sesame seeds roasting in a pan form an interesting texture.

2. Press C for the Crop tool and drag out a rough crop window over the sesame seeds. Select Perspective on the options bar. Then drag each one of the corner handles to more or less match the perspective in the photo (see Figure 6.11). Click the Commit check mark button on the options bar to complete the operation. The resulting texture looks like it was captured straight down, facing the seeds in the pan.

Figure 6.11 Cropping sesame seeds in perspective

3. Choose 3D > New Tiled Painting. The sesame texture is mapped onto a plane and tiled three times in each direction, forming a grid of nine tiles (Figure 6.12).

Figure 6.12 The tiled painting reveals seams needing retouching.

> **Note:** If you are using the standard version of Photoshop, utilize the Offset filter to slide the image over 50 percent in both width and height, rather than using the Tiled Painting 3D feature. The seams you must retouch form a plus symbol in the center of the image.

4. Double-click the Background texture under the word *Diffuse* in the Layers panel (Figure 6.13) to open the texture in a separate document window, which is titled `Layer 0.psb`.

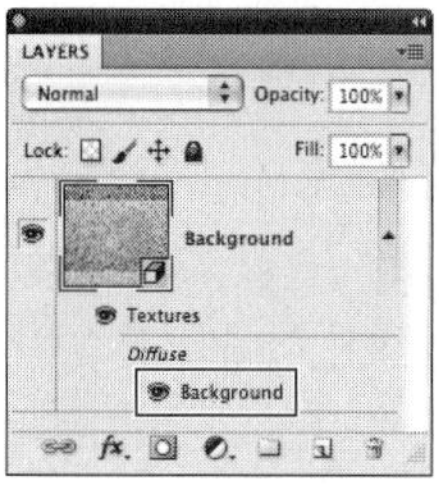

Figure 6.13 Opening a texture map

5. Click the Exposure button in the Adjustments panel. Drag the Exposure slider to –0.75 to darken the image (Figure 6.14).

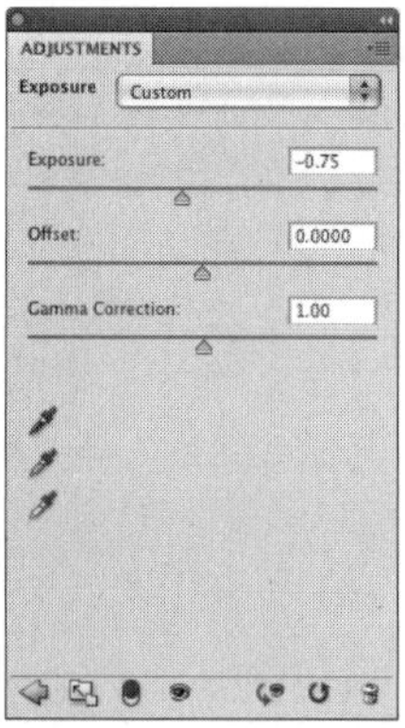

Figure 6.14 Adding an exposure adjustment layer to darken the texture map

6. We don't want the whole texture to be darkened, however. To avoid this, press D, X, and G to set the default colors, exchange foreground and background, and select the Gradient tool. Select Foreground To Transparent from the Gradient drop-down on the options bar. Hold down Shift and drag from the bottom of the document window to the top. The Exposure layer mask is filled with a gradient (Figure 6.15) that fades out the exposure adjustment toward the bottom.

Figure 6.15 Gradient mask

7. Press Cmd+W / Ctrl+W and then Return/Enter to close and save Layer 0.psb. The tiled painting looks much more seamless because the lighting is uniform across the texture. However, there is still more retouching to be done along the edges.

8. Double-click the Background texture under the word *Diffuse* in the Layers panel to reopen the texture map. Choose Layer > Flatten Image to apply the exposure adjustment to the pixels permanently.

9. Choose Image > Image Size and make a note of the width and height dimensions in pixels. The actual size depends on exactly how you cropped the original photo; my image measures 635×565, and yours will be close to these figures. Choose Filter > Other > Offset. Drag the sliders to half the image size, which is 317 horizontally and 282 vertically in this case (see Figure 6.16). Set Undefined Areas to Wrap Around and click OK. The seams we need to retouch now are located in the center of the texture.

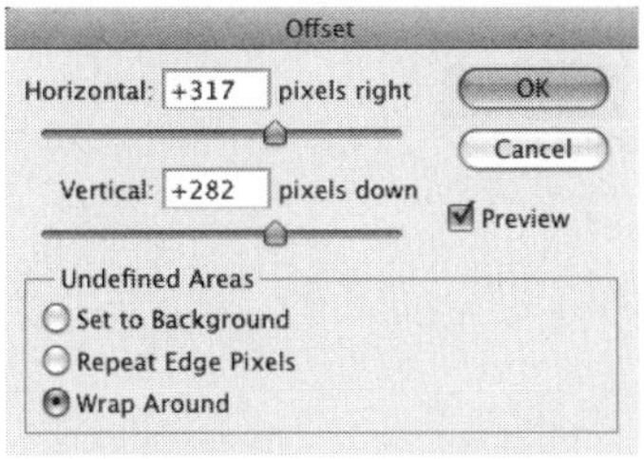

Figure 6.16 Using the Offset filter to bring seams into the center

10. Press J to select the Spot Healing Brush and click the Content Aware radio button on the options bar. Hold down Shift and drag out a horizontal stroke in the center of the image (see Figure 6.17). Follow this with a vertical stroke, again in the center. Both seams are blended.

11. Press Cmd+F / Ctrl+F to repeat the last filter (Offset). The seams are returned to the edges of the texture. Press Cmd +W / Ctrl+W and then Return/Enter to close and save Layer 0.psb. The tiled painting looks as close to seamless as we can get it (Figure 6.18).

Figure 6.17 Using the Spot Healing Brush to blend the seam

Figure 6.18 Seams minimized in the tiled painting

12. Double-click the Background texture under the word *Diffuse* in the Layers panel to reopen the texture map one last time. Save the texture map as SeamlessSesame.jpg.

Harvesting Nontiling Textures from Photos

If you see an object in a photo that you want to reuse as a nonrepeating texture in a 3D model, you can use Photoshop to "harvest" an orthorectified (uniformly scaled) version of the object. Photoshop can correct for distortions inherent in most camera lenses, and you can take it one step further and correct for the diminishment of scale due to perspective. Let's harvest the left framed photo hanging in the hotel room photo included on the DVD for this book.

1. Open Hotel-Room.jpg from the DVD (see Figure 6.19).

Figure 6.19 Hotel room image

2. Choose Filter > Lens Correction. In Photoshop CS5, the Lens Correction filter has a new Auto Correction tab that reads metadata attached to the file and applies corrections appropriate to the specific camera, lens, and aperture used. Go to step 3 if you are using an older version of Photoshop. Check all the options on the Auto Correction tab and press P to toggle the preview on and off so you can see what this filter is doing (see Figure 6.20). Auto Correction removes geometric distortion introduced by the camera lens, but we need to go further to harvest the framed photo on the left.

3. Click the Custom tab to access the parameters that were the only options before CS5. These parameters enable you to correct (or distort) images manually (see Figure 6.21). Drag Vertical Perspective to +20 and Horizontal Perspective to +100 and click OK.

Figure 6.20 Lens Correction's Auto Correction tab

Figure 6.21 Transforming the photo manually with Lens Correction

4. Press P to select the Pen tool. Click each one of the corners of the left photo's frame and then click the corner where you started, clicking to close the path. Press Shift+A for the Direct Selection tool. Select and nudge (by pressing the arrow keys) any of the corners that need slight adjustments.

5. Open the Paths panel and click the Load Path As Selection button along its lower edge. Rename this layer Framed Photo and toggle off Layer 0.

6. Press Cmd+T / Ctrl+T to activate Free Transform mode. Right-click over the framed photo and choose Distort from the contextual menu (see Figure 6.22). Drag the corners of the framed photo to edges on the transparency grid so that each corner forms a 90-degree angle. Press Return/Enter to complete the transformation.

Figure 6.22 Distorting the photo to square out the picture frame

7. Choose Image > Trim, choose the Transparent Pixels radio button, and click OK (see Figure 6.23).

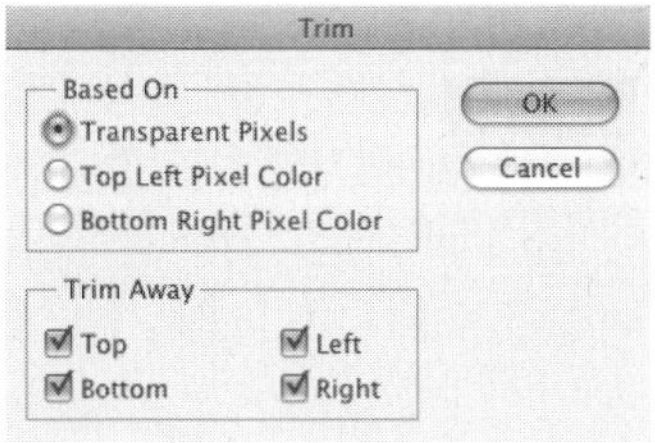

Figure 6.23 Trimming away transparency

8. If any of the transparent background is still visible, choose Select > All. Nudge the marquee by using the arrow keys to crop out transparency and choose Image > Crop. Repeat this procedure if you need to crop another edge with pixel-accurate control.

9. You have now successfully harvested the framed photo from the hotel room so that it could be used as a texture map in a 3D model (see Figure 6.24). Save the image as Framed-Photo.jpg.

Figure 6.24 The framed photo harvested from the hotel room

Extracting Entourage from Photos

The term *entourage* in the context of architectural rendering refers to people, cars, and plants added to illustrations to impart a sense of context and scale. There are many sources of commercially made entourage that a quick Google search will uncover. However, if you own Photoshop and a camera, it's not too difficult to create your own library of entourage appropriate to your locale and industry.

Note: Be aware that if you create entourage with recognizable human faces, it behooves you to procure signed liability release forms.

In this tutorial, you will extract a businesswoman from a photo by using Quick Select, Refine Edge, and mask painting so you can use her in a later photo. Let's give it a try:

1. Open Businesswoman.jpg from the DVD (see Figure 6.25).

PHOTO COURTESY OF ISTOCKPHOTO, © LAJOS REPASI, IMAGE #7144898

Figure 6.25 Businesswoman source photo

2. Press W to activate the Quick Select tool. Select Auto-Enhance on the options bar and use the square bracket keys to adjust the brush size to 6 pixels. Drag over the businesswoman to create a rough selection.

3. Hold the Option/Alt key and drag over any areas that extend beyond her body, to remove them from the selection. It is better to initially exclude areas of partial transparency such as the outer portion of her hair, as shown in Figure 6.26.

4. Click the Refine Edge button on the options bar. You can view the selection against a variety of backgrounds listed in the View drop-down. Press F to cycle through the views and then press B for black (Figure 6.27).

Figure 6.26 Creating a rough selection with the Quick Select tool

5. Click the Zoom tool along the left edge of the Refine Edge dialog box and drag to the right in the document window to zoom in enough so that you see the actual pixels. Hold down the spacebar and drag to pan so that you center her face in the document window.

6. Press E to select the Refine Radius tool within Refine Edge mode. Use the square bracket keys to adjust the brush size and then paint over the areas in her hair where you expect some transparency to appear (the outer edges). Photoshop will perform extra processing in the areas you paint (see Figure 6.28).

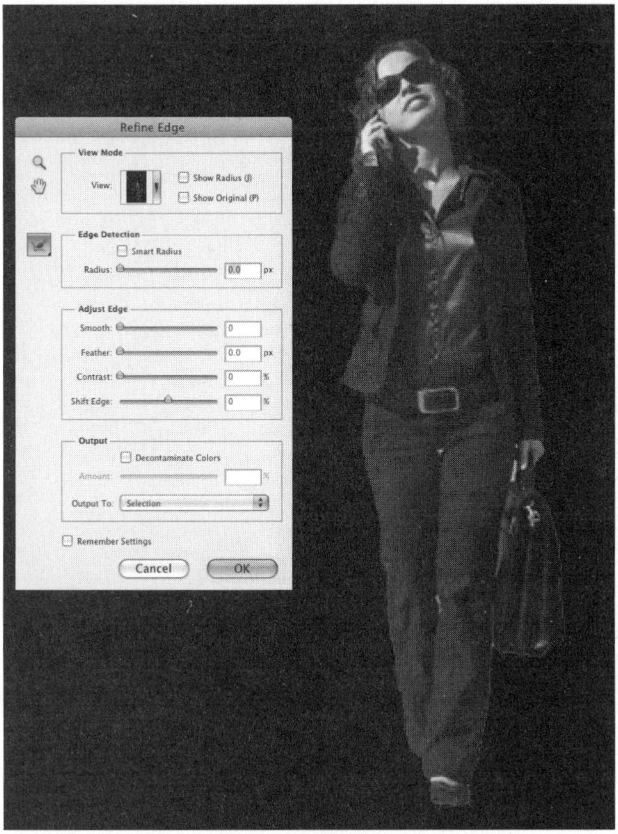

Figure 6.27 Cycling views in the Refine Edge dialog box

Figure 6.28 Refining the radius with Refine Edge tools

7. Press J to see what you've painted (see Figure 6.29) and press J again to toggle Show Radius off. Press Shift+E to select the Erase Refinements tool and paint over any areas where you went too far in the previous step (areas where more than her hair is showing). However, you can't erase parts of the selection that weren't *refinements* to the initial selection.

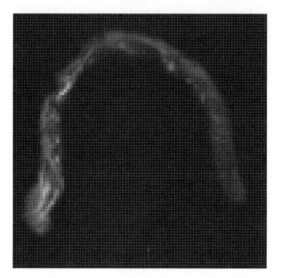

Figure 6.29 Viewing what was painted with the Refine Radius tool

8. Select Decontaminate Colors in the Output area and drag the Amount slider to 100%, as this will eliminate the white fringes around her arms and legs. Select New Layer With Layer Mask from the Output To drop-down and click OK. Rename the new layer Businesswoman.

9. Target the Businesswoman layer mask thumbnail and press B to select the Paintbrush tool. Press D to select the default colors. Paint over any areas you'd like to unmask, such as any curls of hair that were hidden by Refine Edge. Press X to exchange the foreground and background colors, and then paint to remove any areas where you've gone too far. Zoom in and use a small brush size to make any last-minute adjustments.

10. Right-click the Businesswoman layer just to the right of the layer name. Choose Convert To Smart Object from the contextual menu. Now this smart object is ready to be dragged and dropped into your next enhancement project.

11. Double-click the Background layer and click OK in the New Layer dialog box, accepting the name Layer 0. Drag Layer 0 to the Trash icon at the bottom of the Layers panel to get rid of it.

12. Choose Image > Trim, choose the Transparent Pixels radio button, and click OK (see Figure 6.30).

Figure 6.30 Extracted entourage

13. Save the image as Businesswoman.psd.

Compositing Imagery from 3D Applications

Compositing *is the art of creating a new image by combining images from different sources. In the context of a workflow with other 3D applications, compositing involves mixing pre-rendered components in Photoshop to produce a final composition. This chapter uses Autodesk 3ds Max Design 2011 for its examples, but you can use any high-end 3D application. Compositing in Photoshop is much more immediate than rendering in 3D applications because changes are generally updated in real time.*

Chapter Contents

Compositing Render Elements from 3ds Max Design 2011

Render elements is a term used in 3ds Max to refer to separate image components such as shadows, reflections, diffuse colors, Z Depth, and so forth. You will learn how to create render elements separately in this section for eventual recombination in Photoshop in the next section.

We'll be using 3ds Max Design 2011 to render specific image components (a similar procedure will work in many earlier versions of 3ds Max). You can skip over this section if you're not a 3ds Max user or if you want to jump into the actual compositing in Photoshop, because the rendered outputs from 3ds Max are provided on the DVD. If you use Autodesk Maya or another high-end 3D package, you might want to skim this section to understand the issues involved with rendering separate image components. The steps will be different in other programs, but the essence is the same. To render separate image components in 3ds Max Design 2011, follow these steps:

1. Click the large M button in the upper-left corner of the user interface and select Import. Navigate to the DVD and select the BeaverCreekBachelorsGulchRitzCarlton .skp file. This model (which you can see at http://sketchup.google.com/ 3dwarehouse/details?mid=df541864d4601d2dbe2e393d60145630&prevstart=0) was created by 3D Warehouse user Beaver Creek.

2. Click the following check boxes: Skip Hidden Objects, Split Objects By Layer, and Front/Back Materials As Double Sided 3ds Max Materials. Click OK in the Google SketchUp Import dialog box (Figure 7.1).

Figure 7.1 Importing a SketchUp file into 3ds Max Design 2011

3. Click the Create tab of the Command panel. Click the System category button, select Standard from the Type drop-down list, and click the Daylight button.

4. Click Yes when prompted to utilize Photographic Exposure Control (Figure 7.2).

Figure 7.2 Using Photographic Exposure Control

5. Click a point in the viewport and drag to create and size a compass rose. It doesn't matter where you place the rose or what size it is, but I suggest clicking off to the side of the model for maximum clarity (see Figure 7.3).

Figure 7.3 Completed Daylight system showing compass rose and mental ray sun

6. When prompted, click Yes to create a mental ray Sky and mr Physical Sky environment map (Figure 7.4).

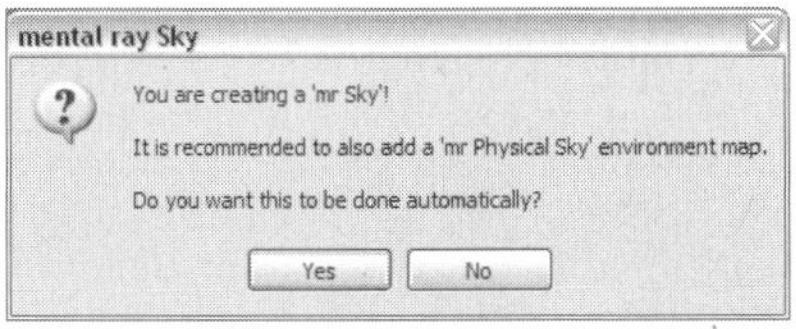

Figure 7.4 Creating a mental ray sky and environment map

7. Drag to the right to increase the orbital scale of the sun, which is linked to the center of the compass rose (as shown previously in Figure 7.3).

8. Click the Get Location button in the Control Parameters rollout on the Command panel. In the Geographic Location dialog box that appears, verify that Nearest Big City is selected and that North America is selected in the Map drop-down. Click inside Colorado or select Boulder, CO from the City list, which is close enough to the site for our purposes (Figure 7.5). Click OK.

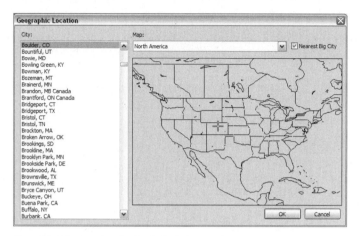

Figure 7.5 Selecting a location for the Daylight system

9. In the Control Parameters rollout, change the time to 14 hours (2 p.m.) by clicking the up-arrow twice (Figure 7.6). The sun correspondingly moves across the sky in the viewport.

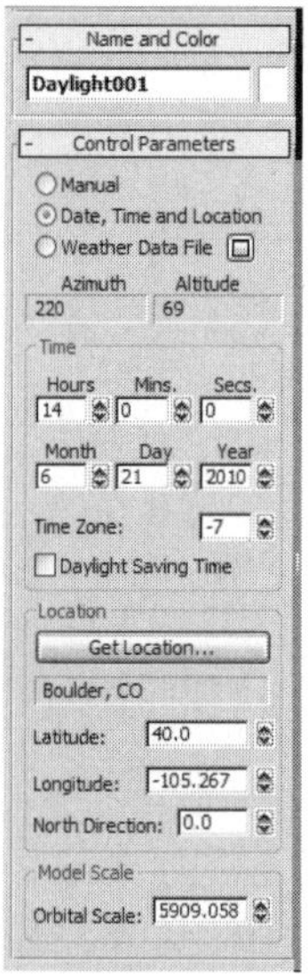

Figure 7.6 Changing the time of day

10. Click off to the side in the viewport to deselect all. Press T on the keyboard to switch to the Top viewport, Z to zoom extents, and G to toggle off the grid.

11. Click the Camera category button on the Create tab. Click the Target button to create a camera with a linked target. Drag from point A to point B (Figure 7.7). Press C on the keyboard to switch to the Camera viewport.

Figure 7.7 Creating a target camera in the Top viewport

12. The camera is actually below ground level at first. Press and hold the mouse wheel button and drag down to pan both the camera and its target upward. Figure 7.8 shows what the Camera viewport displays after this movement.

Figure 7.8 Panning the camera and target upward

13. Press Shift+F to display safe frames, which enable you to match the aspect ratio of the viewport to the output. By default, the output has a 4:3 aspect ratio.

14. Click the Modify tab of the Command panel. Camera001 should still be selected. Click the 24 mm button in the Parameters rollout to change the focal length of the virtual camera lens.

15. Click the Walkthrough icon (it looks like footprints) in the grouping of navigation tools in the lower-right corner of the user interface. Here are the Walkthrough controls:

    • Press the arrow keys to move forward/back and side/side.

    • Hold down Shift and use the up- and down-arrow keys to move up/down.

    • Press the right square bracket key to increase walking speed, or the left square bracket button to decrease walking speed.

16. Frame the building within the middle (cyan-colored) safe frame, as shown in Figure 7.9.

Figure 7.9 Composing a view with interactive walkthrough navigation tools

17. Choose Rendering > Render Setup. On the Common tab of the Render Setup dialog box, click the 800×600 button in the Output Size area.

18. Click the Render Elements tab in the Render Setup dialog box. Click the Add button in the Render Elements rollout. Select mr A&D Level Diffuse (meaning the mental ray renderer's architectural and design material's diffuse color), scroll down to the bottom of the list, and Ctrl+click both Shadow and Z Depth from the long list. Click OK to add these three selected render elements (Figure 7.10).

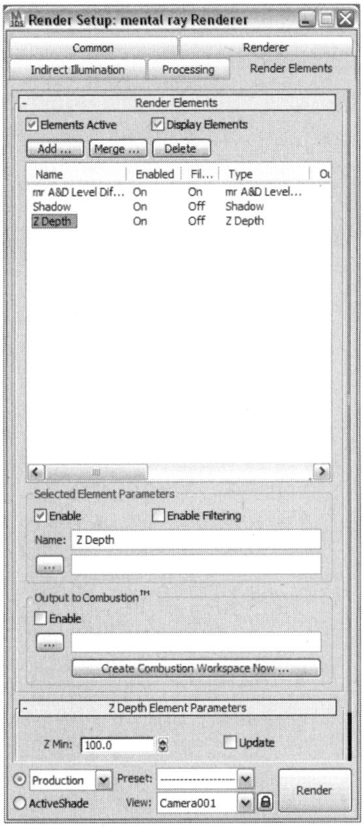

Figure 7.10 Render elements added

19. Click mr A&D Level Diffuse in the Render Elements rollout to make it the selected element. Click the Browse button (ellipsis icon) in the Selected Element Parameters area to open the Render Element Output File dialog box.

20. Navigate to a folder of your choosing (I chose Z:\Scott\BeaverCreek, but this path will likely be different on your system), type **Diffuse** as the filename, and select Targa Image File from the Save As Type drop-down (Figure 7.11). Click OK.

21. In the Targa Image Control dialog box that appears, select 32 bits per pixel, and select the Compress and Pre-Multiplied Alpha check boxes (Figure 7.12). Click OK.

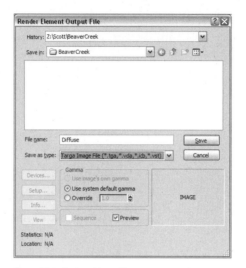

Figure 7.11 Saving a Targa file

Figure 7.12 Setting Targa image output options

Note: Targa image files support alpha channels, and that is why they are often used for compositing.

22. Still on the Render Elements tab of the Render Setup dialog box, deselect Apply Shadows in the Parameters rollout, near the bottom of dialog box (Figure 7.13).

23. Select Shadow in the Render Elements rollout. Click the Browse button in the Selected Element Parameters area to open the Render Element Output File dialog box. Navigate to a folder of your choosing, type **Shadow** as the filename, select Targa Image File from the Save As Type drop-down, and click OK. Click OK to accept the defaults in the Targa Image Control dialog box.

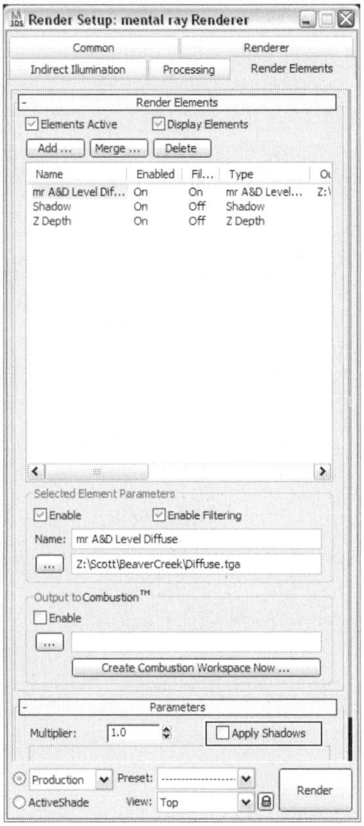

Figure 7.13 Turning off shadow casting for the Diffuse render element

24. Select Z Depth in the Render Elements rollout. Click the Browse button in the Selected Element Parameters area. Navigate to a folder of your choosing, type **ZDepth** as the filename, select Targa Image File from the Save As Type drop-down, and click OK. Click OK to accept the defaults in the Targa Image Control dialog box. Close the Render Setup dialog box by clicking the Close button in the upper-right corner.

25. In order to properly render the Z Depth component, you must measure the distance from the camera to the near and far sides of the building, along the camera-target vector. To do this, press T on the keyboard to select the Top viewport. Click the Create tab of the Command panel. Click the Helpers category icon and click the Tape button. Drag the tape measure from point A to point B, as shown in Figure 7.14, and make a mental note of the Length value shown in the Parameters rollout (approximately 1500). Continue dragging to point C and see that the Length is approximately 5000.

Figure 7.14 Measuring the Z distance in the Top viewport

26. Press C on the keyboard to switch back to the Camera viewport. Press the F10 key to reopen the Render Setup dialog box, and select the Render Elements tab. Select Z Depth in the Render Elements rollout. Scroll down by dragging the narrow, vertical bar along the right edge of the Render Setup dialog box until you see the Z Depth Element Parameters rollout. Type **1500** as the Z Min value and **5000** as the Z Max value (Figure 7.15).

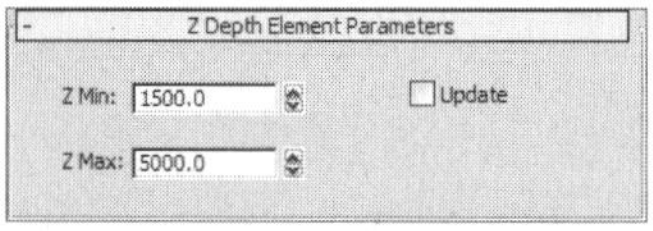

Figure 7.15 Setting Z Depth min and max values

27. Click the Render button in the lower-right corner of the Render Scene dialog box. The rendering process begins, and you can see buckets (small rendered squares) progressively appear. When the rendering is complete, three additional windows appear: mr A&D Level Diffuse (Figure 7.16), Shadow (Figure 7.17), and Z Depth (Figure 7.18). Three Targa files have been automatically saved on your hard drive.

Figure 7.16 mr A&D Level Diffuse render element

Display Alpha Channel button

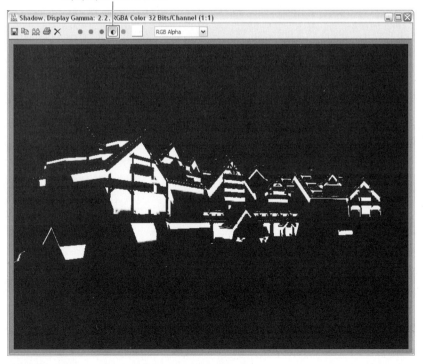

Figure 7.17 Shadow render element (displaying alpha channel)

Figure 7.18 Z Depth render element

28. You might be wondering how shadows are recorded because the image in the Shadow dialog box initially appears completely black. Unlike the other image components, shadows are stored in an alpha channel. Click the Display Alpha Channel button shown in Figure 7.17 to display actual shadows.

You will render one more image containing soft shadows for eventual compositing in Photoshop. The rendering created next isn't technically a render element and thus requires an alternative method for processing that includes the scanline renderer and light tracer. Any rendering you create in your 3D program is a candidate for compositing in Photoshop. Every renderer in 3ds Max is unique in the types of output it can generate. The light tracer is an older renderer known for its efficiency in generating soft shadows on building exteriors. To render this type of output, follow these steps:

1. Select the Common tab of the Render Scene dialog box. Scroll all the way down by dragging the bar along the right edge and expand the Assign Renderer rollout. Click the ellipsis button adjacent to the Production renderer to open the Choose Renderer dialog box, select Default Scanline Renderer (Figure 7.19), and click OK.

2. Select the Render Elements tab and deselect Elements Active.

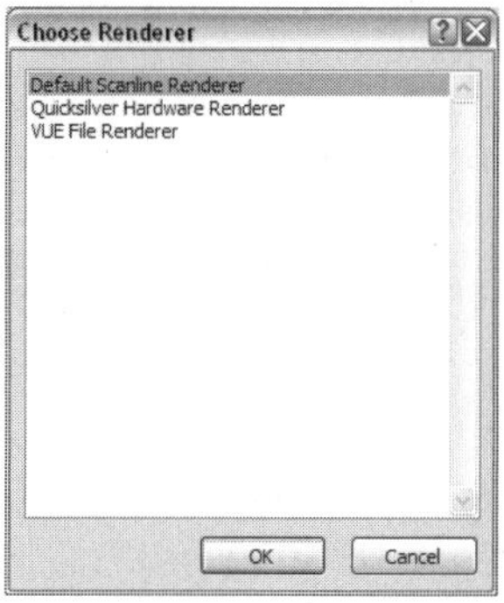

Figure 7.19 Assigning the Default Scanline Renderer

3. Select the Advanced Lighting tab and choose Light Tracer from the drop-down. Change the number of Rays/Sample to 1000 in the Parameters rollout to increase quality (Figure 7.20).

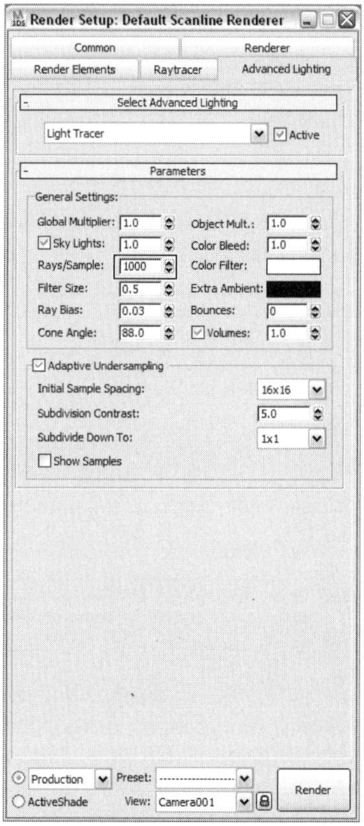

Figure 7.20 Setting up the light tracer

4. Choose Rendering > Material Editor > Compact Material Editor. The top-left material sample slot is active by default and black because Arch & Design materials do not work with the scanline renderer. Change the material type by clicking the Arch & Design button, shown in Figure 7.21.

Figure 7.21 Changing the material type

5. In the Material/Map Browser that appears, expand the Materials and Standard categories, click the Standard material type, and click OK (Figure 7.22).

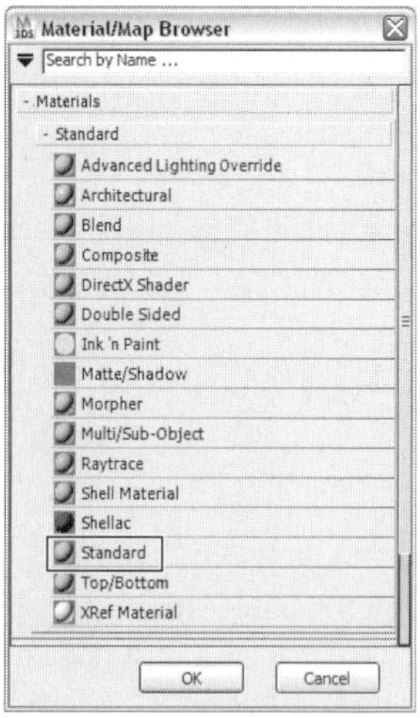

Figure 7.22 Selecting a material type from the browser

6. By default, the Ambient and Diffuse colors are linked in the Blinn Basic Parameters rollout. Click either one of their color swatches to open the Color Picker. Drag the Whiteness slider to the bottom of the gradient to select pure white and click OK (Figure 7.23).

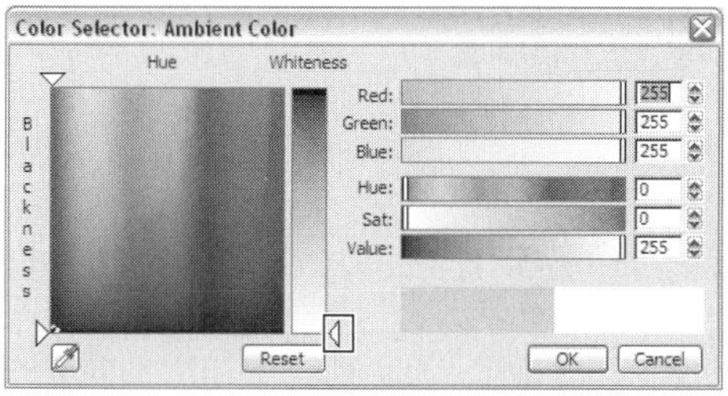

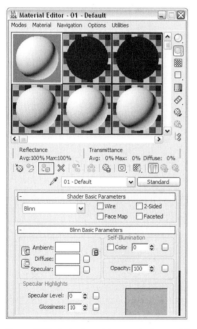

Figure 7.23 Selecting white ambient and diffuse colors

7. Press Ctrl+A to select all objects and then click the Assign Material To Selection button, as shown in Figure 7.24. Press M to close the Compact Material Editor.

Figure 7.24 Assigning white standard material to all

8. Press H on the keyboard to open the Select From Scene dialog box, scroll down to the bottom, expand Compass001, and double-click Daylight001 (Figure 7.25).

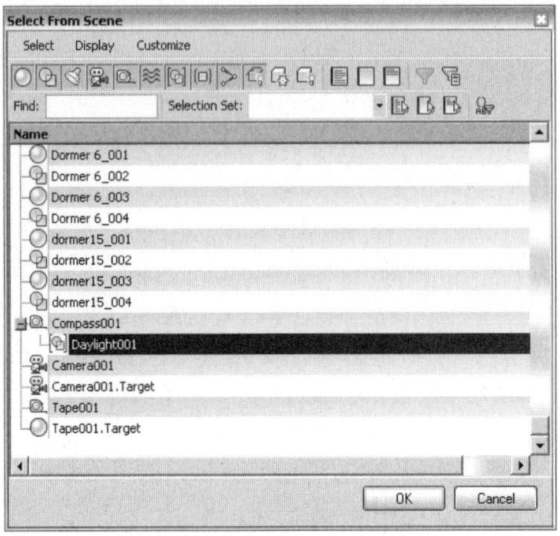

Figure 7.25 Selecting the Daylight node

9. Click the Modify tab of the Command panel, and in the Daylight Parameters rollout deselect Active, which is adjacent to Sunlight. Open the Skylight drop-down and select Skylight (Figure 7.26). Now the scene is illuminated solely by indirect light bouncing off a simulated skydome that is compatible with the scanline renderer.

Figure 7.26 Turning off the sun and illuminating with Skylight

10. Press Shift+Q to render the scene. After a few minutes of processing, you'll see the rendering shown in Figure 7.27.

11. Click the Disk icon in the Rendered Frame window to save the file. In the Save Image dialog box, navigate to the folder of your choosing, type **LightTracer** as the filename, and select Targa Image File from the Save As Type drop-down. Click Save and OK in the Targa Image Control dialog box to accept its defaults.

12. Close 3ds Max Design 2011 without saving the scene unless you want to revisit it later on your own.

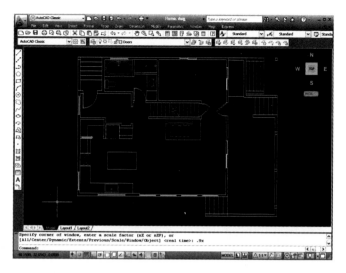

Preparing AutoCAD drawing for enhancement

Drawing enhanced with tone, pattern,
shadow, and lineweight in Photoshop

Original image. Note the construction crane and people on the sidewalk.
PHOTO COURTESY OF ISTOCKPHOTO, ©GUY SARGENT, IMAGE #5100768

Objects removed using the Content-Aware Spot Healing Brush,
Clone Stamp, and Patch tools

The original image's overcast sky and saturated objects are distracting. PHOTO COURTESY OF iSTOCKPHOTO, ©TERRAXPLORER, IMAGE #4213941

The replaced sky and desaturated cars, motorcycles, and signage direct attention back to the architecture.

Original photo of Spanish shoe store PHOTO COURTESY OF iSTOCKPHOTO, ©MLENNY, IMAGE #1000006

Toning down the color focuses attention on the retail space. The image was also straightened.

The original image has an ominous mood due to clouds and shifted color. PHOTO COURTESY OF ISTOCKPHOTO, ©DRUVO, IMAGE #12046126

Color-correcting the image and replacing the sky improves the mood.

The original image is in portrait orientation, which distracts from the pastoral architectural subject matter. PHOTO COURTESY OF ISTOCKPHOTO, ©FONTMONSTER, IMAGE #5167238

Content-aware scale algorithm applied to stretch to landscape orientation without distorting the building

Bracketing photos by shutter speed. No one exposure captures the interior and world outside the windows together. IMAGES COURTESY OF RICHARD TRUEMAN

Bracketed images merged with HDR Pro into a single high dynamic range image

Giving a single image a faux HDR look with the HDR Toning adjustment ORIGINAL PHOTO COURTESY OF iSTOCKPHOTO, ©GUY SARGENT, IMAGE #5100768

Repositioned panoramic photos reveal the strategy of shooting two complete rings at different elevations. IMAGES COURTESY OF RICHARD TRUEMAN

Interactive seamless spherical flash panorama viewed in a web browser

An anaglyph of the author's house requires red/blue 3D glasses to perceive the added dimension of depth. The 3D illusion is created from two images shot side by side.

Assembling a time-lapse video from a series of still images. One can study circulation patterns as people zip around in super speed. VIDEO COURTESY OF ISTOCKPHOTO, ©ADAM WATSON, IMAGE #5657285

Maximum

Mean

Minimum

Range

Skewness

Standard Deviation

Accessing the creative options available when processing multiple exposures with stack modes

Still image from original video clip shows vehicles driving down a busy street. The camera must be stationary in order to alter video with stack modes.
Photo courtesy of iStockphoto, ©Schroptschop, Image #9195349

Altering the video with Range stack mode transforms day into night and the street becomes a river of light in this still image.

Two photos are exposed at different shutter speeds to capture detail in both highlights and shadows. No one exposure can capture the full dynamic range. Images courtesy of Richard Trueman

Creative masking brings the images into a composite whole, which has an increased dynamic range. Unlike HDR Pro, this technique works in the Standard version of Photoshop.

Stucco texture created from scratch in Photoshop

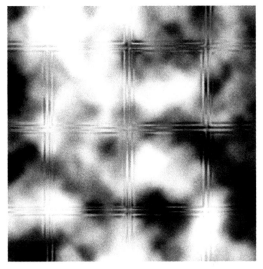

Glass block texture created by altering a few parameters in the Stucco texture

The original photo of a hotel room has framed prints on the wall. Photo courtesy of iStockphoto, ©Brian Raisbeck, Image #6014403

This ortho-rectified framed print from hotel image can be used as a texture map in Photoshop or other 3D applications.

The original photo shows a businesswoman walking down a modern arcade. PHOTOS COURTESY OF ISTOCKPHOTO, © LAJOS REPASI, IMAGE #7144898

The businesswoman extracted from the photo using Quick Select, Refine Edge, and careful mask painting can be used as entourage in future building elevations and perspective projects.

Multiple image components are rendered in 3ds Max 2011. Components include diffuse lighting, hard-edged shadows, and Z depth. MODEL BY 3DWAREHOUSE USER BEAVER CREEK

Image components are composited in Photoshop, where the relative strengths of each component can be mixed in real time without re-rendering.

The original aerial photo of London has a wide depth of field.
PHOTO COURTESY OF ISTOCKPHOTO, ©SEAN RANDALL, IMAGE #13223185

Narrowing the depth of field with the Lens Blur filter and boosting both saturation and contrast enhances the illusion that you are looking at an architectural miniature.

Brooklyn Bridge model opened in SketchUp, where Z-depth information will be rendered out using the **Fog feature** SKETCHUP 3DWAREHOUSE MODEL BY GOOGLE

Z-depth information loaded as an alpha channel in Photoshop; the depth of field is dramatically narrowed using the Lens Blur filter.

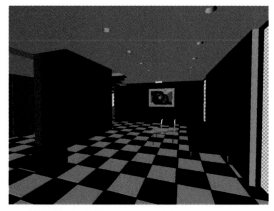

Navigating a 3D model to compose an interior perspective in Photoshop CS5 Extended

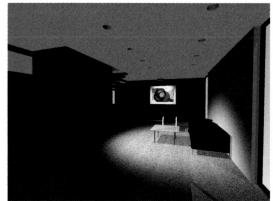

Materials and lighting are added and the scene is rendered.

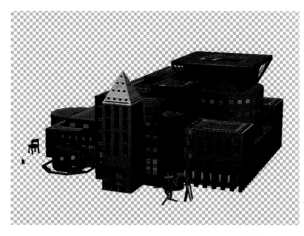

The original 3D model of the Denver Public Library is opened in Photoshop. 3D MODEL BY 3DWAREHOUSE USER CAMELOT. DESIGN BY MICHAEL GRAVES.

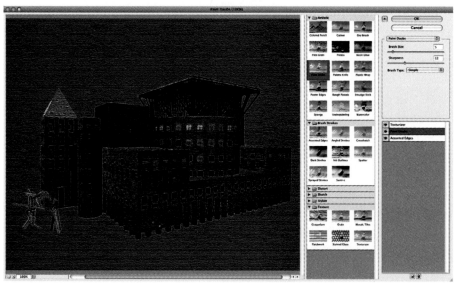

Illustrating the vector model using a combination of smart filters can produce a variety of attractive effects.

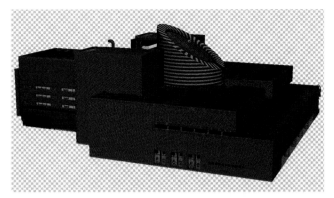

An original 3D model of San Francisco Museum of Modern Art is opened in Photoshop. 3D MODEL BY GOOGLE. DESIGN BY MARIO BOTTA.

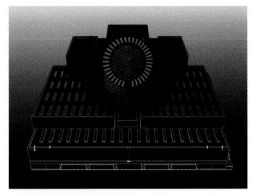

The model is illustrated using a combination of render settings and creative masking.

The original rendering from a 3D model of an old town square shows everything in clear focus.
MODEL BY 3DWAREHOUSE USER DANDIS

Painting with the Art History brush transforms the 3D rendering into a painting and leaves more to the imagination.

The original rendering from a 3D model of the Georgia Aquarium draws attention to the fact it is a low-poly model, which isn't particularly realistic. 3D Warehouse model by Google

Painting with the Mixer Brush softens the obvious faceting on the curtain wall and blends colors organically, making the illustration a more emotive experience than the rendering.

The original photo of a modern condo feels a bit sparse. Photo courtesy of iStockphoto, ©EscoLux, Image #2267151

3D entourage is added in the form of a painting and a side table holding an architectural model. Digital painting ©Scott Onstott, Transamerica Pyramid model by 3D Warehouse user Kevin Girard, Eames stool by 3D Warehouse user SmartFurniture.com

The original photo of the street corner shows an unsightly billboard atop a corner building. Photo courtesy of iStockphoto, ©Tony Tremblay, Image #3581112

A 3D model of a hotel building is integrated into the photo using careful positioning of the 3D camera and precisely painted layer masks. The corner building with the billboard was replaced by a 3D model. Hotel model by 3DWarehouse user Milo Minderbinder

Logo of hypothetical Sol Corporation created with type and a vector shape

Logo colorized and extruded into three dimensions with Repoussé in Photoshop CS5 Extended

The original photo of new retail building is ideally suited to using the Vanishing Point filter because it is boxy and shot at an oblique angle.

Photo courtesy of iStockphoto, © Tony Tremblay, Image #2901986

The Vanishing Point filter allows you to replace textures in perspective, take measurements, and optionally shift the entire perspective of the building by turning photo-mapped surfaces into a 3D model.

Left image   Right image

Original photos of author's house shot adjacent to each other, approximately one foot apart

This stereo pair has an added dimension of depth that is visible when viewed in parallel mode (without crossing your eyes). Stare beyond the page until you see a third image appear, and then slowly bring your eyes' focal plane forward until you perceive the stereographic effect.

The original atrium photo featuring one-point perspective is suitable for turning into an anaglyph. PHOTO COURTESY OF ISTOCKPHOTO, ©TEUN VAN DEN DRIES, IMAGE #3868412

This anaglyph requires red/blue 3D glasses to perceive the added dimension of depth. Mapping the image onto a mesh made from grayscale gradients makes the 3D illusion possible.

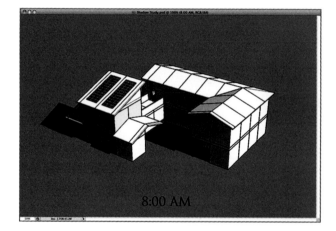

The original conceptual model from SketchUp shows shadows cast at a specific time and place.

This animated GIF shown in a web browser was created frame by frame in Photoshop. The animation allows the massing model's shadows to be qualitatively evaluated over the course of a day. Massing and/or overhangs might have to be adjusted as a result.

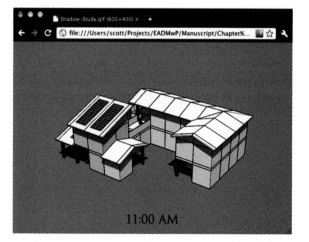

The original video clip smoothly pans across Dubai marina with high-rise buildings in the background. PHOTO COURTESY OF iSTOCKPHOTO, ©THESUPERPH, IMAGE #9269204

Video clip altered globally (rather than frame by frame) with filters and adjustments by first converting it into a smart object

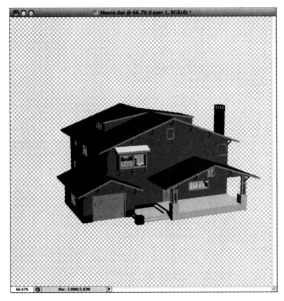

The original 3D house model in Photoshop has interior detail visible through the windows. MODEL BY 3DWAREHOUSE USER J. WALLACE

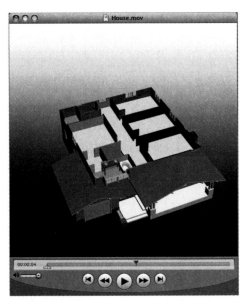

Animating the 3D model's cross section and 3D camera position on the timeline creates the illusion that the house is being built from the ground up right before your eyes.

Figure 7.27 Light tracer rendering

Compositing Image Elements in Photoshop

Now it's time to combine the pre-rendered images in Photoshop to produce an attractive composite illustration. It's okay if you didn't walk through the preceding steps in the 3ds Max Design 2011 section of this chapter, because the images are on the DVD for this book. The purpose of compositing pre-rendered image components in Photoshop is to save time and frustration associated with trying to render perfect output solely in the 3D application. In order to generate output, 3D programs typically require lengthy rendering processing every time a small change to materials, lighting, or shadows is made. Aesthetic decisions are much more pleasant to make when you can get nearly immediate visual feedback in Photoshop.

Lighting and shadow changes in 3ds Max (or any other similar 3D package) typically require re-rendering the entire scene. The tutorial doesn't require an inordinate amount of time to render, but many professional projects have render times measured in hours. Compare that with the amount of time it takes to adjust the opacity of a layer (seconds), and you'll see the value of making aesthetic decisions in Photoshop. Here's how it works:

1. Choose File > Open and select Diffuse.tga either from the folder where you saved it in the previous section or from the DVD.

2. Open the Channels panel and select the Alpha 1 channel. Click the Load Channel As Selection button along the lower edge of the Channels panel (Figure 7.28).

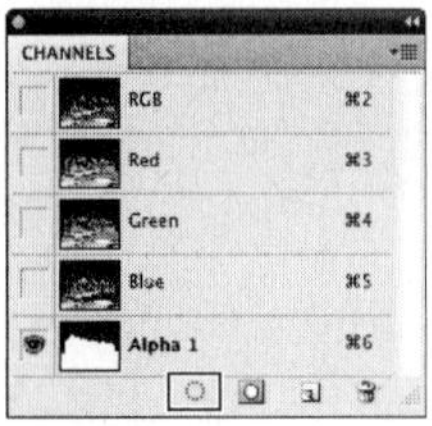

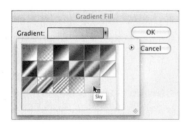

Figure 7.28 Loading the alpha channel as a selection

3. Select the RGB channel at the top of the Channels panel. Notice that the selection you made with the alpha channel remains and that it represents everything but the sky.

4. Choose Select > Inverse to select the sky.

5. Choose Layer > New Fill Layer > Gradient, type **Sky** in the New Layer dialog box, and click OK.

6. Open the Gradient Picker in the Gradient Fill dialog box that appears and select the Sky preset you made in Chapter 3, "Stretching the Photographic Truth" (Figure 7.29).

Figure 7.29 Selecting a gradient preset

7. If you never saved a sky preset, refer to "Replacing the Sky" in Chapter 3 and follow the steps to save a Sky gradient preset. Select the Sky preset, and with the Gradient Fill dialog box still open, drag the gradient upward slightly to brighten the horizon and then click OK (Figure 7.30).

8. Save the image as BeaverCreek.psd.

9. Choose File > Open and select Shadow.tga either from the folder where you saved it in the previous section or from the DVD.

10. Select the Alpha 1 channel in the Channels panel. Press Cmd+A / Ctrl+A and Cmd+C / Ctrl+C to select all and copy it to the clipboard.

11. Close Shadow.tga without saving and switch back to BeaverCreek.psd.

12. Press Cmd+Shift+A / Ctrl+Shift+A, type **Shadow** in the New Layer dialog box, and click OK.

13. Press Cmd+V / Ctrl+V to paste the contents of the clipboard to the Shadow layer. The shadows appear white on a black background, so press Cmd+I / Ctrl+I to invert.

Figure 7.30 Filling the sky with a gradient

14. Change the Shadow layer blend mode to Multiply so that only the darker areas affect the composite. The ray-traced shadows are so dark that they obscure everything in shade. Decrease the Shadow layer opacity to 60% (see Figure 7.31).

Figure 7.31 Adjusting layer opacity and blend mode of the Shadow layer

15. Choose File > Open and select LightTracer.tga either from the folder where you saved it in the previous section or from the DVD.

16. The image lacks punch. To increase contrast and brighten the whites, press Cmd+L / Ctrl+L to invoke the Levels dialog box. Drag the shadow input slider to 100 and gamma to 3 (see Figure 7.32) and click OK.

17. Press Cmd +A / Ctrl+A and Cmd+C / Ctrl+C to select all and copy it to the clipboard. Press Cmd+W / Ctrl+W and then Don't Save / No to close LightTracer.tga without saving.

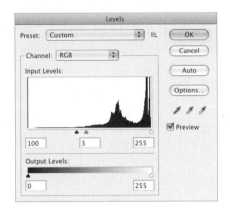

Figure 7.32 Making a levels adjustment

18. Switch back to BeaverCreek.psd and target the Background layer. Press Cmd+ Shift+N / Ctrl+Shift+N to create a new layer, type **LightTracer** in the New Layer dialog box, and click OK.

19. Press Cmd+V / Ctrl+V to paste the contents of the clipboard to the LightTracer layer. Change this layer's blend mode to Multiply and tone down its opacity to 80%. The shadows appear softer, and the building looks arguably more three-dimensional (Figure 7.33).

20. Press Cmd+S / Ctrl+S to save BeaverCreek.psd.

Figure 7.33 Compositing the LightTracer layer adds depth to the rendering.

Narrowing the Depth of Field

In photography the term *depth of field* refers to the extent of the spatial region extending away from the camera that is rendered in sharp focus. Although camera lenses can precisely focus at only one distance, the photographer has manual control over how fast sharpness falls off by adjusting the lens aperture (increasing aperture narrows the depth of field). Narrowing the depth of field naturally focuses attention in the area that remains sharp. You can use this fact to strategically direct viewer attention where you want it.

In this section, you'll narrow the depth of field for your images in Photoshop by using several sources, including photographs, 3ds Max renderings, and SketchUp models.

Using the Lens Blur Filter

You can simulate depth of field with the Lens Blur filter, although what you will be doing in this procedure (blurring the top and bottom image areas) differs from the radial blur produced by a physical lens. The Lens Blur filter simulates depth of field the most effectively with a *depth map*, which is a channel representing spatial information in grayscale. Let's see how this is done:

1. Open the file London.jpg from the DVD (Figure 7.34).

2. Choose Layer > New > Layer, type **Depth map** in the New Layer dialog box, and click OK.

Figure 7.34 Unaltered London photo

PHOTO COURTESY OF ISTOCKPHOTO, © SEAN RANDALL, IMAGE #13223185

3. Press D on the keyboard to set the default colors and X to exchange foreground and background colors so white is in the foreground. Select the Gradient tool in the toolbox and choose the Foreground To Transparent gradient in the picker on the options bar (Figure 7.35).

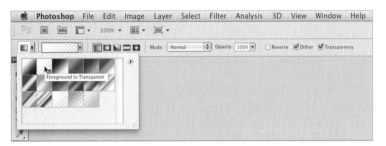

Figure 7.35 Selecting a white-to-transparent gradient

4. Hold down Shift and drag from point A to point B (shown in Figure 7.36) to create a white gradient along the lower edge of the photo. Hold down Shift again and drag from point C to point D to add an upper gradient.

Figure 7.36 Adding white gradients

5. Press Cmd+A / Ctrl+A to select all, and Cmd+C / Ctrl+C to copy the contents of the Depth map layer to the clipboard.

6. Open the Channels panel and click the Create New Channel button along the panel's lower edge. Press Cmd+V / Ctrl+V to paste the pixels from the clipboard to the Alpha 1 channel and press Cmd+D / Ctrl+D to deselect (Figure 7.37). Click the RGB channel to reactivate it.

7. Target the Depth map layer in the Layers panel and press Delete (Mac) / Backspace (PC) to get rid of it.

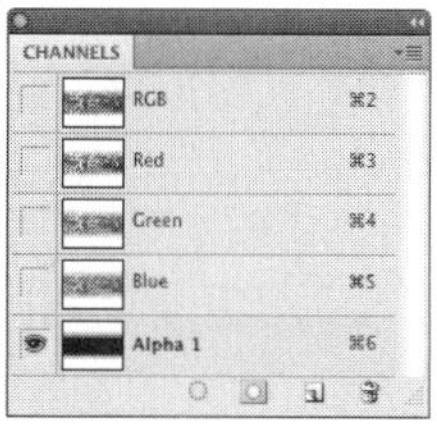

Figure 7.37 Converting a layer to a channel

8. Press Cmd+J / Ctrl+J to copy the Background layer. Rename Layer 1 to Depth of Field.

9. Choose Filter > Blur > Lens Blur. In the Lens Blur dialog box, set the Depth Map source to Alpha 1. Change Iris Shape to Hexagon (6), and move the Radius slider to 11. Drag the Specular Highlight Brightness to 36 and Threshold to 240. Set Noise Amount at the minimal level of 1, click the Gaussian radio button, and select Monochromatic (Figure 7.38). Click OK.

Figure 7.38 Using Alpha 1 as the depth map in the Lens Blur filter

10. Open the Adjustments panel and click the Brightness/Contrast icon. Drag the Contrast slider to the right, to a value of 50.

11. Still in the Adjustments panel, click the Return To Adjustments list button in the lower-left corner and then click the Vibrance icon. Drag the Saturation slider to the right, to a value of +50. Figure 7.39 shows the result.

Figure 7.39 Narrowing the depth of field, and increasing contrast and saturation, gives the illusion of an architectural miniature.

Viewer attention is definitely directed along the Thames from Tower Bridge to the modern mayor of London's office, courtesy of strategic blurring added with the Lens Blur filter. Boosting contrast and saturation enhances the illusion that you're looking at an architectural miniature rather than an aerial photo, resulting in quite an interesting effect.

Using the Z Depth Image Element from 3ds Max to Narrow the Depth of Field

If you are compositing 3ds Max imagery in Photoshop, then a Z Depth rendering is the perfect depth map to use with the Lens Blur filter. The Z Depth image you rendered earlier (see Figure 7.18) depicts objects receding from the camera in ever-darkening grayscale values. Let's see how Z Depth translates into a narrowed depth of field:

1. Open BeaverCreek.psd and ZDepth.tga either from the folder where you saved them earlier or from the DVD.

2. Choose Window > ZDepth.tga and press Cmd+A / Ctrl+A to select all, and Cmd+C / Ctrl+C to copy its contents to the clipboard.

3. Choose Window > BeaverCreek.psd. Open the Channels panel and click the Create New Channel button along the panel's lower edge. Double-click the new channel and rename it **Z Depth**. Press Cmd+V / Ctrl+V to paste the pixels from the clipboard to the new channel (Figure 7.40) and press Cmd+D / Ctrl+D to deselect. Click the RGB channel to reactivate it.

Figure 7.40 Converting the Z Depth image to a channel in `BeaverCreek.psd`

4. Target the Shadow layer in the Layers panel. Press Cmd+Shift+N / Ctrl+Shift+N, type **Depth of Field** in the New Layer dialog box, and click OK.

5. Press C to select the Crop tool. Drag out a crop window as shown in Figure 7.41 and press Return/Enter.

Figure 7.41 Cropping out uninteresting foreground and sky

6. Press Cmd+Opt+Shift+E / Ctrl+Alt+Shift+E to stamp all visible layers onto layer Depth of Field.

7. Choose Filter > Blur > Lens Blur. Select Z Depth as the Depth Map source. Drag Blur Focal Distance to 200 to focus on the tiny structure in front of the resort. Set Iris Shape to Hexagon (6) and drag the Radius slider to 14 (Figure 7.42). Drag all other sliders to zero and click OK.

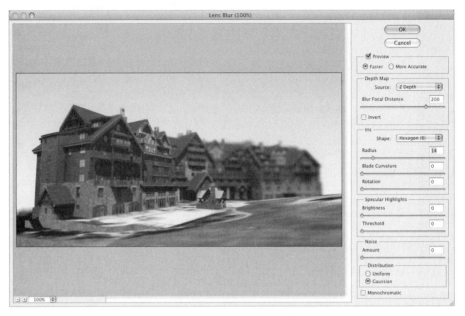

Figure 7.42 Using Lens Blur to narrow the depth of field around a point of interest

8. Save the image as BeaverCreekDone.psd.

Viewer attention is drawn to the smaller structure out in front of the resort because of the narrow depth of field created with Lens Blur and the Z Depth image element. You probably didn't pay much attention to the diminutive building before but are now probably wondering what it is. Given the chimney, maybe it's an elaborate cooking venue? You have the power to direct viewer interest to specific structures by strategically narrowing the depth of field in Photoshop.

Creating Depth Maps with SketchUp 7

Google SketchUp is a popular 3D modeling program known for its ease of use, and is available in both free and Pro versions. SketchUp doesn't allow you to export a Z Depth image directly, as you can in 3ds Max. However, there is a little-known way to coax this type of data out of SketchUp, by using its Fog feature. Let's see how it works:

1. Launch SketchUp. If you don't have a copy, download SketchUp from http://sketchup.google.com. You don't need the Pro version for this tutorial (the free version does everything needed). Install SketchUp on your Mac or PC and then launch the program.

2. Open Brooklyn Bridge.skp from the DVD (Figure 7.43).

3. Choose File > Export > 2D Graphic. Select Tagged Image (*.tif) from the Format drop-down and click the Options button. If you are using the Mac version, select Anti-Alias and Transparent Background in the Export Options dialog box (Figure 7.44) and click OK and then Export. The transparent background works like an alpha channel in isolating the structure from the background. Windows users would have to select the sky in Photoshop (using the Magic Wand tool, for example). However, the sample file you'll use in the next section is saved with transparency, so no selection will be required.

SketchUp 3D Warehouse model by Google

Figure 7.43 Opening the Brooklyn Bridge model in SketchUp

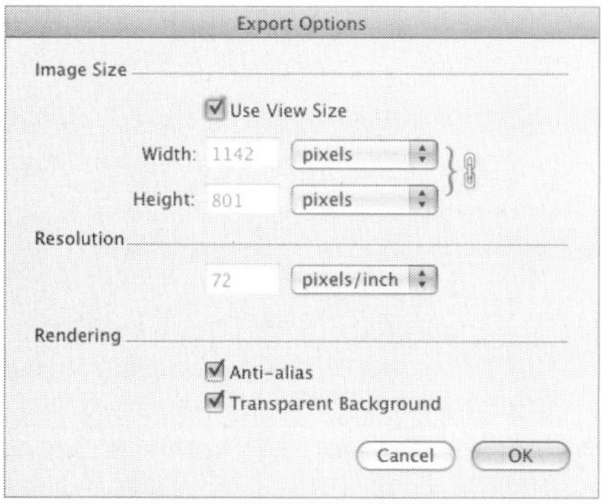

Figure 7.44 Exporting a 2D image with a transparent background from SketchUp

4. Choose Window > Style. There is only one style icon in this scene. Click the Edit button and then click the Face mode button (second icon from the left). Click the second Style button, which is Display In Hidden Line mode (see Figure 7.45).

Click the Front color swatch and select pure white from the Color Picker. Close the Color Picker.

Figure 7.45 Adjusting face style

5. Click the Edge mode button (leftmost icon) and deselect Display Edges (Figure 7.46). Close the Style window.

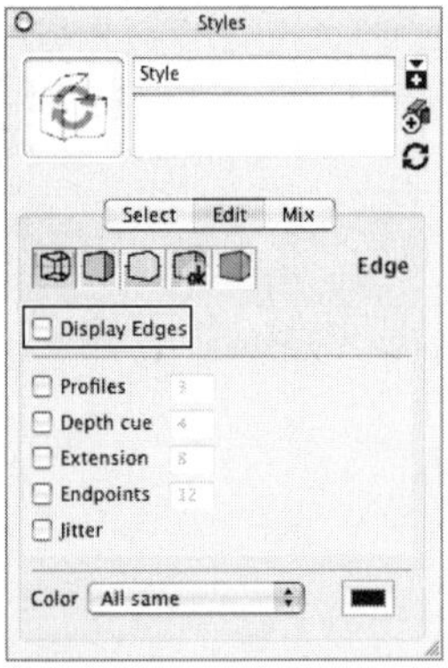

Figure 7.46 Turning edge display off

6. Choose Window > Shadows. Deselect Display Shadows. Close the Shadows window.

7. Choose Window > Fog. Select Display Fog and deselect Use Background Color. Click the color swatch and select pure black from the Color Picker. Close the Color Picker.

8. Drag the distance sliders as shown in Figure 7.47. The top slider controls how far white extends into the scene, and the bottom slider controls how deep black goes. A gradient between black and white exists between the points marked on the sliders' distance scales.

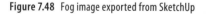

Figure 7.47 Using fog to simulate Z Depth

9. Choose File > Export > 2D Graphic. Click the Options button and deselect Transparent Background. Click OK, change the filename to Brooklyn Bridge Fog.tiff, and then click Export. Figure 7.48 shows the "fog."

10. Quit SketchUp.

Figure 7.48 Fog image exported from SketchUp

Narrowing the Depth of Field in Photoshop

Now that you've exported both textured and fog images from SketchUp, you can narrow the depth of field in Photoshop. Here we go:

1. Launch Photoshop and open Brooklyn Bridge Fog.tif that you just created or open it from the DVD.

2. Press Cmd+A / Ctrl+A to select all, and Cmd+C / Ctrl+C to copy it to the clipboard. Press Cmd+W / Ctrl+W to close the image.

3. Open Brooklyn Bridge Fog.tif. Rename Layer 0 to Bridge.

4. Select the Channels panel and click the Create A New Channel button along its lower edge. Press Cmd+V / Ctrl+V to paste the contents of the clipboard to the new channel. Press Cmd+D / Ctrl+D to deselect. Click the RGB channel to restore it.

5. Choose Layer > New Fill Layer > Gradient. Type **Sky** in the New Layer dialog box and click OK.

6. In the Gradient Fill dialog box that appears, choose the Sky gradient preset from the drop-down (see Chapter 3) and click OK. Press Cmd+Shift+[/ Ctrl+Shift+[to move layer Sky below Bridge so the sky is visible through Bridge's transparency.

7. Chose Layer > Flatten Image.

8. Choose Filter > Blur > Lens Blur. Select Alpha 1 as the Depth Map Source. Drag Blur Focal Distance to zero and select Invert. Set Iris Shape to Hexagon (6) and drag Radius to 15 (Figure 7.49). Set all the other sliders to zero and click OK.

Figure 7.49 Narrowing the depth of field in Photoshop

9. Save the image as Brooklyn Bridge.psd.

In this chapter, you've gotten a taste of the art of compositing. Starting in 3ds Max Design 2011, you exported rendered image elements that you later assembled and adjusted in Photoshop. In addition, you learned how to narrow the depth of field in a photograph, using pre-rendered images from 3ds Max Design 2011 and images exported from SketchUp 7. As you've seen, compositing and narrowing the depth of field can subtly focus viewers' attention on what you want them to see.

Working with Imported 3D Models

Most people don't think of Photoshop when it comes to working with 3D models. However, bare-bones 3D functionality was introduced in CS3 Extended circa 2007. A real breakthrough was made in CS4 Extended, giving independent editing control over meshes, materials, and lights. Photoshop CS5 Extended refines the 3D toolset even more and introduces image-based lighting, material libraries, and more. This chapter teaches you in a continuous tutorial how to work with imported 3D models through the following stages:

Chapter Contents

Transferring 3D models into Photoshop
Navigating in 3D space
Adjusting materials and maps
Illuminating with virtual light
Rendering the model

Transferring 3D Models into Photoshop

After 3D models are imported, you'll be able to navigate in 3D space, adjust materials, tweak lighting, and render the scene to create attractive imagery from the comfort of Photoshop's familiar interface. Although Photoshop has the capability to create basic 3D content in terms of a few preset 3D shapes, 3D postcards, and the mesh from Grayscale and Repoussé features (see Chapter 11, Using Repoussé: 3D modeling in Photoshop), it is not a fully fledged 3D modeling program and is unlikely to ever become one. You must therefore plan to transfer architectural, engineering, and industrial models into Photoshop from content-creation programs such as Google SketchUp or Autodesk's 3ds Max, AutoCAD, Revit, Inventor, and so on.

Since CS3, the Extended version of Photoshop has been able to open five 3D formats:

OBJ—Format of Wavefront Technologies from the late 1980s

3DS—Format of Autodesk 3D Studio DOS from the early 1990s

DAE—Developed by Sony as an interchange format in 2004

KMZ—Google Earth format containing compressed DAE file

U3D—Created by 3D Industry Forum consortium in 2005

No additional 3D formats were added to this short list in Photoshop CS4 Extended or Photoshop CS5 Extended. Considering this history, it seems unlikely that Adobe will add additional formats in the future. Therefore, if you want to transfer 3D models into Photoshop, your content-creation program must export to one of these five formats, or you must use a converter program to translate model data into one of these formats.

The OBJ and 3DS formats have been de facto 3D interchange formats for decades, even though there are numerous technical shortcomings associated with using ancient formats not designed for 3D data exchange. For example, the 3DS format doesn't support texture filenames longer than eight characters (a legacy from DOS), surface normals aren't stored in a modern way (smoothing groups are used instead), and mesh composition is limited to triangles (a serious limitation of polygonal modeling programs).

DAE, KMZ, and U3D were specifically designed as interchange formats, so it makes sense that you'll get better results when using one of these formats to transfer model data into Photoshop. In principle, U3D is an excellent interchange format. However, very few 3D packages support this format, and those that do support it (most notably Bentley MicroStation and Nemetschek Allplan) only export U3D embedded within PDF files. Unfortunately, PDF isn't one of the 3D formats supported by the extended version of Photoshop, so U3D isn't going to work for our purposes. Therefore, DAE and KMZ are the best formats for transferring model data into

Photoshop. For historical reasons, the DAE (Digital Asset Exchange) file format is also known as COLLADA (COLLAborative Design Activity).

> **Note:** Rename any KMZ file as a ZIP file and then double-click it to reveal its contents. KMZ files contain a KML (Keyhole Markup Language) geographic file, and optionally a DAE model and a folder containing associated texture maps.

All Autodesk 3D applications (AutoCAD, Revit, Inventor, 3ds Max, Maya, and so forth) support a proprietary and undocumented file format as Autodesk's preferred 3D interchange mechanism: FBX. Adobe does not support Autodesk's FBX format and probably never will be able to. Fortunately for us, Autodesk has released a free and frequently updated FBX Converter program (available at `http://usa.autodesk.com/adsk/servlet/pc/item?siteID=123112&id=10775855`) that translates between FBX and 3DS, DXF (another ancient de facto exchange format), OBJ, and, most important, DAE. Another bonus is that versions of the Autodesk FBX Converter can run on Windows, Mac, and Linux platforms. Therefore, if you are using Autodesk software to create 3D content, use the program's internal features to export the model to FBX format and then use the stand-alone FBX Converter program to translate FBX to DAE (Figure 8.1). The FBX Converter has no options other than selecting filenames and paths in the process, so it couldn't be any easier.

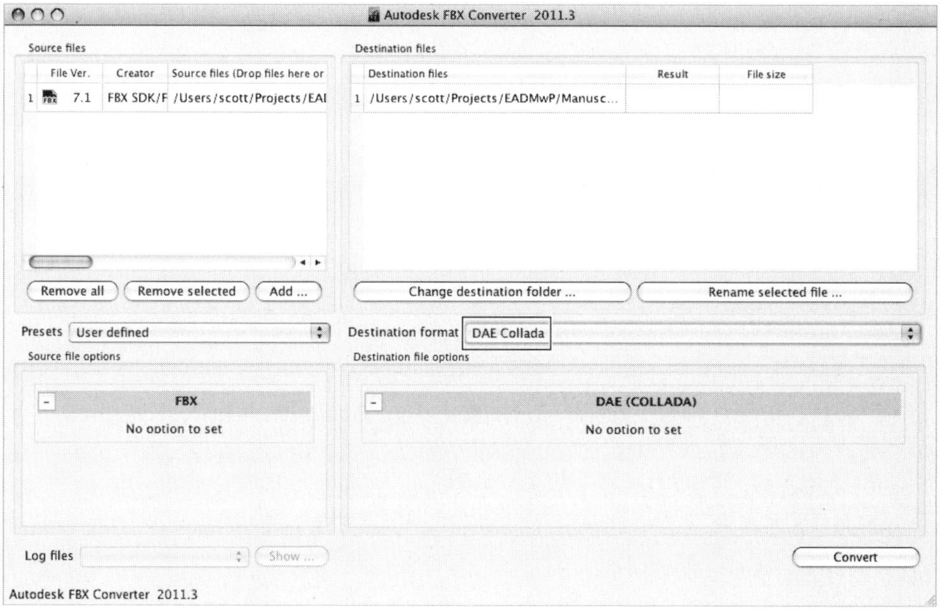

Figure 8.1 Autodesk FBX Converter

Both the free and Pro versions of Google SketchUp allow you to import and export DAE and KMZ files. These can be opened directly in Photoshop. Let's begin the tutorial by exporting a model from SketchUp to the DAE format:

1. Install the free version of Google SketchUp (http://sketchup.google.com) if you haven't already done so. SketchUp is available for Mac and Windows.

2. Launch SketchUp and open ModernRoom.skp from the DVD (Figure 8.2).

Figure 8.2 ModernRoom.skp opened in SketchUp

Note: For best results, explode SketchUp groups and components prior to exporting to DAE or KMZ. This has already been done in the sample file.

3. Choose File > Export > 3D Model.

4. Select COLLADA File (*.dae) from the Format drop-down (Figure 8.3) and navigate to a memorable folder on your hard drive.

5. Click the Options button, select Triangulate All Faces and Export Texture Maps, and deselect all the other options (Figure 8.4). Photoshop will crash if Triangulate All Faces is not selected, and you must select Export Texture Maps if you want these to show up in Photoshop. Click OK in both open dialog boxes to export the DAE file.

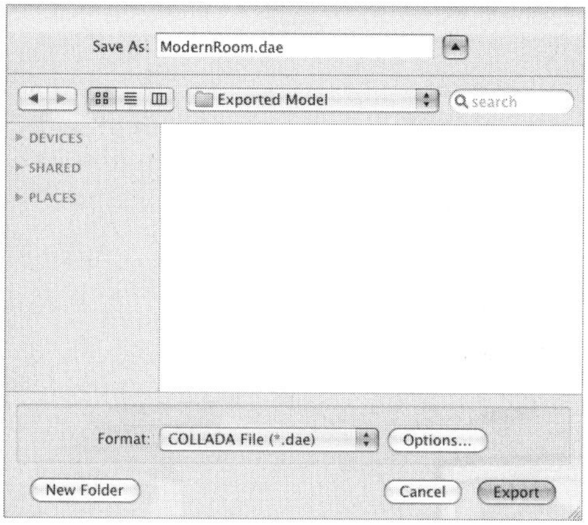

Figure 8.3 Choosing the COLLADA format for export

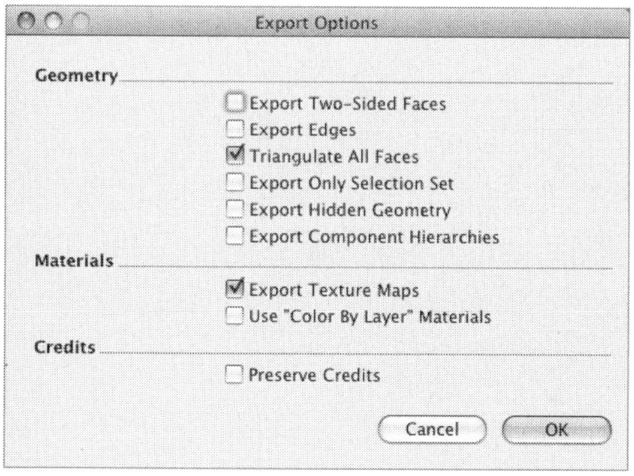

Figure 8.4 Configuring COLLADA options in Photoshop

Figure 8.5 shows the exported ModernRoom.dae file, along with a folder of the same name containing the model's texture maps.

Figure 8.5 DAE file and its associated folder containing texture maps

It is important not to change the path relationship of the DAE file relative to its texture map folder (by placing the DAE file inside the folder, for example). Opening a COLLADA file in a text editor reveals that it is based on a common web technology: XML (Extensible Markup Language). Textures have hard-coded relative paths (see Figure 8.6). You would have to change these paths manually (not recommended) if you wanted to change the location of the DAE file relative to its texture map folder.

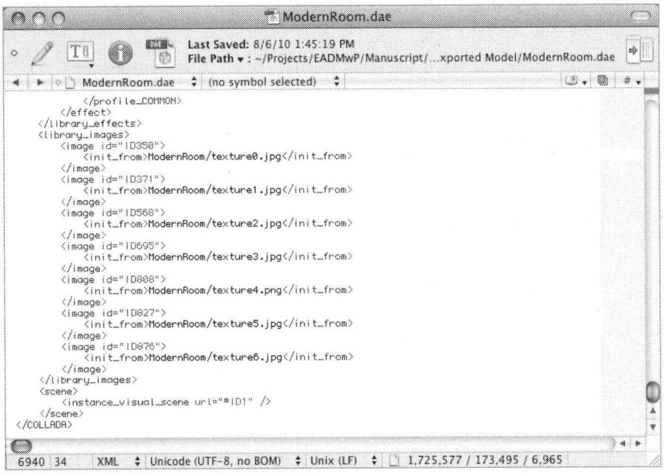

Figure 8.6 COLLADA files are based on XML.

Navigating in 3D Space

In 2D space, you *navigate* (change your point of view) by zooming, panning, or both at the same time by using the Navigator panel. 3D space, on the other hand, requires the use of separate toolsets available for navigating 3D objects and 3D cameras.

It is important not to confuse tools from the 3D Object and 3D Camera toolsets because although they perform functions that are roughly opposite each other, there are important differences too. You'll explore both in the following sections.

Rotating the Model to Match Photoshop's Coordinate System

Let's open the DAE file you created in the preceding section and navigate in 3D to compose an attractive view of the space:

1. Launch Photoshop and open the ModernRoom.dae file you exported from SketchUp.

> **Note:** After importing the 3D model, if you don't see anything in the document window, you likely have a problem with your graphics subsystem. Quitting Photoshop and relaunching won't fix such a low-level problem. You must restart your computer to reinitialize the graphics subsystem.

2. Choose Window > 3D. Click the Toggle Misc 3D Extras button along the lower edge of the 3D panel and choose 3D Ground Plane from the menu that appears. If graphics hardware acceleration is unavailable on a computer that doesn't meet the minimum system requirements, the Toggle Misc 3D Extras button is unavailable. The model is turned on its side because of differences between the coordinate systems of SketchUp and Photoshop (see Figure 8.7).

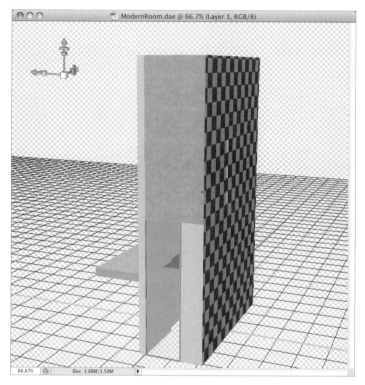

Figure 8.7 The ground plane and room model are mismatched.

3. Press K to select the 3D Object toolset. Select the Rotate The 3D Object tool on the options bar (see Figure 8.8). Target the X orientation text box, type -90, and press Tab twice. Type 90 in the Z orientation box and press Tab. The floor of the room and the ground plane are parallel.

4. Toggle off the 3D ground plane by clicking the Toggle Misc 3D Extras button along the lower edge of the 3D panel. Toggle off the 3D axis as well.

5. Save the file as **ModernRoom.psd**.

196

Return To Original
Object Position

Roll The
3D Object   Slide The
            3D Object

Save The
Current View

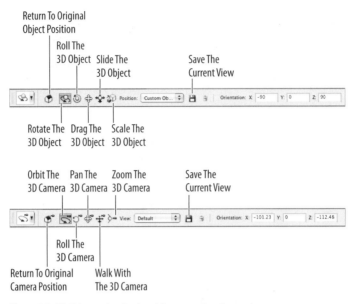

Rotate The   Drag The   Scale The
3D Object   3D Object 3D Object

Orbit The   Pan The   Zoom The
3D Camera   3D Camera   3D Camera

Save The
Current View

Roll The
3D Camera

Return To Original   Walk With
Camera Position   The 3D Camera

Figure 8.8 3D Object toolset (top) and Camera toolset (bottom)

You just used the 3D Object tools to reorient the model with respect to Photoshop's coordinate system. This was appropriate because there was a mismatch between the imported objects' coordinate system (Y up) and Photoshop's coordinate system (Z up). Next you will use the 3D Camera tools to frame a composition.

Using 3D Camera Tools

Think of each 3D layer as a separate 3D camera, and what you see in the document window is what is visible through the lens of the virtual camera. Although it is technically possible to frame a composition by using 3D Object tools (by scaling and repositioning objects), you have more flexibility when using 3D Camera tools to modify the virtual camera's position, orientation, and focal length. Let's give the 3D Camera tools a try:

1. Press N to activate the 3D Camera toolset. Choose Right in the View drop-down menu on the options bar. You see an elevation of the room (Figure 8.9).

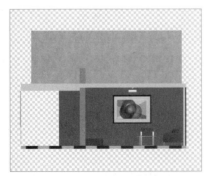

Figure 8.9 Right view of the modern room as seen through the 3D camera

2. Select the Zoom The 3D Camera tool on the options bar. Click the Perspective Camera button. Change the second drop-down on the options bar to mm Lens and type **24** in the Standard Field Of View text box (Figure 8.10). The camera now displays a wide-angle perspective view of the room.

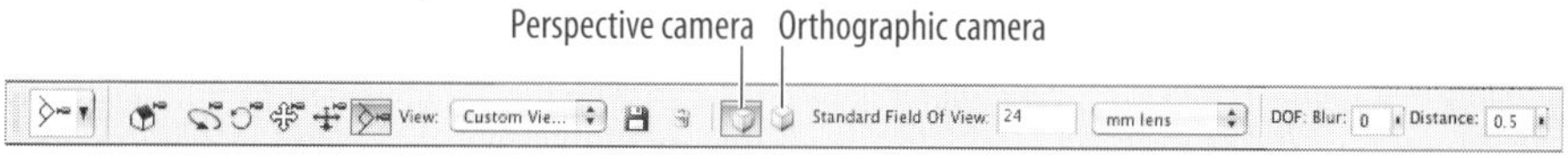

Perspective camera   Orthographic camera

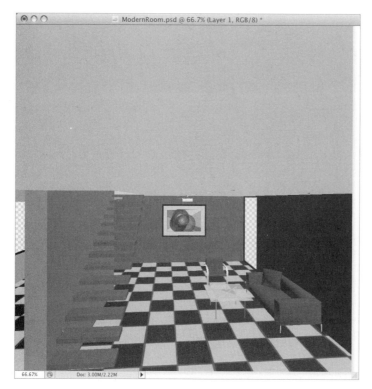

Figure 8.10 Selecting the Perspective camera

3. Select the Walk With The 3D Camera tool on the options bar. Drag upward in the document window to move the camera forward, which allows you to move into the room. The camera is still too high (see Figure 8.11). Dragging to the left or right with the Walk The 3D Camera tool turns the camera.

Figure 8.11 Walking the 3D camera into the room

4. Select the Pan The 3D Camera tool from the options bar. Drag down and to the right in the document window to position the camera at approximately eye level in the right corner of the floor area.

5. The aspect ratio of the document window is square by default—not exactly conducive to a good composition. 3D models are vector in nature, so there's no loss of quality when enlarging or resizing them. Choose Image > Image Size, select Resample Image, and deselect Constrain Proportions. Set the Width and Height drop-downs to pixels, type **1200** in the Width text box and **900** in the Height text box, and click OK (Figure 8.12).

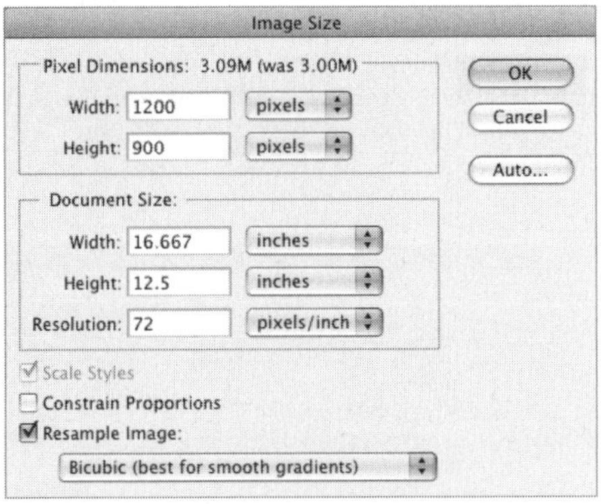

Figure 8.12 Changing the image size without quality loss

6. Take some time practicing with the 3D Camera tools and continue adjusting the camera position and orientation until the 3D camera displays a composition similar to Figure 8.13. However, do not use the Zoom The 3D Camera tool because that would change the field of view from the value set before at 24 mm, which is a wide-angle setting appropriate for an interior space.

 Note: Zooming the 3D Camera is not equivalent to the (2D) Zoom tool in the main toolbox. Zooming the 3D camera changes the focal length of the virtual camera lens. If you want to get closer to a subject, use the Walk The 3D Camera tool instead.

7. Click the Save The Current View icon on the options bar. Accept the default name (Custom View 1) by clicking OK (Figure 8.14).

8. Press Cmd+S / Ctrl+S to save. Leave the file open because you will continue with it in the next section.

ModernRoom.psd @ 100% (Layer 1, RGB/8) *

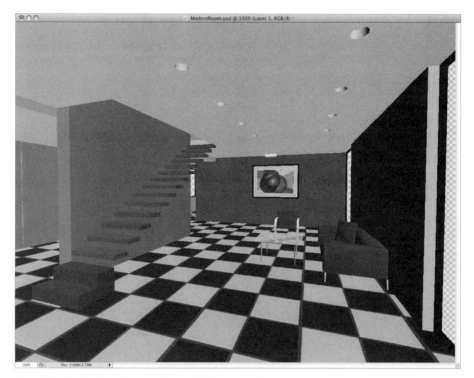

Figure 8.13 Interior of model as seen by a carefully positioned 3D camera

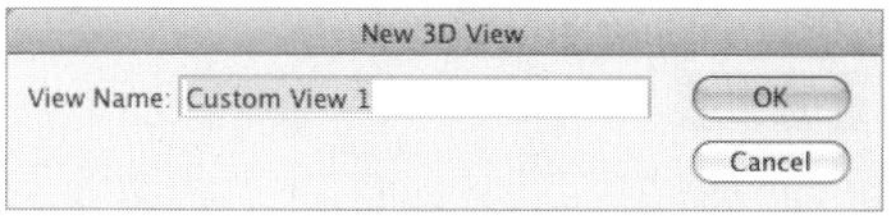

New 3D View
View Name: Custom View 1
OK
Cancel

Figure 8.14 Saving a view after you are pleased with the composition

Adjusting Materials and Maps

Since CS4 Extended, Photoshop has given you control over materials (and any associated maps) assigned to 3D objects. Although materials are assigned to meshes in the 3D software where they were created, materials and maps can be adjusted (or even completely altered) in Photoshop.

Materials are defined by numerous components, including diffuse color, reflection, gloss, bump, and so on. Some of these components can be mapped, which means an image can be stretched over the meshes assigned that material. For example, the checkerboard floor in Figure 8.13 is an image mapped to the diffuse color component of the material that is assigned to the floor mesh. You will change this and many other materials and maps in this section. Let's continue the tutorial:

1. In the Layers panel, rename Layer 1 to **ModernRoom**. Notice the list of Diffuse texture maps belonging to the 3D layer (Figure 8.15).

Figure 8.15 The Modern Room 3D layer, and its associated maps listed underneath

2. Hold the cursor over each diffuse map until its thumbnail appears. As you can see, all the texture maps starting with ID are empty. Let's get rid of these for clarity. The first such map is called ID903.

3. In the 3D panel, click the Filter By: Materials button at the top of the panel. Scroll down and select material ID903 (see Figure 8.16). Notice the folder icons next to many of the material components. The diffuse component has a special icon that means it is mapped. Click this icon and choose Remove Texture from the menu that appears. ID903—Default Texture disappears from the Layers panel.

Figure 8.16 Removing empty textures from specific materials

4. Repeat the preceding step and remove the following diffuse texture maps: ID611, ID603, ID71, ID61, and ID4. Figure 8.17 shows the Layers panel after the empty maps are removed.

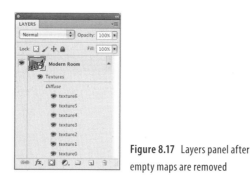

Figure 8.17 Layers panel after empty maps are removed

5. Although it is not possible to rename the texture maps in the Layers panel, it is possible to rename materials so you can make sense of what's what. However, before you can do that, you need to associate materials with meshes. If you are using Photoshop CS5 Extended or later, choose the Select Material tool along the left edge of the 3D panel (it's on the button flyout menu in Figure 8.18) and click the painting in the document window.

Figure 8.18 Using the Select Material tool

6. You may need to scroll down to see that Material ID693 is selected in the 3D panel. Click this material's diffuse map icon and choose Open Texture from the menu that appears (Figure 8.19).

7. A separate document window appears containing the diffuse texture map that was assigned in SketchUp (Figure 8.20). Notice that the title bar identifies this as a dependent PSB file, which functions just like the contents of a smart object (see the "Loading and Manipulating Stacks of Images" section in Chapter 5, "Exploring Multiple-Exposure Tricks"). Press Cmd+W / Ctrl+W to close the PSB file without saving.

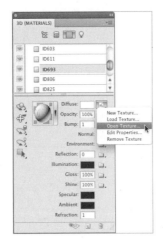

Figure 8.19 Opening a diffuse texture through the material

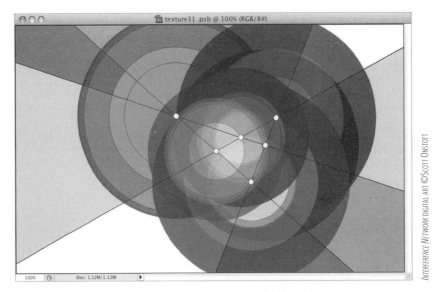

INTERFERENCE NETWORK DIGITAL ART ©SCOTT ONSTOTT

Figure 8.20 Diffuse texture map created in SketchUp and opened in Photoshop

8. Open the Layers panel and hover the cursor over texture3. As you can see, texture3 is the same piece of art (Figure 8.21). The textures in the layers panels are merely shortcuts to the diffuse component within specific materials.

9. In the 3D panel, rename material ID693 to **Painting**.

10. If you are using CS3 Extended or CS4 Extended, you won't have access to the Select Material tool. Here's an alternative method to correlate materials with meshes that works in all Extended versions: Select a material, say the first one (ID4). Position the cursor over the word *Opacity* and observe that the cursor changes to a horizontal arrow. Drag to the left and quickly set opacity to zero (Figure 8.22). The ceiling disappears.

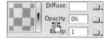

Figure 8.21 Examining texture thumbnails in the Layers panel

Figure 8.22 Quickly adjust Opacity by dragging.

11. Rename material ID4 to **Ceiling**. Position the cursor over the word *Opacity* and drag to the right to set it back to its original value (100%). Repeat this process and identify each material.

12. Rename the materials according to Table 8.1 so they are easier to identify and work with.

▶ **Table 8.1** The Original and New Material Names

Original Name	New Name
ID4	Ceiling
ID61	Red
ID71	White wall
ID121	Not used
ID348	Wood
ID369	Concrete wall
ID566	Metal wall
ID603	Window glazing
ID611	Black frames
ID693	Painting
ID806	Leather
ID825	Floor
ID874	Table legs
ID903	Tabletop
ID1015	Not used

13. Let's assume you want a darker stain on the wooden wall. Double-click texture0 in the Layers panel to open the wooden texture map in its own document window. Open the Adjustments panel and click the Hue/Saturation icon. Select

Colorize and drag the Saturation slider to 25 and Lightness to –15 (Figure 8.23). Press Cmd+W / Ctrl+W to close the document and then press Return/Enter to save. Observe that both the back wall and the stairs are updated in the model. Both of these meshes have the same material assigned.

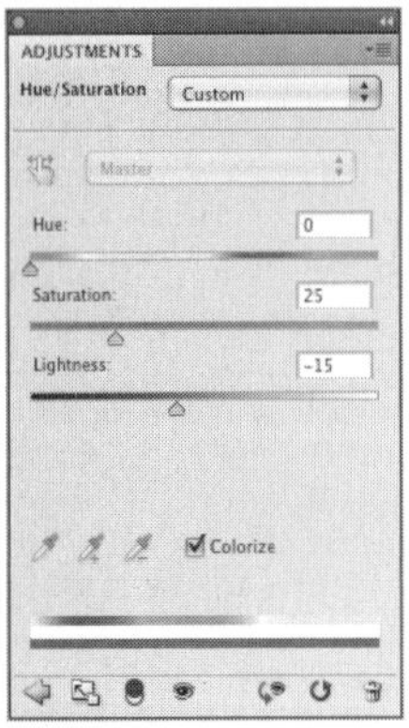

Figure 8.23 Adjusting the saturation and lightness of a texture map

Note: You cannot change material assignment after the 3D model is in Photoshop. Materials can be assigned to meshes only in the 3D-content-creation program.

14. The checkerboard floor is distracting, so you will swap it out for an entirely different texture. Double-click texture5 in the Layers panel to open the checkerboard texture map in its own document window. Open the Terrazzo.jpg sample file from the DVD. You will replace the checkerboard floor with terrazzo.

15. The terrazzo texture is twice as large as the checkerboard texture. Choose Window > texture5.psb and then choose Image > Image Size. In the Image Size dialog box, select Resample Image and Constrain Proportions. Type **512** (pixels) in the Width text box and click OK.

16. Choose Window > Terrazzo.jpg and press Cmd+A / Ctrl+A and then Cmd+C / Ctrl+C to copy the file to the clipboard. Press Cmd+W / Ctrl+W to close Terrazzo.jpg without saving.

17. Press Cmd+V / Ctrl+V to paste the terrazzo texture into texture5.psb. Rename Layer 1 to **Terrazzo**, press Cmd+W / Ctrl+W, and then press Return/Enter to save. The floor texture updates with terrazzo in the model (Figure 8.24).

18. Notice that the chip size is a bit large. You will adjust the mapping coordinates to make the chips composing the terrazzo appear smaller. Click the Filter By: Materials button at the top of the 3D panel if it isn't already selected. Target the Floor material and click the Edit The Diffuse Texture button. Select Edit Properties from the menu that appears.

Figure 8.24 Detail of the new floor texture

19. In the Texture Properties dialog box, change U Scale and V Scale to 2 and click OK. The texture appears.

> **Note:** In 3D-content-creation programs, textures are mapped onto meshes by using texture coordinates, measured in UVW space. The letters *U*, *V*, and *W* were chosen to differentiate texture space from world space (where the meshes are), which is measured in terms of *X*, *Y*, and *Z*. By increasing the scale of *U* and *V*, you are causing the texture to be repeated more frequently on the meshes to which it is mapped, and thus the texture will appear smaller.

20. Architects have long used tie holes as a visual design element in concrete walls, and you will now create this look by adjusting the concrete texture map. Double-click texture1 in the Layers panel to open the concrete texture map in its own document window. This concrete texture was made from scratch in Photoshop by using the technique shown in Chapter 6, "Creating Texture Maps."

21. Press Cmd+R / Ctrl+R to display the rulers. Choose Image > Image Size, deselect Resample Image, and type **12** in the Width text box (Figure 8.25). Click OK.

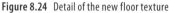

Figure 8.25 Changing document size without changing pixel size

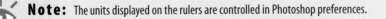

Note: The units displayed on the rulers are controlled in Photoshop preferences.

22. Press V to select the Move tool. Drag guides out from the left ruler and align them at 2, 6, and 10 inches, as shown in Figure 8.26.

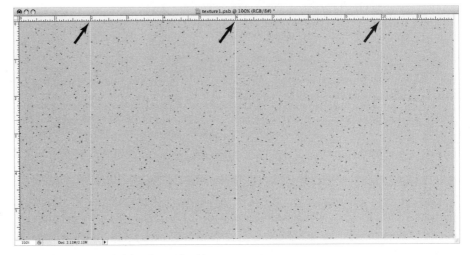

Figure 8.26 Planning tie hole locations with guides

23. Choose Image > Image Size, type **12** in the Height text box, and click OK. The rulers are recalibrated.

24. Drag guides down from the top ruler and align them at 3 and 9 inches, as shown in Figure 8.27. Press Cmd+R / Ctrl+ R to hide the rulers.

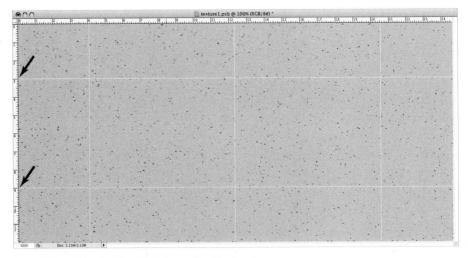

Figure 8.27 Additional guides added after recalibrating the ruler

25. Press U and click the Shape Layers button on the options bar. Click the Ellipse tool and select No Style in the Style drop-down. Click the color swatch on the options bar and select pure black if it's not already selected (see Figure 8.28).

Figure 8.28 Vector drawing tool options

26. Position the cursor over the intersection point of two guides and begin dragging out an ellipse. While you are dragging, hold down Opt+Shift / Alt+Shift, and the ellipse will be created from the center as a circle. Drag a short distance and release the mouse button to draw a small circle representing a tie hole.

27. Press A to select the Direct Selection tool and click the circle you just drew. Press Cmd+C / Ctrl+C and then Cmd+V / Ctrl+V to copy and paste a coincident circle. Drag this new circle to the intersection of two other guides. Repeat this step until you have six circles, one at each guide intersection point (see Figure 8.29).

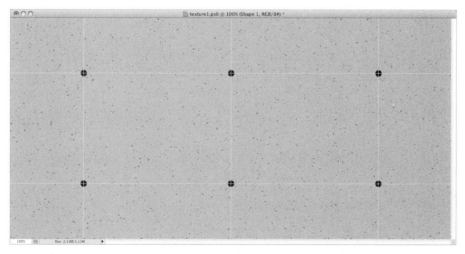

Figure 8.29 Copying and pasting six equally sized circles at guide intersection points

28. Click the fx icon along the lower edge of the Layers panel and choose Bevel And Emboss from the menu that appears. In the Layer Style dialog box that appears, Click the Direction radio button labeled Down and set Size at 6 px (Figure 8.30). Click OK.

29. Double-click the Background layer, type **Concrete** in the New Layer dialog box that appears, and click OK. Double-click just to the right of the word *Concrete* in the Layers panel to open the Layer Style dialog box. Click and highlight the word *Stroke* to open its properties. Choose Inside from the Position drop-down. Target the Size text box and press the down arrow on the keyboard until Size is 3 px (Figure 8.31). Click the Color swatch and select 50% gray by dragging along the left edge of the color ramp until R, G, and B all read 128.

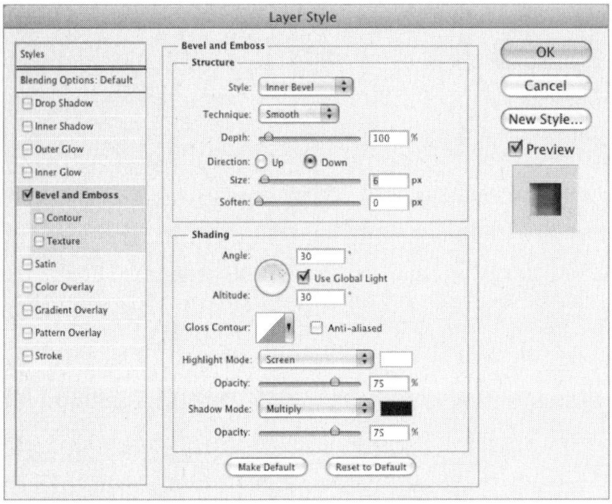

Figure 8.30 Adding depth to tie holes with a layer style effect

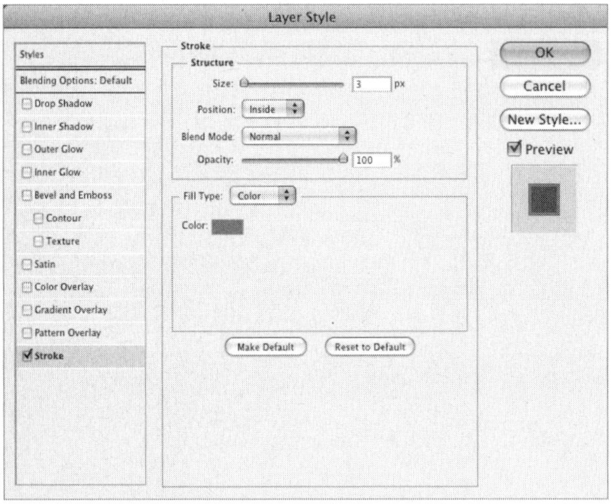

Figure 8.31 Adding a stroke layer style effect

30. Click OK twice to close both dialog boxes. Press Cmd+H / Ctrl+H to hide the guides. Figure 8.32 shows the final result.

31. Press Cmd+W / Ctrl+W and then press Return/Enter to close and save texture1 .psb. The concrete updates on the wall in the model.

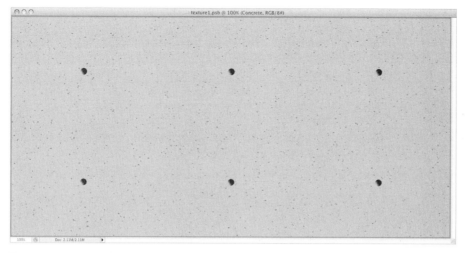

Figure 8.32 Concrete with precisely spaced and inset tie holes characteristic of modern design

32. Choose Layer > New Fill Layer > Gradient. Type **Sky** in the New Layer dialog box that appears and click OK. Select the Sky gradient (created in Chapter 3, "Stretching the Photographic Truth") in the Gradient Fill dialog box and click OK. Press Cmd+Shift+[/ Ctrl+Shift+[to move Sky below the Modern Room layer.

33. Save as ModernRoom2.psd. Figure 8.33 shows the result.

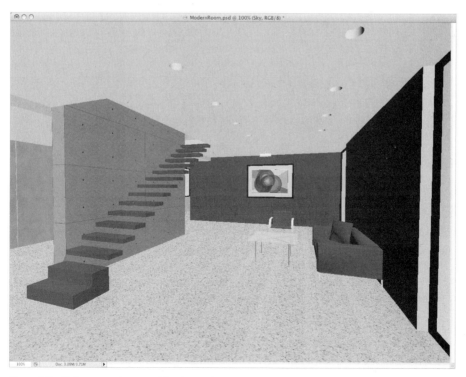

Figure 8.33 Modern room after material and map adjustments

Illuminating with Virtual Light

3D layers are illuminated with two infinite lights by default. These lights are called *infinite* because they simulate sunlight. The sun is actually a point source, casting rays in all directions. However, for all intents and purposes, one can consider the sun's rays parallel because it is so incredibly far away. If a point source were infinitely far away, its rays would truly be parallel.

Photoshop also has *point lights*, which shine in all directions, and *spotlights*, which illuminate in a cone. Photoshop CS5 Extended introduces *image-based lights*, which simulate light coming from the environment as represented by a panoramic image. Let's add some virtual light to the model:

1. Open ModernRoom2.psd from the DVD or continue with the file you've been developing.

2. Click the Filter By: Lights button at the top of the 3D panel. Toggle Infinite Light 1 off by clicking its eye icon. Everything turns black except for the ceiling because this light shines down on the model. Rename Infinite Light 1 to Down and turn it back on. Tone down Intensity to 0.4.

3. Rename Infinite Light 2 to Up. If lights create shadows, their rays stop whenever they hit a surface. Conversely, when lights do not create shadows, they pass through solid objects and illuminate surfaces that lie beyond. Deselect Create Shadows (Figure 8.34). This infinite light will illuminate the ceiling by passing up through the floor. Shadows are visible only in rendered views, which we'll get to in the next section.

4. Let's add a light to illuminate the painting on the wood-clad wall. In order to accurately position the light, you will first move the camera. Press N to select the 3D Camera tools. Select Top from the View drop-down on the options bar. We are looking at the room plan but can't see into the room yet.

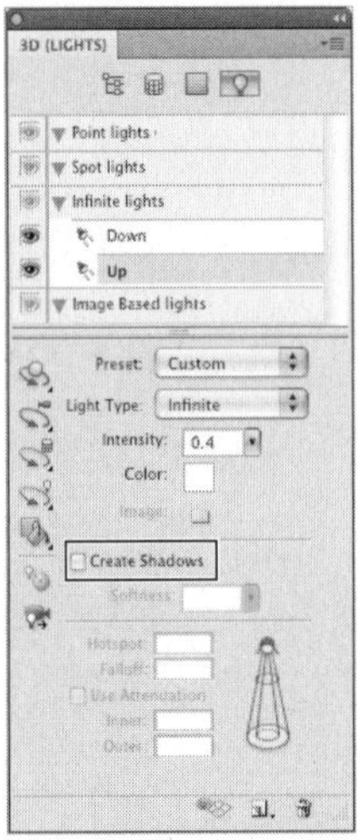

Figure 8.34 Turning off shadow casting for an infinite light enables it to illuminate occluded surfaces.

5. Right-click the ModernRoom layer and choose Render Settings from the contextual menu. Deselect the shaded cube in the 3D Render Settings dialog box that appears. Select the wireframe cube (unavailable without hardware acceleration). Deselect Remove Hidden Lines to see through the ceiling mesh (Figure 8.35). Click OK.

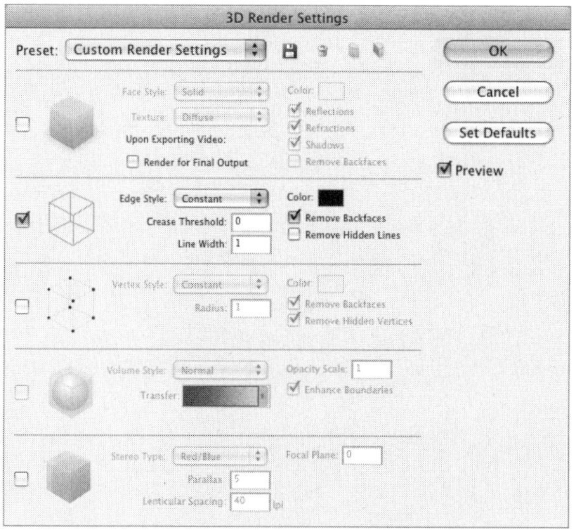

Figure 8.35 Changing render settings to see through the ceiling

6. Click the Create A New Light button and choose New Spot Light from the menu that appears (Figure 8.36).

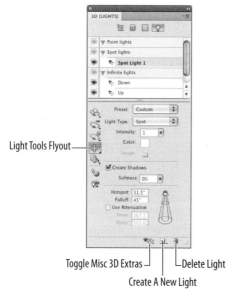

Light Tools Flyout

Toggle Misc 3D Extras — └─Delete Light

Create A New Light

Figure 8.36 3D panel controls

7. Select the Light Pan tool from the Light tools flyout and then click the Toggle Misc 3D Extras button and toggle on 3D Lights. Now you can see the pink wireframe spotlight and the white armature representing its cone of light. Drag the spotlight over the ceiling-mounted fixture, as shown in Figure 8.37.

8. Press N to select the 3D Camera tools. Select Front from the View drop-down on the options bar. From this vantage, you can see that the spot light is way above the ceiling (Figure 8.38). Use the Light Pan tool to move the spot light into the room just below the ceiling-mounted fixture.

9. Select Custom View 1 from the View drop-down to return to the point of view you set up earlier in this chapter, in the "Navigating in 3D Space" section.

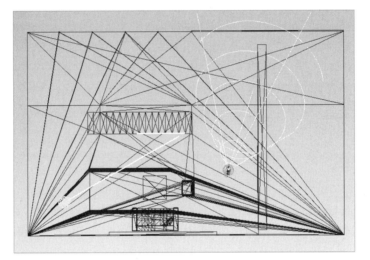

Figure 8.37 Panning a spot light in the plan

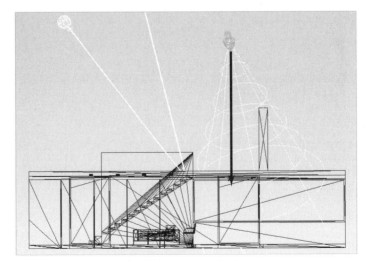

Figure 8.38 Panning a spot light in elevation

10. Click the Filter By: Whole Scene button at the top of the 3D panel. The Scene node should be selected by default at the top of the scene hierarchy. Select Default from the Render Settings drop-down in the lower pane of the 3D panel (Figure 8.39). Shaded textures reappear in the document window, and illumination from the spot light is visible in the space.

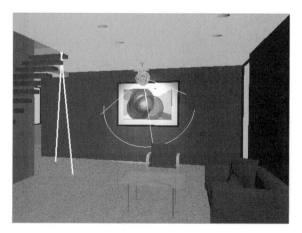

Figure 8.39 Selecting render settings from a drop-down

11. Open the Light tools flyout and select the 3D Light Rotate tool. Drag in the document to reorient the spotlight toward the painting, as shown in Figure 8.40.

Figure 8.40 Orienting a spotlight

12. Scroll to the bottom of the scene hierarchy and select Spot Light 1. Deselect Create Shadows, and set Hotspot to 45 degrees and Falloff to 90 degrees (Figure 8.41). Light is at its full intensity within the hot-spot cone and gradually fades out at the falloff cone, which represents the limit of illumination.

Figure 8.41 Adjusting hot-spot and falloff angles of a spotlight

13. In much the same way as you have done in steps 4–12, create another spotlight to brighten the seating group because it is flat without some variation in lighting intensity. Figure 8.42 shows one such example.

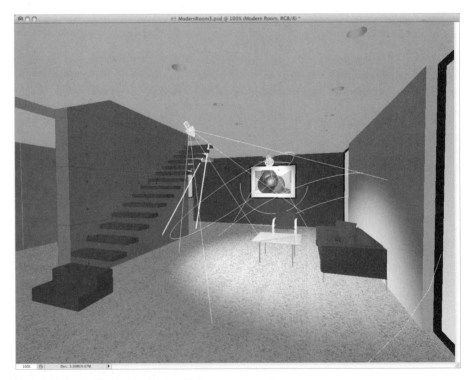

Figure 8.42 Interior illuminated with virtual light

14. Save as ModernRoom3.psd.

Rendering the Model

The shaded materials, maps, and lighting seen in the document window thus far are the result of a quickly calculated approximation that sacrifices quality for interactivity. Greater levels of realism, including shadows, reflection, refraction, and transparency, are possible only when the image is *rendered*. Rendering, or more specifically ray tracing, refers to the often-lengthy process of calculating final values for pixels based on the interaction of meshes, materials, maps, and lights as seen through the 3D Camera.

Note: In the ray-tracing algorithm, rays of light are traced backward from the picture plane, through all object inter-reflections back to the light sources from which the rays emanated. The history of each ray's interaction determines its final pixel color in the rendering. Ray tracing is computationally expensive and can be a lengthy process in complex scenes with many lights.

Photoshop offers two quality levels of ray tracing: draft and final. Instead of waiting forever for high-quality rendering, you'll learn a trick for accelerating the process that harnesses Photoshop's well-known raster editing abilities. Let's give rendering a try:

1. Continue working with the file you've been developing in this chapter or open the ModernRoom3.psd sample file from the DVD.

2. In the 3D panel, click the Toggle Misc 3D Extras button at the bottom of the 3D panel and toggle off 3D Light and any other extras that are selected.

3. Select the Scene node at the top of the unfiltered scene hierarchy. Choose Ray Traced Draft from the Quality drop-down and wait a while as Photoshop renders the scene (Figure 8.43). Click anywhere in the document window to stop the calculation when you feel it isn't getting any better.

Note: Rotate the infinite lights slightly to change the shadow and sunspot angles.

4. Figure 8.44 shows the draft ray-traced rendering. The rendering is too dark. You could add additional lights and re-render the scene but you might be better off rasterizing a copy of the 3D model and working with traditional Photoshop techniques that can be executed in real time. Press Cmd+Shift+N / Ctrl+Shift+N, type **Stamped** in the New Layer dialog box that appears, and click OK. Press Cmd+Opt+Shift+E / Ctrl+Alt+Shift+E to stamp (rasterize) the rendering onto the new layer.

Figure 8.43 Selecting ray-traced quality level

Figure 8.44 Ray-traced rendering in Photoshop

5. Target the ModernRoom layer. In the 3D panel, set the Quality drop-down to Interactive.

6. Target the Stamped layer and change its layer blend mode from Normal to Screen. Adjust its layer opacity to 50%. This layer brings in the shadows and the sun-spot on the floor where the infinite light is shining through the window.

7. The rendering is still a bit too bright. Press Cmd+J / Ctrl+J to duplicate the Stamped layer. Change this new layer's blend mode to Multiply and set its opacity to 20%. There is no waiting when changing a layer's opacity! Darker shadows and more contrast improve the rendering. Figure 8.45 shows the result.

Figure 8.45 Final rendering as modulated by raster blending techniques

Congratulations on completing this lengthy tutorial. You touched on all aspects of working with imported 3D models, from transferring 3D models into Photoshop and navigating in 3D space to adjusting materials and maps. You also learned how to illuminate with virtual light and render the model. In addition, I've shown you a few raster tips that may obviate the need to invest the considerable time necessary to get a "perfect" rendering, when classic Photoshop techniques produce similar results in real time.

Illustrating 3D Models

Creating photo-realistic renderings from 3D models is an extremely complicated and time-consuming process that many architects outsource to experts in 3ds Max, Maya, or other high-end 3D packages. This chapter is about using the Extended version of Photoshop to go in the opposite direction: creating non–photo-realistic illustrations based on 3D models. The bonus is that non–photo-realistic illustration is a relatively fast process. Instead of trying to perfectly simulate reality, there is power in telling your visual story by using abstract and artistic methods.

Chapter Contents

Illustrating with smart filters
Illustrating with render settings
Using painterly approaches to illustrating models

Illustrating with Smart Filters

Filters have been part of Photoshop for 20 years. You have probably used Gaussian Blur, Smart Sharpen, Lens Blur, Lens Correction, and even Vanishing Point occasionally. But have you ever wondered when you'd be able to use one of the literally 100 other filters? Illustrating a 3D model is the perfect opportunity to try some of these classic algorithms out. Here we go:

1. Open `Denver Public Library.dae` from the DVD.

2. Press K to select the 3D Object tools, and click the Rotate The 3D Object tool if it hasn't already been selected. Type **-90** in the X Orientation box and press Return/Enter (Figure 9.1) to match the coordinate system of the SketchUp model to Photoshop's coordinate system.

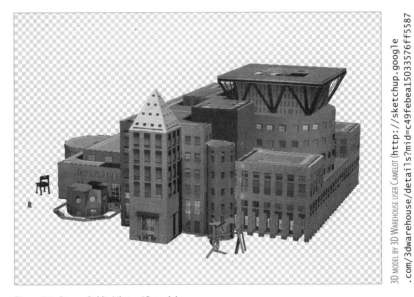

Figure 9.1 Denver Public Library 3D model

3. The document window is square by default. Choose Image > Image Size, select Resample Image, deselect Constrain Proportions, and change the Width unit drop-down to pixels. Type **1200** for Width and **900** for Height (Figure 9.2). Click OK to close the Image Size dialog box. Changing the image size does not adversely affect the quality of a 3D layer as it would a raster layer.

4. Press N to select the 3D Camera tools. Choose Front from the View drop-down on the options bar.

5. Select the Zoom The 3D Camera tool on the options bar, click the Perspective Camera button, change the Standard Field Of View drop-down to mm, and type **24** in the adjacent text box. The full camera choices are detailed in Figure 9.3.

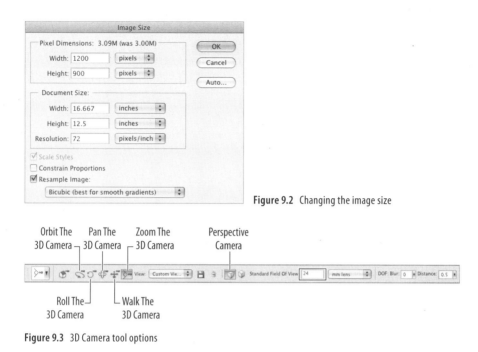

Figure 9.2 Changing the image size

Orbit The
3D Camera

Pan The
3D Camera

Zoom The
3D Camera

Perspective
Camera

Roll The
3D Camera

Walk The
3D Camera

Figure 9.3 3D Camera tool options

6. Select the Orbit The 3D Camera tool on the options bar and drag to the left to get an oblique view of the model. Select the Walk The 3D Camera tool and drag upward to move the camera closer and thus enlarge the size of the model in the document window (see Figure 9.4).

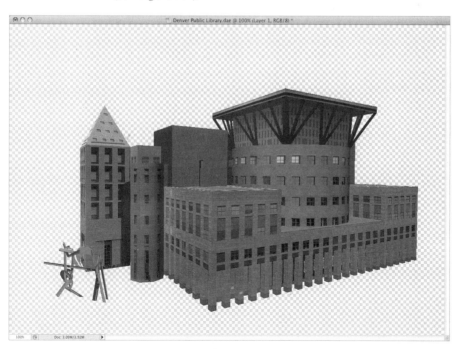

Figure 9.4 Composing a view of the model

7. Click the Add A New Fill Or Adjustment Layer button at the bottom of the Layers panel and select Solid Color from the menu that appears. Select medium gray in the Color Picker by dragging along the left edge of the color ramp until 128 appears in R, G, and B (Figure 9.5). Click OK.

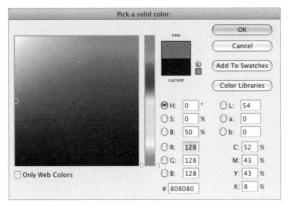

Figure 9.5 Selecting medium gray

8. Press Cmd+[/ Ctrl+[to move the current layer below the 3D layer. Now you have a medium gray backdrop. Rename Color Fill 1 to Backdrop and Layer 1 to 3D Model. Drag Backdrop's layer mask into the Trash at the bottom of the Layers panel to get rid of it.

9. Press Opt+[/ Alt+[to select the 3D model layer. Press Cmd+Shift+N / Ctrl+Shift+N, type **Rasterized** in the New Layer dialog box, and click OK.

10. Press Cmd+Opt+Shift+E / Ctrl+Alt+Shift+E to stamp the visible layers to layer Rasterized. Toggle off layers Backdrop and 3D Model by clicking their eye icons in the Layers panel.

11. Right-click layer Rasterized and choose Convert To Smart Object from the contextual menu (Figure 9.6). By applying filters to a smart object, the changes remain nondestructive and re-editable.

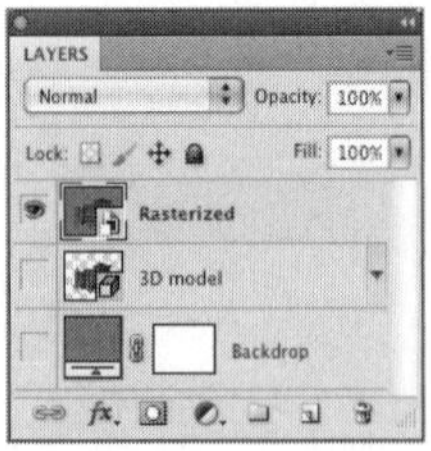

Figure 9.6 Layers panel after creation of stamped Rasterized layer

12. Choose Filter > Filter Gallery. Click the disclosure triangle (Figure 9.7) to expand the categorized list of filters if it's not already open. Open the Brush Strokes category and select Accented Edges. Set Edge Width to 1, Edge Brightness to 15, and Smoothness to 3.

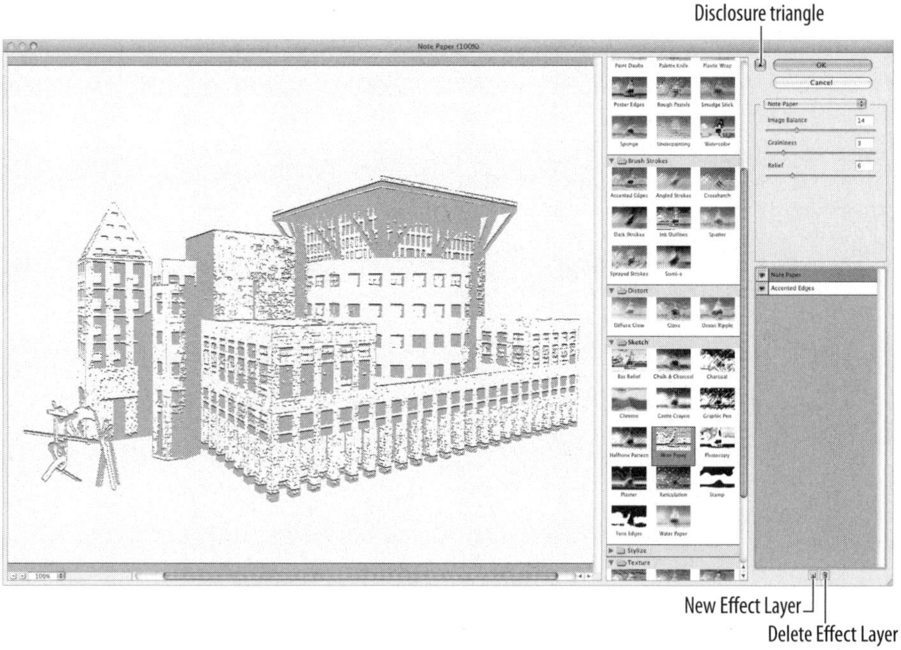

Disclosure triangle

New Effect Layer

Delete Effect Layer

Figure 9.7 Using the Filter Gallery to create an automatic illustration

13. Click the New Effect Layer button at the bottom right of the massive dialog box. Open the Sketch category and select Note Paper (the grayscale thumbnail shows this is a grayscale filter). Set Image Balance to 14, Graininess to 3, and Relief to 6 (Figure 9.7). Click OK to close the Filter Gallery.

14. Press Cmd+Shift+N / Ctrl+Shift+N, type **Illustration 1** in the New Layer dialog box, and click OK.

15. Press Cmd+Opt+Shift+E / Ctrl+Alt+Shift+E to stamp the visible layers to the Illustration 1 layer. Now toggle this layer off.

16. Double-click the words *Filter Gallery* under the Rasterized layer to reopen the large dialog box. Click the Delete Effect Layer button.

17. Open the Artistic category and select Paint Daubs. Set Brush Size to 5, Sharpness to 12, and Brush Type to Simple.

18. Click the New Effect Layer button and click Accented Edges in the Brush Strokes category. Notice that the settings are the same as the last time you applied this effect, in step 12.

19. Click the New Layer Effect button, open the Texture category, and select Texturizer. Select Canvas from the Texture drop-down. Set Scaling to 100% and Relief to 4. Select Top from the Light drop-down, and leave Invert deselected.

20. Drag Paint Daubs above Accented Edges in the effect list. The illustration changes subtly (Figure 9.8). The order of effects can be significant—effects are evaluated in order from bottom to top. Click OK to close the Filter Gallery.

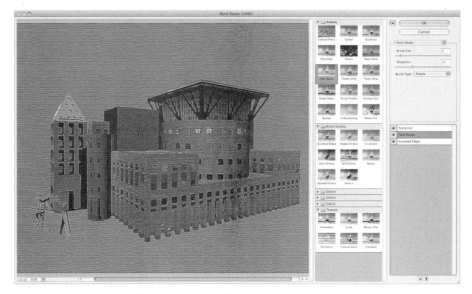

Figure 9.8 Creating an entirely different look with a different combination of filter effects

21. Press Cmd+Shift+N / Ctrl+Shift+N, type **Illustration 2** in the New Layer dialog box, and click OK.

22. Press Cmd+Opt+Shift+E / Ctrl+Alt+Shift+E to stamp the visible layers to the Illustration 2 layer. Now toggle this layer off.

23. Save the image as Library Illustration.psd.

Create another illustration on your own. The Filter Gallery was designed for experimentation. There is seemingly an infinite number of permutations available by combining filter effects. When you're satisfied, create a new layer and stamp the contents of the smart object onto it.

Illustrating with Render Settings

The appearance of 3D layers in the document window is controlled by render settings. By skillfully compositing shaded illustrations, line art, and wireframe views, you can create compelling abstract illustrations. Here's how it's done:

1. Open SF MOMA.dae from the DVD.

2. Press K to select the 3D Object tools and click the Rotate The 3D Object tool if it's not already selected. Type **-90** in the X Orientation box and press Tab twice. Type **-45** in the Z box and press Return/Enter (Figure 9.9).

3. Choose Image > Image Size, select Resample Image, deselect Constrain Proportions, and change the Width unit drop-down to pixels. Type **1200** in the Width box and **900** in the Height box.

4. Press N to select the 3D Camera tools. Choose Front from the View drop-down on the options bar.

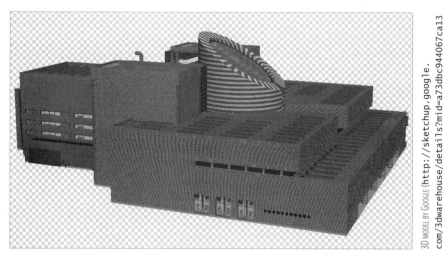

Figure 9.9 San Francisco Museum of Modern Art 3D model

5. Select the Zoom The 3D Camera tool on the options bar and click the Perspective Camera button.

6. Choose the Orbit The 3D Camera tool and drag a short distance straight up to get an aerial view of the museum. Choose the Pan The 3D camera tool and drag down slightly to center the model in the document window (Figure 9.10).

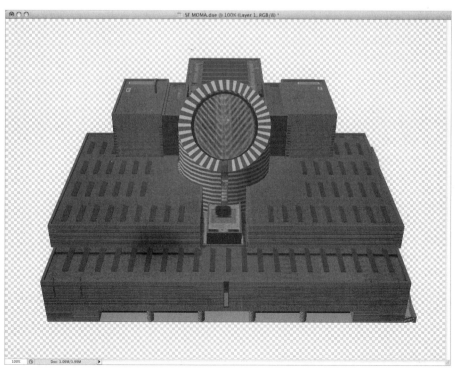

Figure 9.10 Composing a view of the model

7. Choose Window > 3D if the 3D panel isn't already open. Click the Filter By: Whole Scene button at the top of the 3D panel and select the Shaded Illustration preset from the Render Settings drop-down (Figure 9.11).

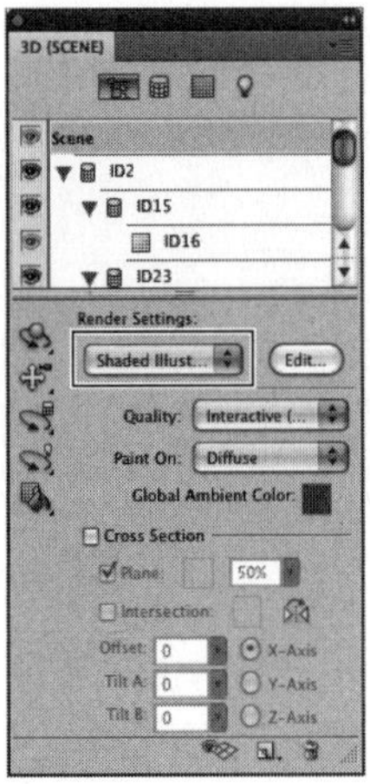

Figure 9.11 Selecting a Render Settings preset

8. Rename Layer 1 to SF MOMA.

9. Press Cmd+Shift+N / Ctrl+Shift+N, type **Shaded Illustration** in the New Layer dialog box, and click OK.

10. Press Cmd+Opt+Shift+E / Ctrl+Alt+Shift+E to stamp what is currently visible onto the Shaded Illustration layer. Now toggle this layer off and target layer SF MOMA.

11. In the 3D panel, select the Wireframe preset from the Render Settings drop-down. The mesh triangulation (Figure 9.12) detracts from the pristine geometry of the design. You will fix this next.

12. Click the Edit button adjacent to the Render Settings drop-down in the 3D panel. In the 3D Render Settings dialog box that appears, set Crease Threshold to 2 and set Line Width to 3 (Figure 9.13). Click OK. The triangulation is gone, and the wireframe is thicker.

13. Press Cmd+Shift+N / Ctrl+Shift+N, type **Wireframe** in the New Layer dialog box, and click OK.

14. Press Cmd+Opt+Shift+E / Ctrl+Alt+Shift+E to stamp what is currently visible onto the Wireframe layer. Now toggle this layer off and target layer SF MOMA once again.

15. In the 3D panel, select the Line Illustration preset from the Render Settings drop-down.

16. Press Cmd+Shift+N / Ctrl+Shift+N, type **Line Illustration** in the New Layer dialog box, and click OK.

Figure 9.12 The Wireframe preset suffers from mesh triangulation.

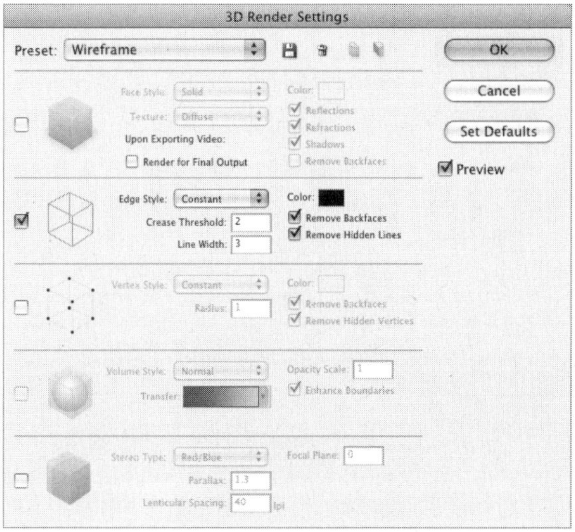

Figure 9.13 Customizing render settings

17. Press Cmd+Opt+Shift+E / Ctrl+Alt+Shift+E to stamp what is currently visible onto the Line Illustration layer.

18. Choose Layer > New Fill Layer > Gradient, type **Backdrop** in the New Layer dialog box that appears, and click OK.

19. Select the Black, White gradient in the Gradient Fill dialog box and increase Scale to 150% to soften the transition from black to white (Figure 9.14). Click OK.

Figure 9.14 Customizing the backdrop gradient

20. Drag layer Backdrop to the bottom of the layer stack in the Layers panel. Drag Backdrop's layer mask to the Trash icon in the lower-right corner of the Layers panel.

21. Toggle off layer SF MOMA. Toggle on layers Line Illustration and Wireframe. Target layer Wireframe.

22. The black wireframe on layer Wireframe blots out the white wireframe on Line Illustration. You can combine these effects with a layer mask. Click the Add Layer Mask button at the bottom of the Layers panel.

23. Select the Gradient tool from the main toolbox (press Shift+G to cycle between it and the Paint Bucket tool). Press D to select the default colors and then X to exchange foreground with background so that black is in the foreground.

24. On the options bar, open the Gradient Picker and select Foreground To Transparent. Select the Linear Gradient button and select Dither and Transparency (Figure 9.15).

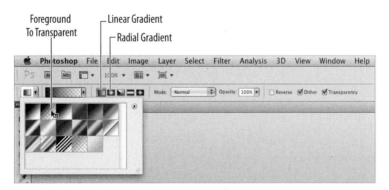

Figure 9.15 Selecting gradient options

25. Hold down Shift and drag from the bottom of the building to the top (Figure 9.16). The wireframe gradually transitions from white to black.

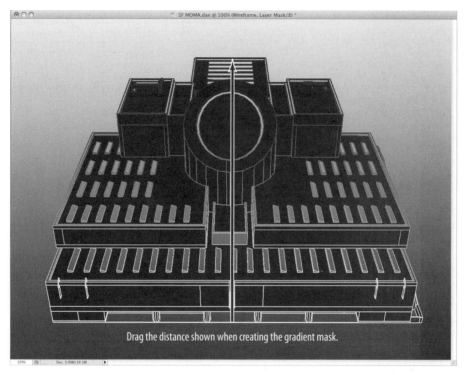

Drag the distance shown when creating the gradient mask.

Figure 9.16 Creating a gradient mask on layer `Wireframe` that gradually reveals the `Line Illustration` layer

26. Toggle on layer `Shaded Illustration` and target this layer. Opt+click / Alt+click the Add Layer Mask button at the bottom of the Layers panel to add a black mask that completely obscures this layer. You will reveal the `Shaded Illustration` layer in stages.

27. Press G to select the Gradient tool. Click the Radial Gradient button on the options bar and press X so that White is the foreground color.

28. Hold down Shift and drag from the center of the glass atrium to the edge of the building, as shown in Figure 9.17. Perform this step twice more to progressively brighten the gradient and thus reveal more of the `Shaded Illustration` layer.

29. Press B to select the Paintbrush tool. Press the F5 key to open the Brushes panel. Select the Round Fan bristle brush (new in CS5 Extended), shown in Figure 9.18.

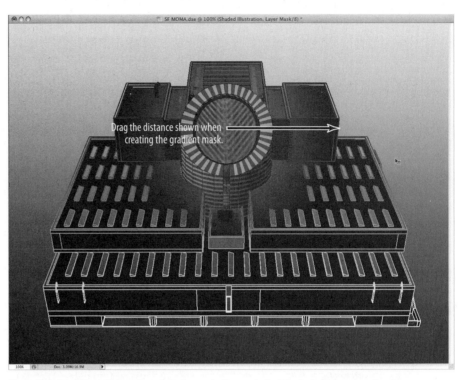

Figure 9.17 Creating a radial gradient mask that gradually reveals the Shaded Illustration layer

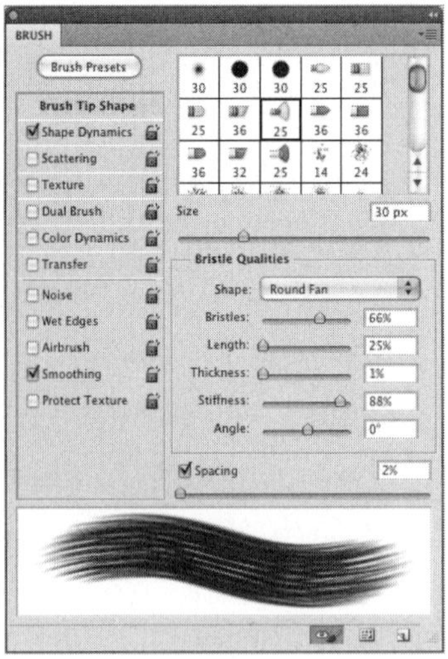

Figure 9.18 Selecting one of the new bristle brushes

30. You'll use the bristle brush to reveal some of the brick on the front of the building by painting in white on Shaded Illustration's layer mask. The bristle brush is especially nice as brushstrokes are evident in the individual bristle tips. Paint across the façade as shown in Figure 9.19. Hold down Shift after you begin painting to ensure that the brush strokes are perfectly horizontal. The arrows in Figure 9.19 indicate the direction and extents of brushstrokes made to partially reveal the brick texture.

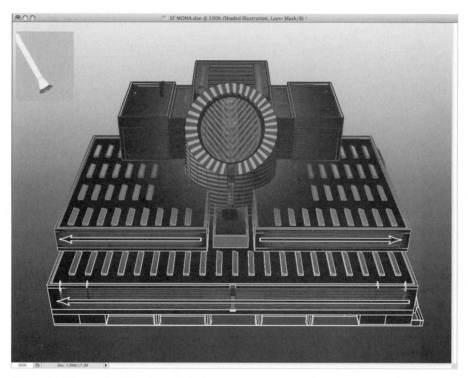

Figure 9.19 Selecting a bristle brush to paint on the layer mask and reveal selected parts of the shaded illustration

31. Save the image as **SF MOMA.psd**. Compare Figure 9.20 with Figure 9.10 to see how far you've come from the 3D model. The result has a unique abstract quality you don't normally see in 3D models. Variations on this technique have great potential for generating attractive illustrations.

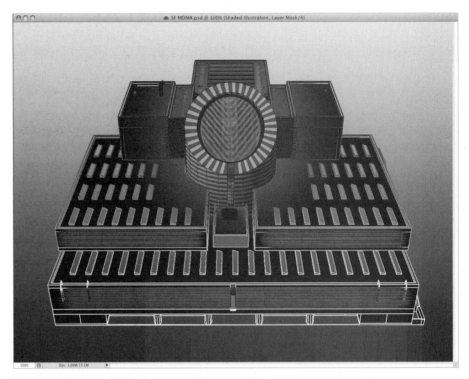

Figure 9.20 Composite of 3D render settings makes an attractive illustration

Using Painterly Approaches to Illustrating Models

Using brush tools to create an illustration can result in a handmade look typically associated with traditional media. However, I'm not suggesting you paint an illustration completely from scratch unless you happen to have an innate talent or desire to take up digital painting as a hobby. It is much faster and more efficient to start with a 3D model as the basis of your "painting."

In this section, you'll explore two painterly tools: the Art History Brush (introduced in Photoshop 5.5) and the Mixer Brush (new in Photoshop CS5 Extended). Both brushes help you simulate the look of traditional paintings by using markedly different methods. The Art History Brush uses gestural algorithms to simulate the way the hand typically moves a brush, whereas the Mixer Brush blends pixels by simulating physical bristles interacting with paint on the canvas.

Art History 101

What does art history have to do with Photoshop? The Art History Brush is related to the History Brush, and you don't need to know anything about Renoir or Monet to use these tools. Both tools source their paint from a history state (marking a step you took in Photoshop). The Art History Brush differs from the History Brush by adding gesture to the brushstroke through a variety of algorithms. Let's give it a try:

1. Open Old Town Square.jpg from the DVD (Figure 9.21). This image was exported from a SketchUp 3D model.

Figure 9.21 Old Town Square 3D model exported from SketchUp

2. Press Cmd+Shift+N / Ctrl+Shift+N, type **Underpainting** in the New Layer dialog box that appears, and click OK.

3. Press Shift+F5 to invoke the Fill dialog box. Select 50% Gray from the Use drop-down (Figure 9.22), and click OK. Think of this gray as your canvas.

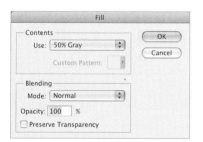

Figure 9.22 Filling a blank layer with 50% gray

4. Press Shift+Y to cycle to the Art History Brush (it's on a flyout with the History Brush). Select a 30-pixel soft round brush from the picker on the options bar. Select Tight Medium from the Style drop-down, type **50 px** in the Area box, and click the Tablet Pressure Controls Size button if you are using a tablet (Figure 9.23). If you are using a mouse, you can adjust brush size with the [and] keys.

Figure 9.23 Setting Art History Brush options

Note: Although it is possible to paint with more-complex brushes including bristle tips while using the Art History Brush (for more-interesting facture), my MacBook Pro bogs down and the strokes appear only after a lag of several seconds. Perhaps in the future, computers will be able to keep up in real time and thus enable more-complex painterly effects. For now, I recommend sticking with the soft round brush, whose effects are calculated much faster.

5. Starting with a larger brush (pushing hard on the stylus on a pressure-sensitive tablet), paint a few brush strokes and observe the Art History Brush in action (Figure 9.24). Large strokes appear with dynamic tight medium curls.

Figure 9.24 Painting a few brushstrokes with the Art History Brush

6. Using the same large brush, cover the entire canvas with brushstrokes (Figure 9.25).

7. Press Cmd+Shift+N / Ctrl+Shift+N, type **Overpainting** in the New Layer dialog box that appears, and click OK.

8. Paint with a smaller brush and add finer detail (press lightly on the stylus or press the [key to reduce brush diameter) to draw attention to the buildings surrounding the square and to the square itself.

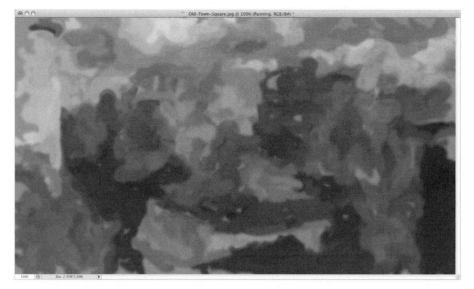

Figure 9.25 Creating a multicolored underpainting

9. Choose Filter > Sharpen > Smart Sharpen. Set Amount at 100%, set Radius at 1.0 px, and choose Gaussian Blur from the Remove drop-down (Figure 9.26). Click OK.

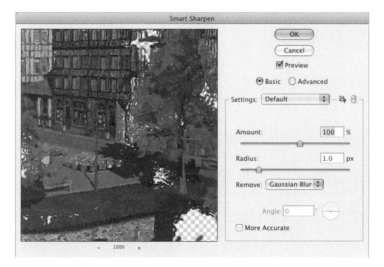

Figure 9.26 Sharpening the overpainting increases clarity.

10. Decrease the opacity of the Overpainting layer and blend it with layer Underpainting. The opacity amount to select is entirely subjective (I chose 76%). Figure 9.27 shows my unique painting.

Figure 9.27 This illustration made with the Art History Brush has a traditional look.

Experiment with the styles on the options bar to develop a feel for the Art History Brush and find your own style. There is no "right way" to paint, and that is part of the beauty of this technique: Every artist's painting is a unique original based on the same 3D model.

Painting with the Mixer Brush

The Mixer Brush differs from the Paintbrush tool in its capability to mix paint that's already on the canvas with the foreground color in any percentage. You can even choose not to apply new paint at all but instead treat the paint that's already on the canvas as wet. The Mixer Brush can spread this "wet paint" around just as you'd expect a real brush to behave on a physical canvas.

We will use the Mixer Brush to convert a 3D rendering to something that has hand-painted appeal. Whereas the Art History Brush uses an algorithm to style the brushstroke, the Mixer Brush offers full manual control. Those with real painting experience will likely get better results with the Mixer Brush because it was designed to be a physical analogue. Having a pressure-sensitive tablet to better simulate brush feel is a great boon as well. Regardless of your painting experience, give the Mixer Brush a try:

1. Open GeorgiaAquarium.tif from the DVD. This image was exported from a SketchUp 3D model (Figure 9.28).

2. The rendered image has transparency information (rather than an alpha channel) that you will use to reveal a sky gradient. Choose Layer > New Fill Layer > Gradient, type **Sky** in the New Layer dialog box, and click OK.

3D Warehouse model by Google (http://sketchup.google.com/3dwarehouse/details?mid=22b4b1889f701ac9be2e393d60145630&prevstart=0)

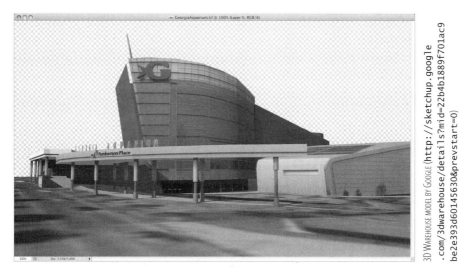

Figure 9.28 Georgia Aquarium model exported from SketchUp

3. Choose the Sky gradient (created in Chapter 3, "Stretching the Photographic Truth") in the Gradient Fill dialog box (Figure 9.29) and click OK.

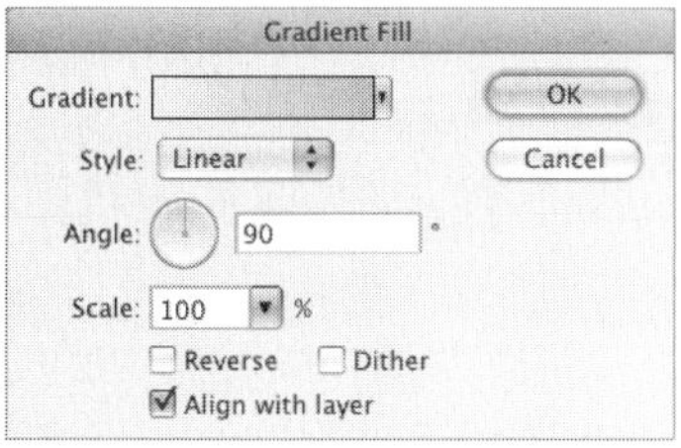

Figure 9.29 Creating a Sky gradient

4. Press Cmd+[/ Ctrl+[to move the `Sky` layer below `Layer 0`. Rename `Layer 0` to `3D Rendering`.
5. First you will set up the Mixer Brush for spreading wet paint without introducing new color. Choose the Mixer Brush from the brush flyout in the Tools panel. On the options bar, click the Load The Brush After Each Stroke button to turn off this mode. Set Wet to 100%, Load to 1%, Mix to 100%, and Flow to 100%. Deselect Sample All Layers, and if you are using a tablet, click the Tablet Pressure Controls Size button (Figure 9.30).

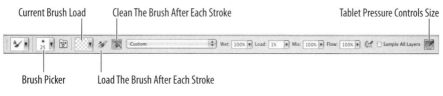

Figure 9.30 Selecting Mixer Brush options

6. Select a 25 px soft round brush from the Brush Picker on the options bar. Keep your strokes parallel to framing, reveals, and any other linear elements. Trace over all edges to give them a hand-painted look. If you are using a mouse, adjust the brush size by using the [and] keys for more-subtle results. If you are using a tablet, press lightly for a smaller brush and press more firmly for a wider brush. Figure 9.31 shows my unique painting.

Figure 9.31 The Mixer Brush gives 3D rendering a hand-painted look.

7. Cmd+click / Ctrl+click the New Layer icon at the bottom of the Layers panel to add a new layer under the 3D Rendering layer. Rename Layer 1 to Clouds.

8. Press D to select the default colors and then press X to exchange foreground and background swatches so that white is in the foreground.

9. Press Shift+B to select the Paintbrush tool. Select the Round Fan bristle brush from the Brush Picker on the options bar. Paint in some clouds. Select a very light gray and paint over the cloud bottoms to give them depth. Figure 9.32 shows my unique clouds (and contrail).

10. Perform these last steps only if you have a tablet. Open the Swatches panel and select pure red by clicking the upper-left swatch. Target the 3D Rendering layer and press Cmd+Shift+N / Ctrl+Shift+N, type **Cars** in the New Layer dialog box, and click OK.

11. Select a small, soft, round brush on the options bar. Enable both Tablet Pressure Controls Opacity and Tablet Pressure Controls Size on the options bar (Figure 9.33).

Figure 9.32 Clouds add interest to an otherwise featureless sky.

Tablet Pressure   Tablet Pressure
Controls Opacity   Controls Size

Figure 9.33 Selecting Paintbrush options

12. Drag from left to right with increasing pressure to paint in some time-lapse car taillights in the parking lot. These streaks help add interest to the large gray expanse at the bottom of the painting. Figure 9.34 shows my completed painting.

Figure 9.34 Red streaks representing cars help balance the composition.

Compare Figure 9.28 with Figure 9.34 to appreciate how the painting leaves more to the imagination as compared with the 3D model. Consider the immortal words of Albert Einstein:

Imagination is more important than knowledge.

By simulating reality as closely as possible, photo-realistic 3D computer renderings made with programs such as 3ds Max leave little to the imagination, and sometimes visually conveying accurate project knowledge is precisely the intent. However, the non–photo-realistic techniques presented in this chapter offer the viewer a looser interpretation of reality that provides a space to stimulate the imagination. Consider employing non–photo-realistic techniques early in the design process and photo-realistic techniques later on as forms and details become increasingly carved in stone.

Integrating 3D Models with Photos

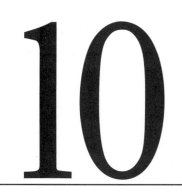

Your mastery of Photoshop won't be complete until you learn how to integrate images from the world of photography with 3D computer-generated imagery. 3D models can be integrated as entourage (that is, furnishings, art, and so forth) within photographic interiors, or as virtual buildings on real streets. The Extended version is required to practice the following types of image alchemy:

Chapter Contents

Adding 3D entourage to photos

Merging 3D buildings with photos

Adding 3D Entourage to Photos

In Chapter 6, "Creating Texture Maps," you learned how to extract a piece of raster entourage (in the shape of a businesswoman) from a photo. One advantage 3D entourage has over its raster cousin is there is no need to extract images from the surrounding pixels. Please note that you'll need the Extended version of Photoshop to work with 3D models.

Although there is no need to extract a 3D model from a photographic background, integrating 3D entourage into a photograph can still be challenging. There are some tricks, however, to streamlining this process. One is to draw temporary lines to help match the perspective of the virtual camera with the lines of perspective in the photo. You'll sometimes need to get creative with light and shadow to make 3D models seem like they belong in photographs.

Adding a 3D Painting to a Wall

The first procedure is to place a 3D painting on a wall in a photo. You'll begin by drawing lines to highlight the perspective implied in the photo and then you'll position the 3D painting relative to these lines. The following steps show how to add a 3D painting to a wall:

1. Open the Condo.jpg sample file from the DVD (Figure 10.1).

Figure 10.1 Original photo of condominium interior

2. Press U to select the vector drawing toolset, click the Shape Layers button, and select the Line tool on the options bar. Make sure no style is selected in the drop-down and select a bright red color. Target the Weight text box and then repeatedly press the up- and/or down-arrow keys to change the weight value

until it reads 3 px (Figure 10.2). The first time you draw a line, the Create New Shape Layer mode will be selected by default (all other modes are grayed out).

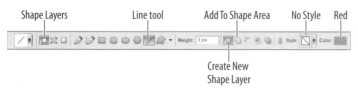

Figure 10.2 Selecting drawing-tool options

3. Lines that run horizontally or vertically in the real world are fair game for tracing in the photo because they reveal the lines of perspective. Draw a line along one of the subtle horizontal ridges in the concrete wall (left from the formwork), as shown in Figure 10.3. Rename layer Shape 1 to **Perspective**.

Figure 10.3 Drawing a line of perspective

4. Click the Add To Shape Area button on the options bar (see Figure 10.2) so that all the lines you draw will be on a single shape layer. Draw additional lines to indicate more lines of perspective found along the concrete wall in the photo (Figure 10.4).

> **Note:** Click the vector mask thumbnail on a shape layer to toggle vector highlighting off or on. It is easier to see the lines when vector highlighting is off, but you'll need highlighting on if you want the Add To Shape button enabled or to adjust any of the lines with the Direct Selection tool.

Figure 10.4 Lines of perspective highlighted on the wall to receive 3D entourage

5. Choose 3D > New Layer From 3D File. Select Painting.dae from the DVD (Figure 10.5). One of the author's paintings appears as a framed 3D model.

Figure 10.5 Creating a piece of 3D entourage from Painting.dae

6. Press N to select the 3D Camera toolset. Interiors are typically photographed with slightly wide-angle lenses. Click the Zoom The Camera tool on the options bar, type **32** in the Standard Field Of View text box, and press Tab (Figure 10.6).

Zoom The 3D Camera

Figure 10.6 Matching virtual camera focal length to the physical lens

7. Using a combination of the Orbit, Roll, Pan, and Walk The 3D Camera tools on the options bar, match the perspective of the 3D model of the painting to the lines drawn on layer Perspective. Use Figure 10.7 as a guide.

Figure 10.7 The 3D painting hung on the photographic wall

8. Toggle off layer Perspective to hide the red lines.

9. Adding a drop shadow will make the painting appear more realistic. Double-click layer Painting just to the right of its name. Click and select the Drop Shadow page in the left pane of the Layer Style dialog box that appears. Change Angle to 140 degrees and set Distance to 3 px (Figure 10.8). Click OK.

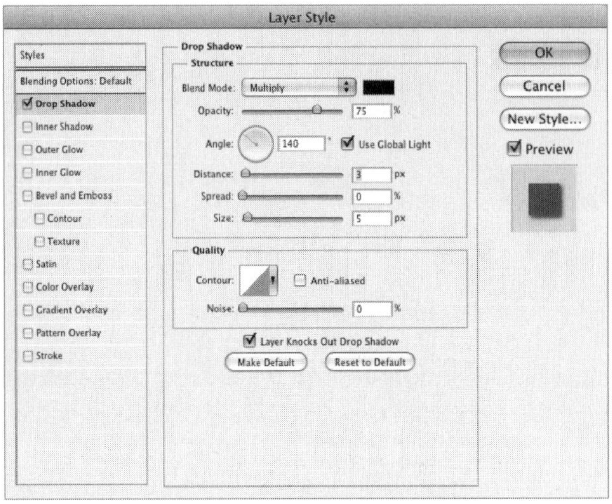

Figure 10.8 Adding a drop shadow to the Painting 3D layer

10. Choose Window > 3D. Click the Filter By: Whole Scene button at the top of the panel if it's not already selected. Change the Quality drop-down to Ray Traced Final (Figure 10.9). The aliasing (undesirable pixelated stair-stepping) along the edges of the frame disappear after the processing is complete.

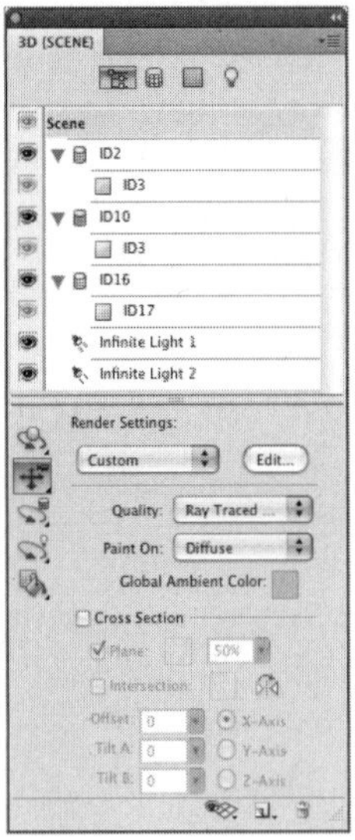

Figure 10.9 Ray tracing the Painting layer

Adding 3D Furniture with Shadows

In this procedure, you will add to the photo a stool holding an architectural miniature, add a light source, and then cast shadows by rendering. The following steps show how to add 3D furniture and shadows:

1. Now you'll add another piece of 3D entourage. Choose 3D > New Layer From 3D File. Select `ArchModel.dae` from the DVD. The model comes in sideways.

2. Press K to select the 3D Object toolset. Type **-90** in the X Orientation text box and press Tab to straighten the model (Figure 10.10).

Figure 10.10 An architectural model on a stool brought into Photoshop as 3D entourage

Transamerica Pyramid (`http://sketchup.google.com/3dwarehouse/details?mid=e9f105619b1989fb7c1c5 059db53898f`). Design by Kévin Girard.

Eames stool (`http://sketchup.google.com/3dwarehouse/details?mid=d90421754178a7f45102fd96313 3c627`). Design by Herman Miller.

3. Using a combination of the Orbit, Roll, Pan, and Walk The 3D Camera tools on the options bar, match the perspective of the 3D model to the space. Use Figure 10.11 as a guide and be aware that object alignment is much more of an art than a science.

4. Select the Light Rotate tool along the left edge of the 3D panel (this enables the Misc 3D Extras option). Click the Toggle Misc 3D Extras button on the lower edge of the 3D panel and choose 3D Light from the menu that appears (Figure 10.12).

Figure 10.11 The model after alignment

Light Rotate tool

Toggle Misc 3D Extras

Figure 10.12 Visualizing lights by toggling 3D extras

5. Click the Filter By: Lights button at the top of the 3D panel. Drag Infinite Light 1's directional vector (selected by default) over the lamp adjacent to the architectural model on the stool (Figure 10.13).

Infinite
Light 1

Bright
spot

Figure 10.13 Rotating a 3D light to match the illumination in the photo

6. Click Infinite Light 1's color swatch in the 3D panel to open the Color Picker. However, instead of selecting a color in the picker, click the bright spot on the concrete wall next to the lamp (see Figure 10.13). A pale, bright yellow color is selected. Click OK to close the Select Light Color dialog box.

7. Click the Toggle Misc 3D Extras button on the lower edge of the 3D panel and turn off 3D Lights. Click the same button again and turn on 3D Ground Plane.

8. Choose 3D > Snap Object To Ground Plane. The model jumps up so that the stool's base rests on the 3D ground plane (Figure 10.14). In order for the model to cast shadows properly, it must be on the ground plane.

9. Choose 3D > Ground Plane Shadow Catcher to turn this mode on. Click OK after reading the text in the dialog box that appears. Shadows are visible only in ray-traced renderings. Toggle the 3D Ground Plane off.

10. Press N to select the 3D Camera tools again. Reposition the model so it appears to rest on the floor of the room next to the table lamp, as it did before in Figure 10.11.

11. Click the Filter By: Whole Scene button at the top of the 3D panel. Change the Quality drop-down to Ray Traced Final, as you did in step 10 in the previous procedure. After a processing delay, the object is anti-aliased and a shadow appears behind the stool (Figure 10.15).

Figure 10.14 Snapping the object to the 3D ground plane causes it to change position.

Figure 10.15 A ray-traced shadow appears behind the 3D entourage

Masking Unrealistic Ray-Traced Shadows

In some cases, you may have to mask ray-traced shadows that don't appear particularly realistic. Such shadows can occur because only a small portion of the image is represented as a 3D model, and shadows can be projected only on 3D surfaces or the ground plane defined in the 3D layer. The following steps show how to mask unrealistic ray-traced shadows:

1. The ArchModel 3D layer isn't "aware" of the window wall behind the object because it's not part of the 3D model. You must therefore mask the parts of the shadow that aren't realistic. Click the Add Layer Mask button at the bottom of the Layers panel.

2. Press X to exchange the default colors and press B to select the paintbrush. Zoom in and mask out any portions of the shadow that don't belong, such as shadows on the glazing (Figure 10.16).

Figure 10.16 Masking out portions of the shadow that don't suit the photo

Painting Shadows and Fading Them with a Gradient Mask

Painting shadows is an acceptable alternative to ray tracing shadows, especially where subtle effects are desired that go beyond the realism of the ray-tracing engine. For example, the shadow of the stool on the hardwood floor should be soft and fade out the farther it is from the object (just as the adjacent shadows do). The following steps show how to paint shadows and fade them out with a gradient mask:

1. If the ArchModel image were real, the stool holding the model would cast a soft shadow on the floor from the overcast sky, much like the table and stools do on the left. Instead of rotating a shadow-casting 3D light and ray tracing again, it is sometimes more expedient to paint shadows manually. For this task, you will

need a new layer. Press Cmd+Shift+N / Ctrl+Shift+N, type **Shadow** in the New Layer dialog box, and click OK.

2. Paint in what you think the shadow might look like under the stool. It doesn't have to be perfect (Figure 10.17).

Figure 10.17 Manually painting a shadow

3. Obviously, the painted shadow doesn't look realistic yet. Decrease the Shadow layer opacity to 20%.

4. Click the Add Layer Mask button at the bottom of the Layers panel.

5. Press Shift+G once or twice until the Gradient tool is selected. Select the Foreground To Transparent gradient from the picker on the options bar and choose Linear Gradient if it's not already selected. Select Dither and Transparency (Figure 10.18).

Figure 10.18 Selecting gradient options

6. Drag from the tip of the shadow to the base of the stool. Repeat this once more to reduce the strength of the shadow as it fades; this fading will become more noticeable the farther the shadow gets from the shadow-casting object (as shadows do in the real world). Figure 10.19 shows the result.

Figure 10.19 Completed integration of the 3D entourage with the photograph

7. Save the image as **Condo.psd**.

Merging 3D Buildings with Photos

Just as 3D objects can be convincingly placed inside buildings, entire 3D buildings can be merged into street photos to show how proposed projects might look in their real-world context. In addition to careful perspective matching, you'll usually also have some precise masking to do before the illusion is complete.

Adding a New 3D Building

The first task is to add a new building in the form of a 3D model to the photograph of the street. You'll find that this is easier said than done because matching the perspective of a virtual camera to a real one can be a challenging process. I recommend making subtle rather than gross adjustments with the 3D Camera tools. Mastering the art of perspective matching requires practice. The following steps will show you how to add a new 3D building to a photo:

1. Open Street-Corner.jpg from the DVD (Figure 10.20).

Figure 10.20 Original photo

2. Choose Window > Swatches and click the red color swatch in the upper-left corner.

3. Press U and select the Line tool on the options bar. Verify that no style is selected in the Style drop-down and that Weight is set to 3 px (as shown in Figure 10.2 earlier).

4. Draw a line along one of the horizontal or vertical edges of the corner building to emphasize the lines of perspective in the photo.

5. Click the Add To Shape Layer button on the options bar and draw all the lines shown in Figure 10.21.

6. Rename layer Shape 1 to **Perspective**.

7. Choose 3D > New Layer From 3D File and select Hotel.dae from the DVD.

8. Press K, type -90 in the X orientation text box, press Tab twice, type 90 in the Z orientation text box, and press Tab again to match the coordinate system of the model to Photoshop's coordinate system (Figure 10.22).

9. Press N to select the 3D Camera tools and click the Zoom The 3D Camera tool on the options bar. Verify that the Standard Field Of View drop-down is set to "mm lens." Type 12 in the adjacent text box (Figure 10.23) and press Tab to set the value. The sloping verticals in the photo indicate it was shot with a wide-angle lens.

Figure 10.21 Drawing lines of perspective over the corner building

Figure 10.22 The hotel 3D model brought into the photo

HOTEL MODEL BY 3D WAREHOUSE USER MILO MINDERBINDER (`http://sketchup.google.com/3dwarehouse/details?mid=f0b0b96d3b00ca3e31a50841704a69bf&prevstart=108`)

Figure 10.23 Selecting 3D Camera tool options

10. Using a combination of the Orbit, Roll, Pan, and Walk The 3D Camera tools on the options bar, match the perspective of the 3D building model to the lines drawn on layer Perspective. Although this is much easier said than done, with enough practice, you will get it. The process of positioning the camera will be familiar to those experienced with other 3D programs. Use Figure 10.24 as a guide. Toggle off layer Perspective when you are finished.

Figure 10.24 The 3D building's perspective matched to the photo

11. Save the image as **Street-Corner-Aligned.psd**.

Note: The Orbit, Roll, Pan, and Walk tools must each be mastered to precisely position the 3D camera. Here's a description of each:

- The Orbit tool is used to rotate the camera along an imaginary line connected to the center of the virtual space. Use it to roughly position the model with respect to the photo.

- Roll turns a model about the same imaginary line connecting the camera to the center of the space. The Roll tool should be used sparingly and only to correct a building that appears to be tilted.

- The Pan tool is used to slide the camera up, down, right, and left.

- The Walk tool is used to move the camera forward and backward in space in addition to sliding left and right.

Adding a Masked Sky Gradient

The new 3D building in this project is smaller than the photographic building it is replacing (especially because of the billboard mounted atop the existing building), so it is necessary to deal with a large portion of sky that needs to be fabricated. Gradients are good at simulating the natural variation in the sky, and you'll mask the gradient to bring some of the original clouds back in. The following steps show how to add a masked sky gradient:

1. Continue with the file you developed in the preceding section or open the file `Street-Corner-Aligned.psd` from the DVD.

2. You will next cover the original building with a sky gradient. Target the `Background` layer. Press Shift+W until the Quick Select tool is chosen. Select Auto-Enhance on the options bar and drag across the sky to make an initial selection. Adjust the brush size with the square bracket keys (larger for areas of low contrast, and smaller for areas with finer details) and continue forming a selection that encompasses the entire sky plus the portion of the original corner building not obscured by the Hotel layer (Figure 10.25).

Figure 10.25 Selecting the sky and the building to be removed

---

Note: Hold the Opt/Alt key to temporarily enter Subtract From Selection mode.

3. Click the Refine Edge button on the options bar. Set Contrast at 30% and Shift Edge to +10%. Verify that the Output To drop-down is set to Selection (Figure 10.26). Click OK.

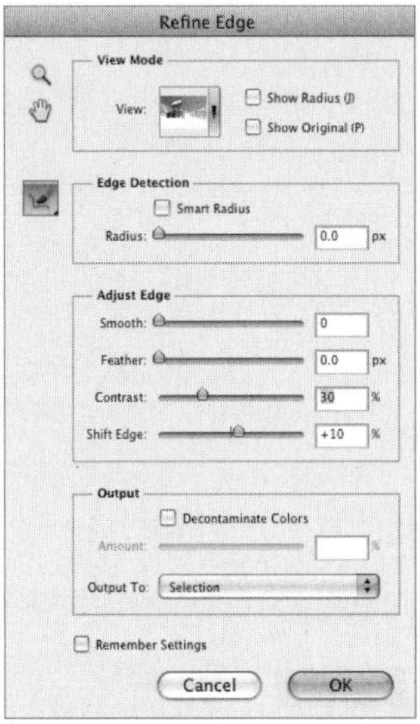

Figure 10.26 Refining the selection edge

4. Click the Create New Fill Or Adjustment Layer button on the lower edge of the Layers panel and select Gradient from the contextual menu that appears. In the Gradient Fill dialog box, select the Black, White gradient in the Gradient drop-down (Figure 10.27) and click OK. The selection is transformed into a gradient.

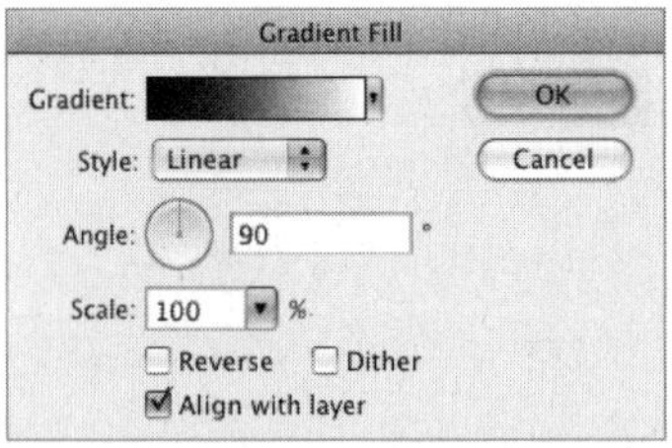

Figure 10.27 Selecting a base gradient for the sky

5. Rename layer Gradient Fill 1 to **Sky**. Toggle off the Sky layer by clicking its eye icon.

6. Double-click the Sky layer swatch to reopen the Gradient Fill dialog box. Click the Black, White gradient swatch itself (not the drop-down arrow) to open the Gradient Editor (Figure 10.28). Click the lower-left stop and then click the color swatch in the Stops area to open the Color Picker. Instead of selecting a color

in the picker, sample the lightest portion of blue sky in the image. Click OK to close the Select Stop Color dialog box.

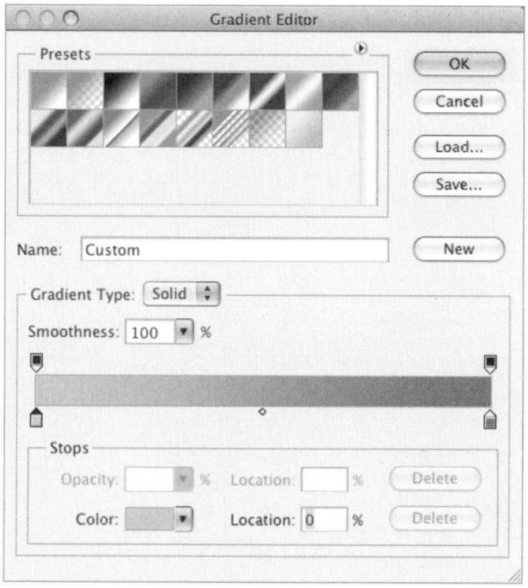

Figure 10.28 Customizing a gradient by sampling the sky

7. Click the lower-right stop and then click the color swatch in the Stops area to open the Color Picker. Sample the darkest portion of blue sky in the image. Click OK to close the Select Stop Color dialog box. Click OK twice more to close the open dialog boxes and toggle on layer Sky. Figure 10.29 shows the result.

Figure 10.29 The original building, billboard, and sky replaced by the gradient

8. The Sky layer isn't perfect, so you will improve it by painting on its mask. Toggle off the Hotel layer and zoom into the large street lamp near the corner of the original building.

Note: Painting in black on a layer mask reveals the underlying layer, and painting in white hides it. Press X to quickly trade black for white or vice versa.

9. Press R for the Rotate View tool. Drag left or right to rotate the canvas. Sometimes it is easier to paint over an edge when your elbow joint's arc of rotation is parallel with the work area. Target the Sky layer mask and press B for the Brush tool. Paint in black over the street lamp to reveal it (Figure 10.30). Don't worry about painting too large a swath. Press R and click the Reset View button on the options bar to restore the canvas to its original orientation.

Figure 10.30 Revealing the street lamp by painting in black on the Sky layer mask

10. Press X to exchange black for white. Press B for the Brush tool, decrease the brush size, and mask out the pixels surrounding the street lamp that aren't part of the street lamp. Repeat in the areas indicated in Figure 10.31.

11. Paint on the Sky layer mask in shades of gray to partially reveal the clouds so that they blend in with the sky gradient. The darker the gray, the more the clouds will show through the mask. Use Figure 10.32 as a guide.

Figure 10.31 Cleaning up the mask by carefully painting along narrow edges

Figure 10.32 Revealing clouds but not the original building by painting on the mask in grayscale

12.   Press the Opt/Alt key and click the Sky layer mask thumbnail to view the mask by itself (Figure 10.33). It can be helpful to see what you've actually painted in grayscale. Opt+click / Alt+click the layer mask thumbnail again to restore its normal functionality as a mask that hides parts of the Sky layer.

Figure 10.33 Viewing the actual layer mask in a document window

> 👁 **Note:** Shift+click a layer mask to toggle it off and on.

Merging the 3D Building with Neighboring Structures in the Photo

The areas where 3D models meet neighboring structures often require special attention to ensure seamless continuity between the virtual and the real. The following steps show how to merge the 3D building with its neighbors:

1. Target the Hotel layer, toggle it on, and click the Add Layer Mask button at the bottom of the Layers panel.

2. Zoom into the hotel and paint in black to hide portions of the hotel and reveal the Background layer. You can think of this process as bringing objects forward. Bring the cars, newspaper boxes, and street lamps forward (Figure 10.34).

3. The shading on the hotel doesn't quite match the shading in the photo. Choose Window > 3D if the 3D panel isn't already open and click the Filter By: Lights button. Click the Light Rotate tool along the panel's left edge and then toggle on 3D Lights display from the Misc 3D Extras menu.

4. Drag Infinite Light 1 to the right a short distance until the shading on the hotel's left edge darkens to match the lighting on the adjacent brick building on the left (Figure 10.35). Toggle off 3D Lights display.

Figure 10.34 Bringing objects in the photo forward by painting over them on the 3D layer mask

Figure 10.35 Rotating 3D lights to match the shading in the photo

5. The hotel edges still look jagged. Click the Filter By: Whole Scene button along the top edge of the 3D panel. Chose Ray Traced Final from the Quality drop-down. After a processing delay, the edges are anti-aliased and the shadows are cast. Figure 10.36 shows the result.

Figure 10.36 Ray-traced rendering of the Hotel 3D layer smoothes its edges and casts shadows

6. The last areas that need attention are where the hotel abuts the adjacent build-ings. The building on the right was clipped where the original building stood. Create a new layer by pressing Cmd+Shift+N / Ctrl+Shift+N, type **Neighbor 1** in the New Layer dialog box, and click OK.

7. Press M to select the Marquee tool, and drag out a small selection on the brick in shadow on the side of the neighboring building on the right. Choose Edit > Define Pattern, type **Shadow Brick** in the Pattern Name dialog box (Figure 10.37), and click OK. Press Cmd+D / Ctrl+D to deselect.

8. Zoom into the area where you made the selection in the previous step. Press P to select the Pen tool. Click three points, forming a triangle at the top of the hotel to represent the portion of the neighboring building, as shown in Figure 10.38.

Figure 10.37 Defining the shadow brick pattern

Figure 10.38 Drawing a vector path to represent a missing part of the neighboring building

9. Choose Layer > New Fill Layer > Pattern. Click OK in the Pattern Fill dialog box (the Shadow Brick pattern is selected by default). The path clips the pattern; it functions very much like a raster layer mask in this way, but with a path we call it a vector mask. Press Shift+A to choose the Direct Selection tool, target the Neighbor 1 vector mask, and adjust the path if necessary by selecting an individual vertex and nudging with the arrow keys 1 pixel at a time. The building should appear to extend into the block, as shown in Figure 10.39.

Figure 10.39 Extending the existing building where it was obscured by the original building

10. Create one final layer by pressing Cmd+Shift+N / Ctrl+Shift+N, type **Neighbor 2** in the New Layer dialog box, and click OK. Zoom into the area on the left edge of the hotel where it interfaces with the neighboring building and the remainder of the original building.

11. Drag `Neighbor 2` below the `Hotel` layer so the new building will cover this new layer (Figure 10.40).

12. Press S to select the Clone Stamp tool. Select Current & Below from the Sample drop-down on the options bar. Hold the Opt/Alt key and click a point on the neighboring building, such as the top of one of its windows.

13. Clone in new windows along the edge of the brick building and try to paint in a convincing illusion of the building's edge that was partially obscured by the original building.

Figure 10.40 Ordering layers

14. Press C to select the Crop tool. Crop out some of the sky. Unfortunately, this causes the ray tracer to re-render the Hotel layer. After a final processing delay, the image is complete. Figure 10.41 shows the result. Compare it with Figure 10.21 to appreciate how far you've come in this tutorial.

Figure 10.41 The 3D building merged with the photo

Congratulations on completing what amounted to delicate image surgery to create this illusion. Being able to merge the unreal with the real is one of the most valuable skills to develop in visualizing architecture.

Playing with Depth Perception

Computer-generated visualizations displayed in print or onscreen must flatten three-dimensional reality onto two-dimensional surfaces, so obviously a lot gets lost in translation. Fortunately, Photoshop offers many illusions for simulating an extra dimension by playing with depth perception. Use the following techniques to add depth to 2D imagery in order to give the viewer a richer visualization experience:

11

Chapter Contents

Using Repoussé: 3D modeling in Photoshop

Maximizing vanishing point

Shooting and perceiving stereographic images

Creating anaglyphic imagery for 3D-glasses experiences

Using Repoussé: 3D Modeling in Photoshop

Repoussé is the name Adobe has chosen for a new 3D modeling tool inside Photoshop CS5 Extended. The French term comes from a traditional metalworking technique whereby malleable metal is shaped by hammering from the reverse side. In addition to creating objects in low relief, Repoussé can model anything from extruded text to 3D corporate logos, all without leaving Photoshop. The following steps show how to use Repoussé:

1. Choose File > New. Type **Logo** in the Name box within the New dialog box. Set the unit drop-downs to pixels, and type **800** in the Width box and **300** in the Height box. Set Background Contents to White (Figure 11.1) and click OK.

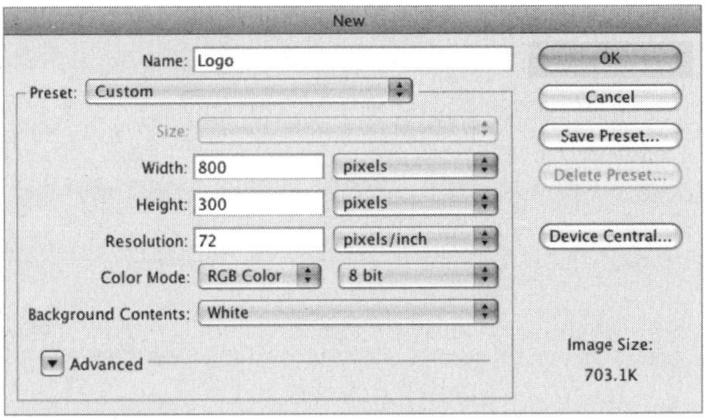

Figure 11.1 Starting a logo from scratch

2. Press U to select the vector drawing toolset. Select the Custom Shape tool on the options bar, open the Custom Shape Picker, and click the Picker menu. Choose Nature from the shape library list that appears and click OK when prompted to replace the current shapes with the shapes from Nature. Select the sun shape indicated in Figure 11.2 from the picker.

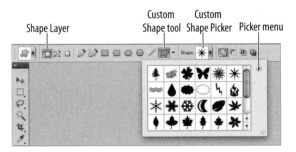

Figure 11.2 Picking a custom shape

3. Starting approximately in the middle of the canvas, start dragging and then, as you are dragging, press and hold Opt+Shift / Alt+Shift to both create the shape from its center and constrain its proportions horizontally and vertically. Drag along a 45-degree angle until the sun fills the document window and then release the mouse button (Figure 11.3).

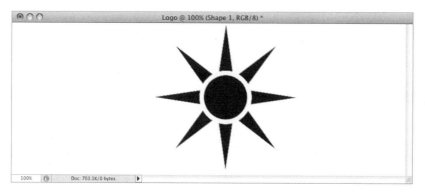

Figure 11.3 Drawing a custom shape precisely

Note: Custom corporate logos can be drawn in Photoshop with the vector toolset or placed as smart objects from Adobe Illustrator. In Photoshop, choose File > Place to import a logo from Illustrator.

4. Press Cmd+A / Ctrl+A to select all. Press V to select the Move tool and then click the Align Vertical Centers and Align Horizontal Centers buttons on the options bar (Figure 11.4). The logo is centered. Press Cmd+D / Ctrl+D to deselect.

Figure 11.4 Centering the logo within the document window

5. Press T to select the Horizontal Type tool. Type Shift+S and Shift+L to create uppercase letters separated by a few spaces. The aim is to create a logo for a hypothetical company called Sol. You can select whichever font you prefer to accomplish this. (I chose Helvetica Neue, Bold, 300 pt, Sharp anti-aliasing on the options bar.) Figure 11.5 shows my result.

Note: You can move text onscreen as you are typing it. Position the cursor outside the text object, and when the cursor changes to the Move icon, you can drag the text and reposition it.

Figure 11.5 Hypothetical logo for the Sol corporation

6. Save the image as **Logo.psd**. This file is provided on the DVD for your convenience. Another font will be substituted for Helvetica Neue, however, if it is not on your system.

7. Right-click the text layer and choose Create Work Path from the menu that appears.

8. Target the Shape 1 layer's vector mask containing the custom shape. Press A to select the Path Selection tool. Click the sun logo in the document window and press Cmd+C / Ctrl+C to copy it to the clipboard.

9. Open the Paths panel and target the Work path. Press Cmd+V / Ctrl+V to paste the path from the clipboard to the work path. You should see the entire logo on the work path now (Figure 11.6).

Figure 11.6 Converting text and the custom shape to the work path

10. Open the Layers panel if the Paths panel obscures it. Target the top layer, which is the text layer in this case. Press Cmd+Shift+N / Ctrl+Shift+N, type **Logo** in the New Layer dialog box, and click OK.

11. Open the Swatches panel and click on an orange swatch to set it as the foreground color.

12. Open the Paths panel and click the Fill Path With Foreground Color button (leftmost along the panel's lower edge). The logo turns orange.

13. Choose 3D > Repoussé > Selected Path. The Repoussé dialog box has many options, but we are going to start by extruding and beveling the logo. In the Extrude area, set Depth to 0.1 and Scale to 1. In the Bevel area, set Height to 6 and Width to 6. Select the Cone-shaped contour from the Contour Picker (Figure 11.7) and click OK.

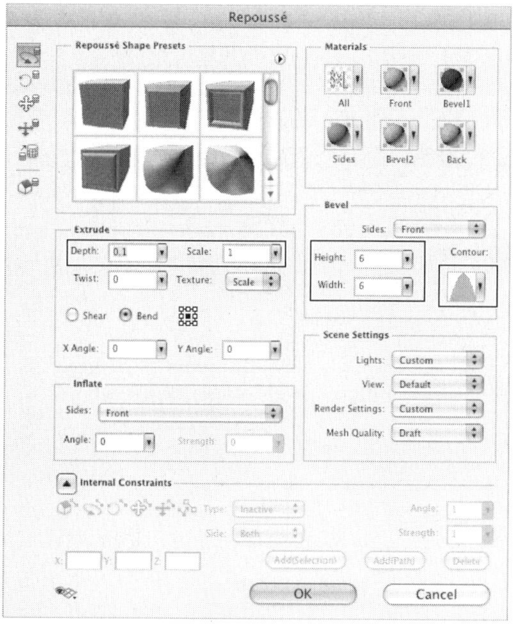

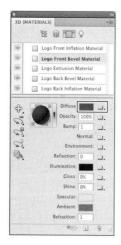

Figure 11.7 Repoussé interface

14. Open the 3D panel and click the Filter By: Materials button at the top of the panel. Target the Logo Front Bevel Material. Materials can either have texture maps or colors but not both. Click the icon next to the Diffuse color swatch and choose Remove Texture from the menu. Click the Diffuse color swatch and choose dark gray in the Color Picker and click OK (Figure 11.8). The bevels stand out.

Figure 11.8 Customizing a material to control the appearance of the Repoussé object

15. Target the Logo Extrusion Material in the 3D panel. Change its Diffuse color to brown to make the parts receding from the viewer darker. Figure 11.9 shows the resulting logo.

Figure 11.9 3D logo after customizing its materials

16. Click the Filter By: Lights button in the 3D panel. Turn off Infinite Lights 2 and 3 by clicking their eye icons. Click the Create A New Light button at the bottom of the 3D panel and click New Spot Light in the menu that appears.

17. Select the Light Slide tool from the flyout along the left edge of the 3D panel (Figure 11.10) and drag in the document window to slide the spot upward so that it fully illuminates the sun in the logo but only partially lights up the letters *S* and *L*.

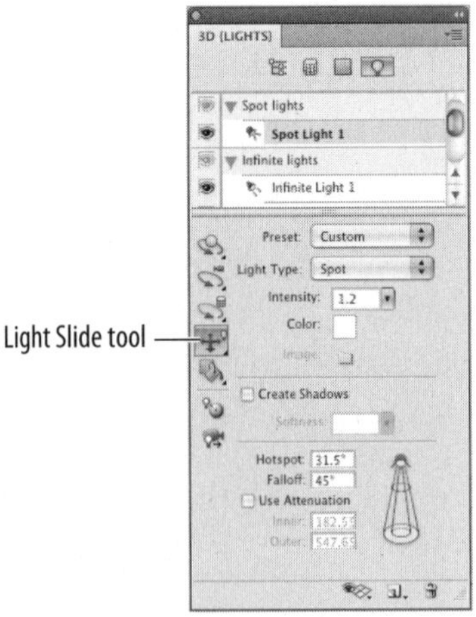

Light Slide tool —

Figure 11.10 Sliding a spotlight into position

18. Set the Intensity of Spot Light 1 to 1.2 and deselect Create Shadows. This makes the spotlight's contribution more pronounced.

19. Click the Filter By: Whole Scene button at the top of the 3D panel. Select Ray Traced Final from the Quality drop-down and wait for Photoshop to process the rendering. Clicking anywhere in the document window interrupts the rendering process (feel free to prematurely stop the rendering process when the results look acceptable).

20. Choose Layer > New Fill Layer > Gradient, type **Backdrop** in the New Layer dialog box, and click OK. Choose the Violet, Orange gradient in the Gradient Fill dialog box and click the Radial Gradient button on the options bar. Click OK and then drag layer Backdrop to the bottom of the layer stack (just above the empty Background layer). Figure 11.11 shows the result.

Figure 11.11 Custom logo given 3D depth with Repoussé

Maximizing Vanishing Point

Vanishing Point is an amazing filter that lets you "teach" Photoshop about the perspective implied in a photo. Once Photoshop has this "understanding," a vista of possibilities open up, including replacing textures, painting and measuring in perspective, and even shifting perspective by generating a texture-mapped 3D model. Vanishing Point is great for exploring what-if scenarios in photos. You'll start by replacing textures in perspective.

Replacing Textures in Perspective

If you try to replace building textures in a photo, you run directly into the problem of perspective. Objects appear to diminish in size the farther they are away from us. Figure 11.12 shows that the illusion of perspective is generated by projecting objects seen by a viewer onto a plane. We take perspective for granted and generally don't think of it as an illusion because it is how we see, but perspective is not reality.

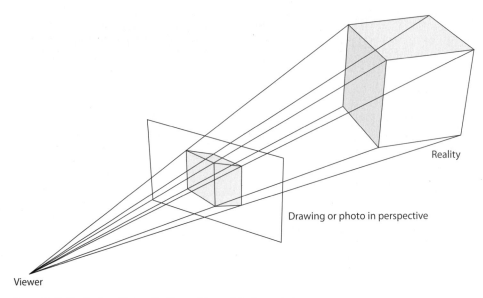

Reality

Drawing or photo in perspective

Viewer

Figure 11.12 The illusion of perspective is something we take for granted.

In a technique perfected in the Renaissance, artists and architects painstakingly constructed perspective drawings by projecting parallel lines in the real world along guide lines that converge at distant points on the horizon called vanishing points (Figure 11.13).

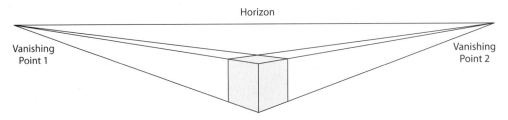

Horizon

Vanishing
Point 1

Vanishing
Point 2

Figure 11.13 Traditional projection method for constructing a two-point perspective drawing

Textures in perspective drawings or photos also diminish in scale the farther they are from the viewer, making it very difficult to replace these with texture maps.

The Vanishing Point filter handles the mechanics of perspective if we first "educate" it about a few parallel and perpendicular surfaces. After this is done, it is very easy to replace perspective surfaces in photos with texture maps. The following steps show how to replace textures in perspective:

1. Open `Retail.jpg` from the DVD (Figure 11.14).

2. Choose Filter > Vanishing Point. Review the toolset along the Vanishing Point dialog box's left edge. Select the Create Plane tool and click the four points shown in Figure 11.15 to create your first plane.

CHAPTER 11: PLAYING WITH DEPTH PERCEPTION

Figure 11.14 Original photo of a retail building

Tools:

Vanishing Point menu

Edit Plane
Create Plane
Marquee
Stamp
Brush
Transform
Eyedropper
Measure
Hand
Zoom

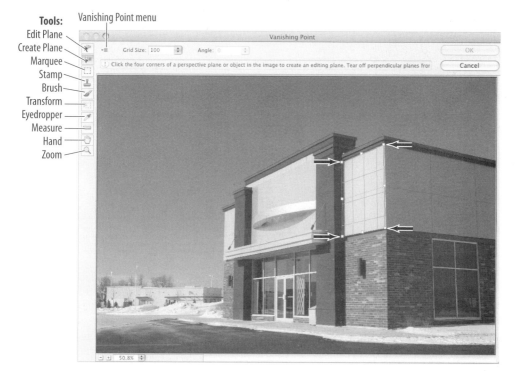

Figure 11.15 Vanishing Point interface

3. Select the Zoom tool and click a few times to zoom into the upper corners of the plane you sketched in the preceding step. Select the Edit Plane tool and drag each corner to better fit the photo (Figure 11.16). Use the Hand tool or the scroll bars along the edges of the Vanishing Point dialog box to see the lower corners. Match the remaining corners of the plane to the rectangular surface in the photo.

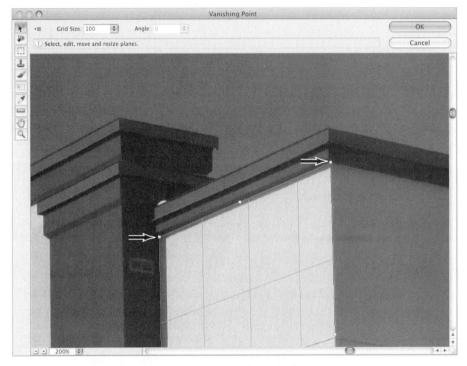

Figure 11.16 Zooming in to better match the plane to the surface in the photo

Note: If the plane you are drawing in Vanishing Point turns yellow or red, Photoshop is warning you about an unlikely or unrealistic perspective angle. Planes shown in blue are more likely to be realistic.

4. Double-click the Hand tool to make the entire image fit within the dialog box. Using the Edit Plane tool, drag the lower-middle handle down until the plane reaches the ground. Middle handles scale planes but do not change their perspective angles.

5. Hold down Cmd/Ctrl and drag the middle-right handle to the right to generate a perpendicular plane on the right side. Enlarge the Vanishing Point dialog box if necessary so a gap appears between the edge of the image and the window frame.

6. Hold Opt/Alt and drag the middle-right handle of the new plane to rotate it in an effort to better match the perspective lines in the photo. An angle of 281 degrees is about right for this photo (Figure 11.17). Although we "know" the building has a 270-degree corner angle (which is an increment of 90 degrees), the photo was evidently taken using a wide-angle lens that distorts perspective lines. Click OK.

Opt/Alt+drag this handle to rotate the new plane.

Figure 11.17 Generating a perpendicular plane and adjusting its angle to match the perspective lines in the photo

7. Press Cmd+Opt+V / Ctrl+Alt+V to reopen the Vanishing Point dialog box. Observe that the work you've done drawing planes is not lost and is in fact stored with the file.

8. Hold down Cmd/Ctrl and drag the middle-left handle to the left to create another perpendicular plane (Figure 11.18). Drag this handle to match the width of the pilaster that juts out beyond the initial surface you mapped.

9. Hold Cmd/Ctrl and drag this new plane's upper-middle handle upward to generate a perpendicular surface (See the A section of Figure 11.19). Type **180** in the Angle text box to rotate the perpendicular plane into a parallel one (B). Drag the new plane's right handle to the right until it covers the cornice (C).

Figure 11.18 Pulling off another plane to match the geometry of the building

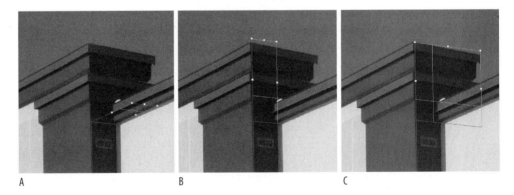

A   B   C

Figure 11.19 The stages of creating a perpendicular plane (A), rotating it (B), and resizing it to encompass the cornice (C)

Note: You do not have to create a perfect model of a building with grids in Vanishing Point. Aim instead to quickly cover all surfaces with grids, whether they are spatially correct or not. It is always a balancing act between mapping planes perfectly and getting the job done quickly. If you need an accurate texture-mapped 3D model, consider using SketchUp or 3ds Max. Vanishing Point is more like a 2.5D solution.

10. Hold Cmd/Ctrl and drag the middle-left handle of the tall narrow plane on the pilaster to the left. To save time, cover the rest of the building with this one plane. Drag its upper-middle handle upward until it covers the cornice line on top (Figure 11.20). Click OK.

Figure 11.20 Mapping the final plane to approximate the rest of the building

11. Save the image as **Retail.psd**.

12. Open **Brick.jpg** from the DVD. It is a seamless tiling texture map (Figure 11.21).

Figure 11.21 Brick texture map

13. Press Cmd+A / Ctrl+A to select all and Cmd+C / Ctrl+C to copy it to the clipboard. Press Cmd+W / Ctrl+W to close Brick.jpg.

14. In Retail.psd, press Cmd+Shift+N / Ctrl+Shift+N, type **Brick** in the New Layer dialog box, and click OK. The work you do in Vanishing Point will output to this layer.

15. Press Cmd+Opt+V / Ctrl+Alt+V to reopen the Vanishing Point dialog box. Press Cmd+V / Ctrl+V to paste the brick pattern from the clipboard. The brick pattern appears surrounded by a marquee in the upper-left corner of the Vanishing Point dialog box.

16. Position the cursor inside the marquee containing the brick pattern and drag over the building. The pattern automatically adheres and wraps around the grids you have drawn (Figure 11.22).

Figure 11.22 Sliding brick along the perspective grids

17. Select the Transform tool along the left edge of the Vanishing Point dialog box. Drag the lower-left handle of the pattern, hold down Shift to constrain proportions, and scale the pattern to fit on the wall, as shown in Figure 11.23.

18. Zoom in and position the cursor inside the selection; hold Cmd/Ctrl and drag downward to duplicate the selected pixels. Release the Cmd/Ctrl key and then hold Shift to constrain movement vertically or horizontally. Drag down until brick replaces all the stucco on the first wall you drew a grid on in step 2.

Figure 11.23 Transforming the selection

19. Repeat the procedure in the previous step and replace all the stucco on the right side of the building, then click OK (Figure 11.24).

Figure 11.24 Replacing stucco with brick in the perspective photo

20. In order to replace the rest of the stucco on the building, you will make selections that match the aspect ratio of the areas you want to replace. Press Cmd+Opt+V / Ctrl+Alt+V to reopen the Vanishing Point dialog box.

21. Select the Marquee tool along the left edge. Drag out a selection that covers the long narrow strip of stucco at the top of the building. Position the cursor inside the selection and drag over the stucco you've already replaced with brick. It's acceptable for the marquee to wrap around the corner.

22. Press Cmd+C / Ctrl+C to copy the selection to the clipboard and then press Cmd+V / Ctrl+V to paste it in place (on top of the existing selection).

23. Position the cursor inside the selection and drag the marquee over the long narrow strip of stucco at the top of the building (Figure 11.25).

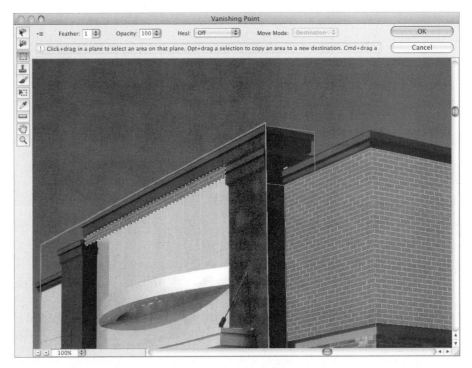

Figure 11.25 Replacing a textured area by copying and pasting a selection

24. Repeat steps 21–23 for the remaining stucco along the building's left edge. Do not worry if some of the pasted brick texture obscures parts of the building, because you will mask these areas next. Click OK to close the Vanishing Point dialog box. Figure 11.26 shows the result.

Figure 11.26 Stucco replaced with brick

25. Click the Add Layer Mask button at the bottom of the Layers panel. Press D to set the default colors and B to select the Brush tool. Press X to exchange background and foreground colors so that Black is in the foreground. Zoom in by pressing Cmd/Ctrl and paint over any portions of the Brick layer that cover parts of the building that should be visible, such as the awning, its cable support, and the top of the left pilaster. Don't worry if you mask too much at first (see the left side of Figure 11.27).

Figure 11.27 Initially masking too much of the Brick layer (left) and then cleaning up the mask (right)

26. Press X to exchange foreground and background colors so that White is in the foreground. Reduce the brush size by pressing the left bracket key. Paint over areas on the mask where you took too much away (see the right side of Figure 11.27).

27. You can easily change the color of the replaced texture because it exists on its own layer. Click the Hue/Saturation button in the Adjustments panel. Click the Adjustment Clips Layer button (third from the left, along the lower panel edge) and select Colorize. Drag the sliders to Hue 225, Saturation 25, and Lightness 0 (Figure 11.28).

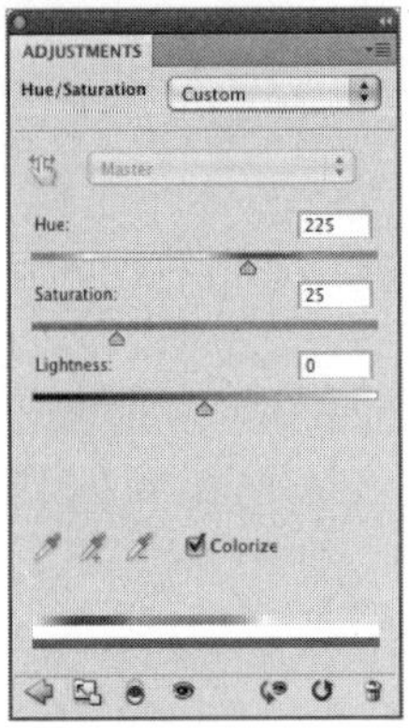

Figure 11.28 Shifting the texture color with a Hue/Saturation adjustment

28. Although the brick pattern covers up all the stucco, the shading on the brick is still not right because the right portion of the building is in shadow. Press Cmd+Shift+N / Ctrl+Shift+N, type **Shadow** in the New Layer dialog box, and click OK.

29. Press Cmd+Opt+V / Ctrl+Alt+V to reopen the Vanishing Point dialog box. Zoom into the part of the building in shadow on the right. Select the Brush tool and click the Brush Color swatch, then choose Black in the picker. Decrease brush size to 30.

30. Position the cursor in the upper-left corner of the surface in question, hold Shift, and drag to the right. The brush is constrained along the perspective edge. Repeat this procedure for each of the edges to outline the surface in black. Increase the brush size by pressing the right bracket key repeatedly and paint the interior of the surface freehand (Figure 11.29). Click OK.

31. Decrease the opacity of the Shadow layer to 65% to match the shading with the illumination level in the photo. Figure 11.30 shows the result. Leave the file open for work in the next section.

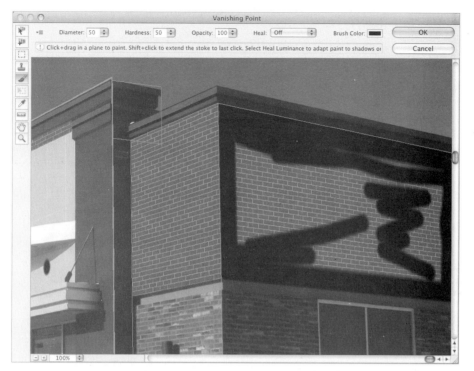

Figure 11.29 Painting in perspective

Figure 11.30 Texture replacement, masking, and shading complete

Measuring in Perspective

After you've aligned surfaces in Vanishing Point, it is straightforward to take measurements off the grids you've drawn. Be aware that the distances in Vanishing Point aren't laser-accurate but they can be useful as estimates. The following steps show how to make measurements in perspective:

1. Press Cmd+Shift+N / Ctrl+Shift+N, type **Measurements** in the New Layer dialog box, and click OK.

2. Choose Filter > Vanishing Point. Select the Measure tool. Drag a measurement from the top of the door to the ground. There are two tags on the measurement: an angle and a distance. Try to get the angle to read as close to zero or 90 degrees as possible (Figure 11.31).

Figure 11.31 Making the first measurement in Vanishing Point

3. The first measurement you make is the basis for all subsequent measurements made in Vanishing Point. You measured the door because door heights are generally known. It is safe to assume doors are approximately 7 feet in height. Type **7.00** in the Length text box at the top of the Vanishing Point dialog box. The Length text box is unitless, so if you are using metric, you might type **215** (cm).

4. Make several more measurements by dragging with the Measure tool. Try each time to get the angle as close as possible to zero or 90 degrees so that the dimensions are horizontal or vertical (Figure 11.32). The building is approximately 58 feet wide and 21 feet high.

Figure 11.32 Making additional measurements in perspective

5. Click the Vanishing Point menu and choose Render Measurements To Photoshop. Click OK, and the measurements you just made are returned as pixels on the Measurements layer. You could save this layer as a record and even print out the image with dimensional estimates overlaid. Leave the file open for work in the next section.

Shifting Perspective

Another advantage to aligning surfaces in Vanishing Point is the ability to project the photo itself onto these surfaces and create a very simple 3D model. This photo-model can be rotated to alter the perspective angle and give the viewer a better view of a façade, for example. The following steps show how to shift the perspective of the entire building:

1. Toggle off the Measurements layer so it will not be part of the photo-model.

2. Press Cmd+Shift+N / Ctrl+Shift+N, type **Stamped** in the New Layer dialog box, and click OK. Press Cmd+Opt+Shift+E / Ctrl+Alt+Shift+E to stamp the visible layers onto layer Stamped.

3. Choose Filter > Vanishing Point. Click the Vanishing Point menu and choose Return 3D Layer To Photoshop. Click OK. After a few moments, a 3D layer appears called temp. Rename temp to Photomodel.

4. Press N to select the 3D Camera tools. Orbit the camera to the left, walk forward, and pan the camera downward so the photo-model completely covers the original photo on the Background layer.

5. Right-click layer Photomodel and chose Rasterize 3D.

6. Press E to select the Eraser tool. Erase any halos that appear along the outer edges of the texture maps where the Photomodel layer meets the sky. Figure 11.33 shows the result. Compare with Figure 11.14 to see how far you've come.

Figure 11.33 Returning a 3D model to Photoshop allows you to shift the perspective.

7. Save and close the file.

Shooting and Perceiving Stereographic Images

The history of art is in some sense the history of playing with human perception. A perception of depth called a *stereogram* arises in your mind when viewing two similar but slightly different images. Stereograms were very popular at the birth of photography in Victorian times, and stereographic perception is currently enjoying a renaissance in popular films such as *Avatar* and with the recent introduction of new stereographic camera and television technology. Stereographic perception adds a dimension beyond

3D computer-generated imagery that is as close as we can get to actually "being there" without really being on site. With a little practice, anyone with two eyes can perceive stereographic imagery.

Shooting stereo pairs couldn't be any easier. All you have to do is shoot two exposures separated by a short distance horizontally. In other words, shoot one exposure, slide horizontally, and shoot another exposure while aiming the camera at the same subject. If you are creating a macro stereogram of a small subject such as an architectural model, move a short distance such as the distance between your eyes (approximately 2.5 inches). If you are shooting a distant subject such as a building exterior, it's reasonable to sidestep a foot or two in between exposures.

Plan to keep track of which image in the stereo pair was shot on the left and which was shot on the right. I recommend always shooting the left image first and the right image second so you don't get mixed up later when transferring the images from camera to computer. Figure 11.34 shows a stereogram example.

Left image   Right image

Figure 11.34 Stereo pair of the author's house

There are two modes for perceiving stereographic image pairs: parallel or cross-eyed. If the left image is displayed on the left and the right image on the right, the perceptual mode is parallel. If the images are reversed, the perceptual mode is cross-eyed.

Most people find it easier to perceive parallel mode, wherein you defocus your gaze and allow your mind to form a third image in between the pair. As your eyes refocus on the central illusory image, they will naturally converge on a plane deeper than the surface of the monitor and perceive an added dimension of depth. Stare at Figure 11.37, which appears a little later in the procedure, and see if you can perceive the parallel-mode stereogram right away. You'll know it when you see it! Don't get discouraged if you don't see it right away, because learning new modes of perception can take a little practice. The following steps show how to create and perceive this illusion:

1. Open the files House-Left.jpg and House-right.jpg from the DVD.

2. Choose Window > Arrange > Float All In Windows (document windows that is, not the operating system).

3. Target House-Left's document window and choose Image > Canvas Size. Change the Width and Height drop-down menus to percent, type **205** in the Width text box, and click the middle-left anchor button (Figure 11.35). Select Black as the Canvas Extension Color and click OK.

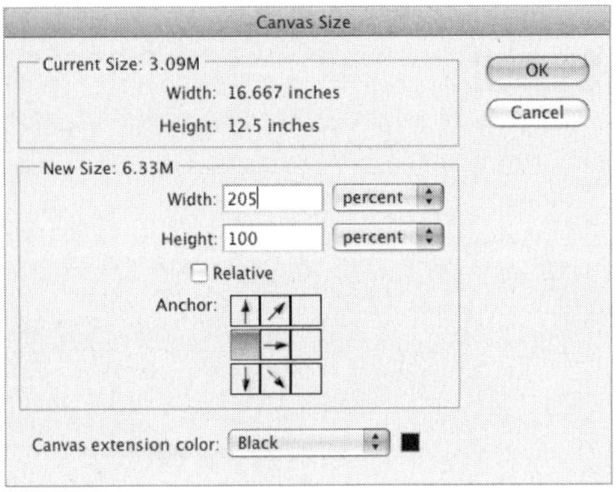

Figure 11.35 Increasing the canvas size to accommodate two side-by-side images with a gap in between

4. On the Mac, choose Photoshop > Preferences > General. On Windows, choose Edit > Preferences > General. Select the Zoom Resizes Windows option in the Preferences dialog box if it is not already selected (Figure 11.36). Click OK.

5. Target House-Right's document window, press V to select the Move tool, and then drag from House-Right's document window into House-Left's document window to create a new layer there. Rename layer 1 to **Right**. Close House-Right.jpg without saving.

6. Drag layer Right into position on the right-hand side of the canvas, leaving a narrow, vertical, black space in between the images. Press Cmd+- / Ctrl+- a few times to zoom out to 25% magnification and thus shrink the document window (Figure 11.37).

7. Press F to center the document window on your screen. Stare beyond the two images and let your eyes blur. After a few moments, you may notice a third image appear in between the two images that are really there. This is your mind beginning to perceive the stereogram. When you see the blurry central image, slowly try to focus your eyes on it. When you do see the stereogram, the effect is unmistakably three-dimensional. Eureka!

Figure 11.36 Changing a preference

Figure 11.37 Parallel-mode stereogram

Note: The parallel mode of perceiving stereo pairs works only when the distance between the photos is equal to or less than the distance between your eyes. Try holding the book farther away from you if you have trouble getting into the illusion.

8. Double-click the Background layer, type **Left** in the New Layer dialog box that appears, and click OK.

9. Drag the image of layer Left to the right edge of the document window underneath layer Right.

10. Target layer Right and drag it to the left edge of the document window so that the image is where layer Left was previously.

11. Press D to set the default colors. Press Shift+G to select the Paint Bucket tool. Click in between the images in the document window to fill the narrow space with Black.

12. Double-click the Hand tool in the toolbox to enlarge the document window to the maximum size that will fit on your screen. Press the Tab key to hide the panels.

13. Cross your eyes slightly and try to focus on the third image that you may eventually perceive in between the images that are really there. When this image comes into focus, you will see the same stereographic effect you saw before but with greater resolution (Figure 11.38). Don't be discouraged if this illusion eludes you. More people seem to have trouble with the cross-eyed perceptual mode as compared with the parallel mode. However, the advantage of crossing image inputs is that stereograms perceived in this mode can be much larger, without being limited by the distance between our eyes.

Figure 11.38 Cross-eyed-mode stereogram

14. Press Shift+F to return to Standard Screen mode.

Creating Anaglyphic Imagery for 3D-Glasses Experiences

Whereas stereograms require the viewer to learn new perceptual modes, anaglyphic imagery is immediately visible to anyone wearing red/cyan "3D glasses" (assuming the viewer has two eyes). You can pick up a pair of paper red/cyan glasses for less than $1 or get a more durable plastic set without breaking the bank. Search Amazon.com for 3D glasses and you'll see what I mean. Although it might sound preposterous to ask your clients to put on 3D glasses (and it may have been before *Avatar*), getting the most immersive 3D experience without learning a new mode of perception currently requires the viewer to don a pair of 3D glasses.

3D glasses present different images to each eye by filtering what is delivered by color. The left eye has a red filter, so the red channel is all the left eye sees. The right eye actually has a cyan filter (rather than blue, as it's often called), so the right eye sees the green and blue channels (because cyan = green + blue).

Once equipped with your pair of red/cyan glasses (differentially polarized glasses from recent blockbuster movies won't work for our purposes as they use polarization to separate the images each eye sees), you are ready to go. There are a few ways of creating anaglyph images in Photoshop:

- With a pair of stereo photos

- With a 3D model (required for the method listed next)

- With only a single photo (for this you will build a 3D model)

Turning a Pair of Stereo Photos into an Anaglyph

You can convert a pair of stereo photos (see "Shooting and Perceiving Stereographic Images" earlier in this chapter) into a single anaglyph image very easily. Anaglyphs and 3D glasses enable viewers to perceive an added dimension of depth without any special perceptual training. The following shows how to create an anaglyph from two image inputs:

1. Choose File > Scripts > Load Files Into Stack. In the Load Layers dialog box that appears, click the Browse button and select House-Left.jpg and House-Right.jpg from the DVD (Figure 11.39). Click OK in the Load Layers dialog box. After a few moments a single document window will appear, containing two layers.

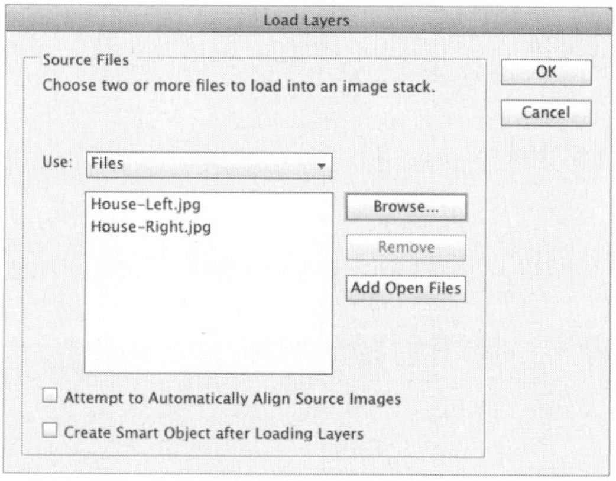

Figure 11.39 Loading two files into a stack

2. Double-click the top layer just to the right of the name House-Left.jpg to open the Layer Style dialog box. In the Advanced Blending area under Channels, deselect both G and B check boxes. Now layer House-Left.jpg is delivering information

in the red channel only, and the layer underneath (House-Right.jpg) is delivering green and blue info only (Figure 11.40). Click OK.

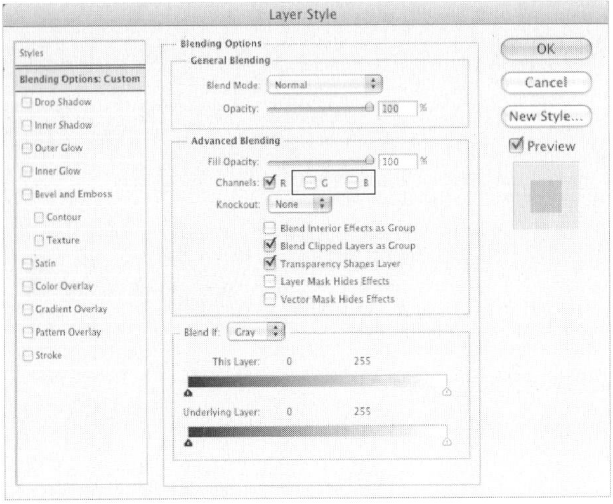

Figure 11.40 Controlling which color channels are displayed with Advanced Blending features

3. Put on your red/cyan 3D glasses and view my house in all its 3D glory (Figure 11.41). Consider how novel (and fashionable) it might be to hand out 3D glasses in your next client presentation.

Figure 11.41 This anaglyph image doesn't work in grayscale, but you can observe its shifted channels carrying depth information. See the color section for the actual anaglyph.

Turning a Single Image into an Anaglyph

You can convert a single photo exhibiting one-point perspective (having a single vanishing point) into an anaglyph. However, instead of automatically gleaning depth information from a second photo (as you did in the previous section), you must build depth information manually with gradients, create a 3D model from the gradients, and project the image as a texture map onto the model. The following steps show how to create an anaglyph from a single image:

1. Open Atrium.jpg from the DVD (Figure 11.42).

Figure 11.42 Original atrium image exhibiting one-point perspective

2. Press Cmd+Shift+N / Ctrl+Shift+N to create a new layer, type **Depth map** in the New Layer dialog box, and click OK.

3. Enlarge the document window by dragging its lower-right corner handle outward (you must be in Standard Screen mode to see a document window) so that a space appears between the image and the window frame.

4. Press Shift+L (several times if necessary) to select the Polygonal Lasso tool. Click the four points shown in Figure 11.43 to create a precise selection.

5. Press Shift+G (twice if necessary) to select the Gradient tool. Select the Black, White gradient from the picker on the options bar and make sure the Linear gradient button is selected. Drag from point A to point B as shown in Figure 11.44 to create a gradient. Press Cmd+D / Ctrl+D to deselect.

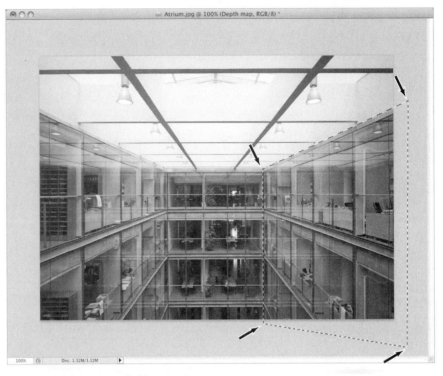

Figure 11.43 Selecting one wall of the atrium

Figure 11.44 Adding a gradient to represent a wall receding in perspective

6. Press Cmd+J / Ctrl+J to duplicate the current layer. Choose Edit > Transform > Flip Horizontal. Press V to select the Move tool and drag the gradient over to the left side of the image.

7. Press Cmd+T / Ctrl+T, type **104%** in the Height box on the option bar, and press Return/Enter. Use the arrow keys to nudge the gradient into position to represent the left wall and press Return/Enter (Figure 11.45).

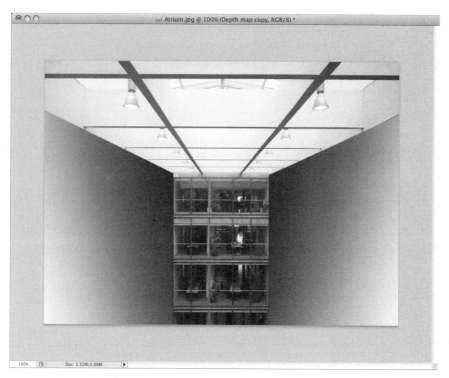

Figure 11.45 Duplicating the gradient along the left wall

8. Press L to activate the Polygonal Lasso tool. Click the six points shown in Figure 11.46 to create another selection along the ceiling. Click the Create A New Layer button on the lower edge of the Layers panel. Don't worry about naming the layer at this time.

9. Press G to select the Gradient tool. Drag a gradient from the vanishing point at point A to point C (Figure 11.47). Press Cmd+D / Ctrl+D to deselect.

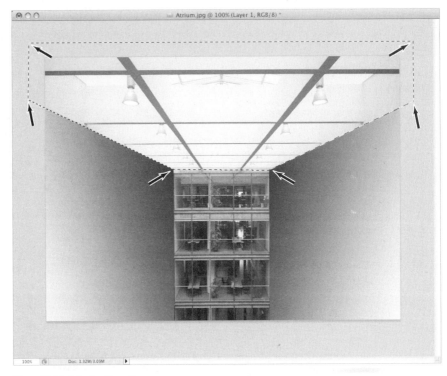

Figure 11.46 Selecting the ceiling

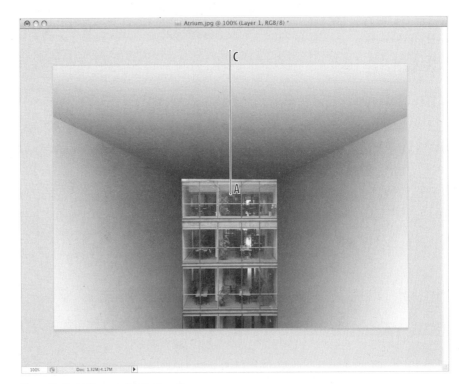

Figure 11.47 Adding a gradient to the ceiling

10. Press U to select the vector tools and click the Shape Layers button and Rectangle tool on the options bar. Draw in a rectangle that covers the far wall. Double-click the Shape 1 layer's color swatch and select a black with approximately 8% brightness so that it's just darker than the surrounding gradients (Figure 11.48).

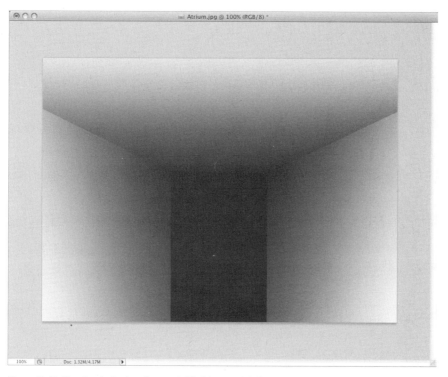

Figure 11.48 Drawing the back wall as nearly black because it is far away

11. Shift+click all four layers above the Background layer. Press Cmd+E / Ctrl+E to merge these layers into one (Figure 11.49). Rename this layer **Model**.

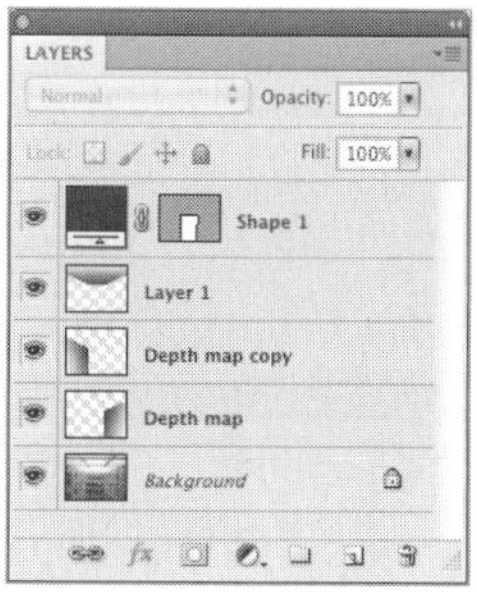

Figure 11.49 Selecting and merging all grayscale layers

12. Choose 3D > New Mesh From Grayscale > Plane. Photoshop converts the grayscale information into a simple 3D model where darker values are farther away (Figure 11.50).

Figure 11.50 New mesh created from grayscale layer

13. Press N to select the 3D Camera tools and select the Zoom The 3D Camera tool on the options bar. Type 70 in the Standard Field Of View text box on the options bar (Figure 11.51) and press Return/Enter.

Figure 11.51 Changing the field of view of the 3D camera to fit the model to the photo

14. Toggle off the Model layer and target the Background layer. Press Cmd+A / Ctrl+A to select all and Cmd+C / Ctrl+C to copy it to the clipboard. Press Cmd+D / Ctrl+D to deselect.

15. Toggle on the Model layer and double-click the Model diffuse map to open it in a separate document window (Figure 11.52). Press Cmd+V / Ctrl+V to paste the photo from the clipboard into this document. Press Cmd+W / Ctrl+W to close and press Return/Enter to save.

Figure 11.52 Opening the texture map (not the depth map)

16. Open the 3D panel and click the Filter By: Whole Scene button at the top of the panel if it's not already selected. Click the Edit button in the Render Settings area.

17. In the 3D Render Settings dialog box that appears, select Unlit Texture from the Face Style drop-down so the 3D lights don't influence the composition. Select the last category to enable stereographic display. Set Parallax at its maximum value of 100 (Figure 11.53) for the deepest 3D effect and click OK.

Figure 11.53 Enabling stereo rendering in the 3D Settings dialog box

Note: Creating anaglyphs from imported 3D models is trivial because all you need to do is enable stereo rendering in the 3D Render Settings dialog box.

18. Put on a pair of 3D glasses and enjoy the atrium with the illusion of added depth (Figure 11.54). This is especially amazing considering you generated the extra dimension from perspective cues in a single photo. Note that this anaglyph image doesn't work in grayscale, but you can observe its shifted channels carrying depth information. See the color section for the actual anaglyph.

Figure 11.54 The final anaglyphic atrium

In this chapter, you've gone far beyond the traditional 2D picture by learning multiple techniques that play with depth perception. You've learned how to extrude text and shapes into 3D objects, how to harness the vanishing point to replace textures in perspective, estimate distances in perspective, and even shift the entire perspective by generating a photo model. In addition, you've explored the fascinating world of stereographic image pairs and anaglyph imagery to craft memorable 3D experiences that are sure to impress your clients.

Working with Animation and Video

As the name suggests, most people assume Photoshop is just for editing photos. Although that's been true for more than 20 years, with the introduction of the Extended version, Photoshop is also for video editing and timeline animation. Frame-based animation features go even further back (before the Creative Suite) to the companion program ImageReady, whose features have long been integrated into Photoshop. So now there's clearly no excuse for not harnessing the power of animation and video.

Chapter Contents
Animating one frame at a time
Animating using the timeline
Altering videos the smart way
Animating 3D models on the timeline

Animating One Frame at a Time

The simplest way to create an animation is to work on it one frame at a time. Much like a childhood flip-book animation, you can create the illusion of motion by changing something incrementally in each frame. In the following steps, you will put together a shadow study animation one frame at a time.

Creating a Frame-Based Animation

You will begin by loading all the individual images into a single document and then you'll convert these layers into frames of an animation. Here is how to create a basic frame-based animation:

1. Choose File > Scripts > Load Files Into Stack. Click the Browse button in the Load Layers dialog box and select all 18 files in the Shadow Study folder on the DVD (Figure 12.1). Click OK. These files were generated in SketchUp, showing the movement of shadows in half-hour increments.

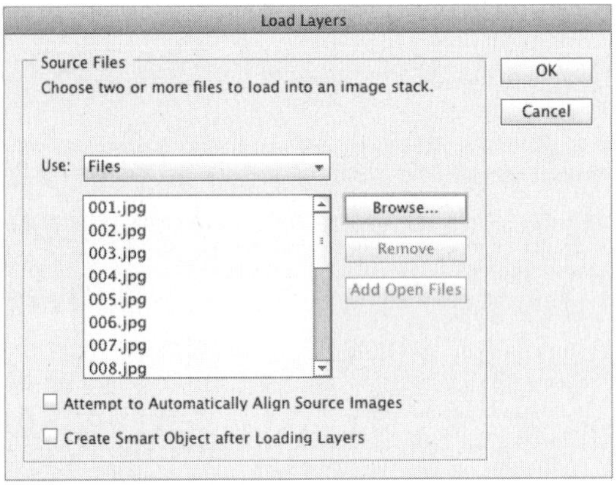

Figure 12.1 Loading shadow study images into a stack

2. Choose Window > Animation. By default the Animation panel appears in Timeline mode, which you'll use in the next section. Click the Convert To Frame Animation button in the lower-right corner to access the older mode (Figure 12.2). A single frame appears in the Animation panel.

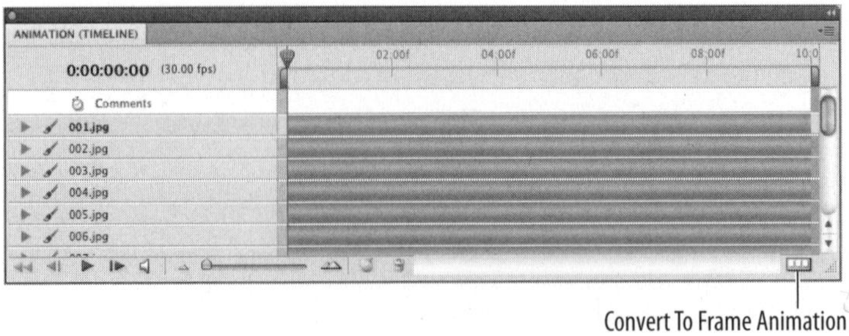

Convert To Frame Animation

Figure 12.2 Converting the Animation panel to Frame Animation mode

3. Click the Animation panel menu (button at the upper right) and select Make Frames From Layers in the menu. Eighteen frames appear in the panel, one for each layer (Figure 12.3).

Figure 12.3 Layers appear as frames in the Animation panel.

4. Notice that the duration of frame 1 is 10 sec, and all the other frames are 0 sec. To make the animation play smoothly, you need to equalize the duration of all frames. With frame 1 selected (it should be by default), scroll all the way to the right, hold down Shift, and click frame 18. Click the duration on any one of the frames and set it to 0.5 sec (Figure 12.4).

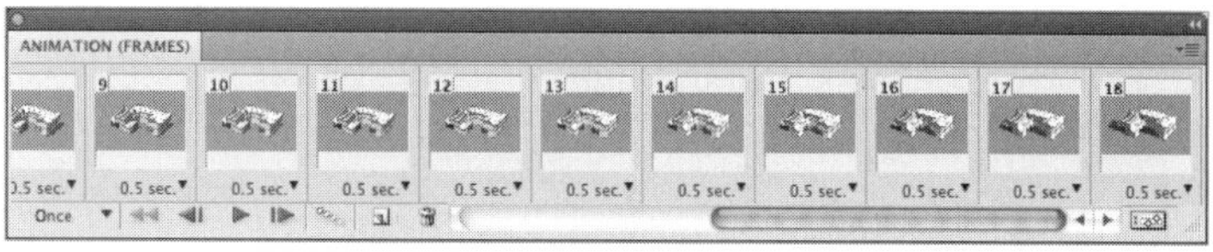

Figure 12.4 Setting the frame duration for all frames

5. Click the Play button in the Animation panel and watch the animation. The animation plays backward compared to the layer order. Press the spacebar to toggle playback.

6. Click the Animation panel menu and choose Reverse Frames from the menu.

7. Click the word Once in the loop menu in the lower-left corner of the Animation panel and select Forever on the menu that appears.

8. Change frame 18's duration to 5 sec. Now the animation will play through, pause at the end, and then loop all over again, forever.

9. Save the file as **Shadow Study.psd**.

Adding Changing Text to the Animation

Each frame records the visibility state of all the layers in the Layers panel (much like layer comps). To add changing text, you must create a series of layers and then toggle visibility states for each frame. Here is how to add changing text to a frame-based animation:

1. Target frame 1 in the Animation panel.

2. Press T to select the Type tool. Press D to set the default colors. Click a point under the building and type **8:00 AM**. Click the Center Justify button on the options bar. Highlight the text and adjust its size to 50 pt, and click the Commit button at the right end of the options bar to complete the text-creation process (Figure 12.5).

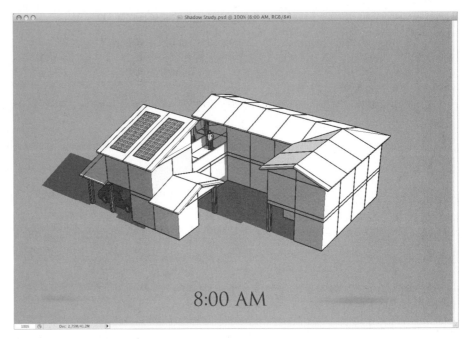

Figure 12.5 Adding time reference text

3. Press Cmd+A / Ctrl+A to select all. Press V to select the Move tool. Click the Align Horizontal Centers button on the options bar (Figure 12.6) to horizontally center the text in the document window. Press Cmd+D / Ctrl+D to deselect.

Align Horizontal Centers

Figure 12.6 Centering text in the document window

4. Press Cmd+J / Ctrl+J to copy the current layer. Toggle off the layer underneath the new layer. Press T to select the Type tool and edit the text onscreen to read **8:30 AM**. Click the Commit button on the options bar.

5. Repeat step 4 to create individual layers for times ranging from 9:00 a.m. to 4:30 p.m. in half-hour increments. Figure 12.7 shows the resulting layers.

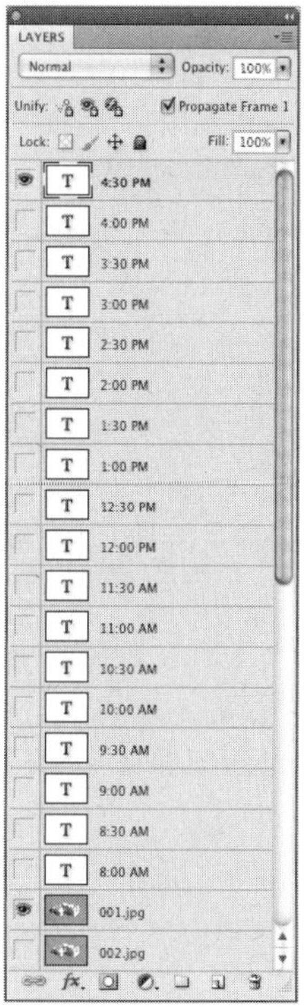

Figure 12.7 Creating text layers
for each time coordinate

6. Toggle off layer 4:30 PM and toggle on layer 8:00 AM. Verify that frame 1 is targeted and that only 001.jpg and 8:00 AM are toggled on.

7. Target frames 2 through 18 and toggle off 8:00 AM and 001.jpg for each frame so that only the JPEG layer matching the frame number remains toggled on and visible.

8. Target frames 2 through 18 again, toggling on the next time layer in each successive frame. Play the animation and verify that the shadows and time increments are in step with each other.

9. Choose File > Save For Web & Devices. In the Save For Web & Devices dialog box, select the GIF 64 Dithered preset from the top-right drop-down menu. In the Image Size area in the lower-right corner, type 50 in the Percent text box. Select Bicubic Sharper from the Quality drop-down (Figure 12.8).

10. Use the playback controls in the lower-right corner of the Save For Web & Devices dialog box to preview the animated output. Click the Save button and save with the default name of Shadow-Study.gif (click Save when prompted).

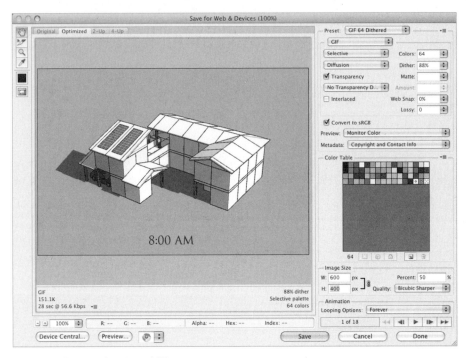

Figure 12.8 Exporting the animated GIF

11. Open Shadow-Study.gif in your default web browser (Figure 12.9) and enjoy the animation (this file is provided on the DVD for your convenience). GIF files work in all browsers without plug-ins.

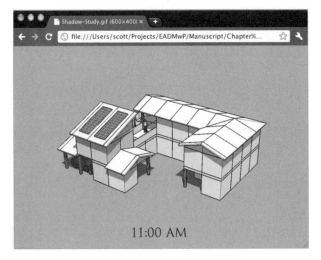

Figure 12.9 Animated GIF plays in a web browser (Google Chrome shown here)

Animating Using the Timeline

Timeline animation brings the Extended version of Photoshop up to speed with the way animation and video editing are done in other professional programs. In the method known as *keyframing*, specific states (such as layer opacity, mask position, and many others) are stored on the timeline as keys. Photoshop automatically interpolates, or blends, the frames in between the keys to create the illusion of smooth motion.

In the following tutorial, you will take a snapshot in NASA World Wind and then animate a moving path on the 3D map using Photoshop CS3 Extended, Photoshop CS4 Extended, or Photoshop CS5 Extended. These steps show how to animate using the timeline:

1. Point your browser to http://worldwind.arc.nasa.gov/java/demos/ and download ApplicationTemplate.jnlp. This Java Network Launching Protocol (JNLP) file requires a Java Virtual Machine to run, which you must also download from http://java.com if it is not already installed on your system.

2. Double-click the ApplicationTemplate.jnlp file and wait for the interface to appear (it must download components the first time it is run). Zoom into an area of interest. This could be anywhere in the world: a project site you are working on, your home, or a famous locale. If you want to use the same example as this tutorial, zoom into San Francisco.

> **Note:** You might rename ApplicationTemplate.jnlp to **NASA World Wind.jnlp** so you can better identify it on your system.

3. Select USGS Urban Area Ortho to load a map layer with high-resolution imagery of selected cities. United States Geological Survey (USGS) satellite imagery is in the public domain and may be used for commercial purposes. MS Virtual Earth Aerial imagery is proprietary, so leave it unselected.

4. Drag the mouse to move around the city, roll the wheel to zoom, and drag the wheel to orbit into a point of view that simulates aerial photography. You may optionally try to match the point of view in Figure 12.10, although this is not necessary.

5. Copy the contents of the screen to the clipboard. Press Control+Shift+Cmd+3 (Mac) or press the Print Screen key (Windows).

6. Quit NASA World Wind and launch your Extended version of Photoshop. Press Cmd+N / Ctrl+N and click the OK button in the New dialog box. Press Cmd+V / Ctrl+V to paste the image from the clipboard into the new document.

Figure 12.10 NASA World Wind Java interface

7. Press C to select the Crop tool, drag a crop window around the satellite imagery, and click the Commit button on the options bar. Save the image as **Map.jpg**. This file is provided on the DVD for your convenience. Open Map.jpg if you are jumping in here.

8. Press P to select the Pen tool. Draw a path by clicking to create a series of anchor points along the streets connecting any two sites. In this case, I will draw a path connecting the Transamerica Pyramid with Saints Peter and Paul Church at Washington Square (Figure 12.11). The towers of this church have the same forms as the Transamerica Pyramid.

Note: To see the Transamerica Pyramid and Saints Peter and Paul Church juxtaposed next to each other, see the photo gallery at http://thepyramidcenter.com.

9. Press Cmd+Shift+N / Ctrl+Shift+N to create a new layer, type **Route** in the New Layer dialog box, and click OK.

10. Open the Swatches panel and click the red swatch to set it as the foreground color. Press B to select the Brush tool and then press the square bracket keys to adjust the brush size to a reasonable value to stroke the path (8 px in this case).

Figure 12.11 Drawing a path on the map connecting two sites

11. Open the Paths panel and click the Stroke Path With Brush button (Figure 12.12). Figure 12.11 is the result.

Stroke Path With Brush

Figure 12.12 Stroking a path with the Brush

12. Click below the Work Path in the Paths panel to deselect it. The thin vector path at the center of the red stroke disappears in the document window.

13. Click the Add Layer Mask button at the bottom of the Layers panel. Press Shift+G until the Gradient tool is selected. Select the Foreground, Transparent gradient in the picker on the options bar and verify that Linear Gradient mode and Transparency are selected (Figure 12.13).

Foreground, Transparent gradient

Transparency

Linear Gradient

Figure 12.13 Selecting gradient options

14. Drag a gradient from point A to point B, as shown in Figure 12.14. The route is now completely masked, and a small portion of the mask remains white.

Figure 12.14 Applying gradients to initially hide the route

15. Unlink layer ROUTE from its mask by clicking the link between their thumbnails (Figure 12.15).

16. Choose Window > Animation to open the Animation panel if it's not already open. Click the Convert To Timeline Animation button in the lower-right corner if the Animation panel is still in Frame-based mode.

17. Expand the Route track and click the stopwatch icon in the Layer Mask Position track. A key is created at time zero (Figure 12.16).

Click here to unlink the mask.

Figure 12.15 Unlinking the mask from the Route layer

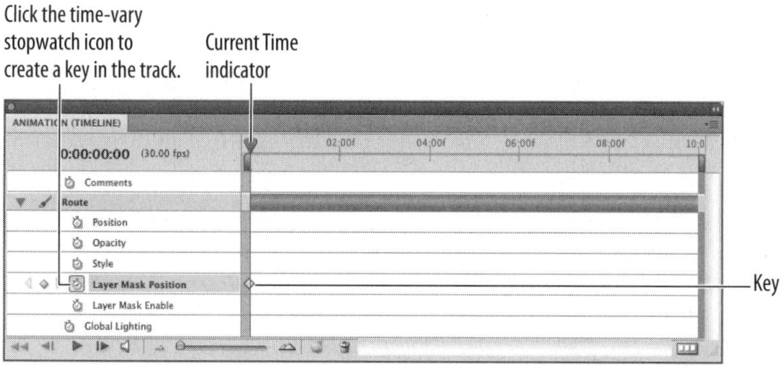

Click the time-vary stopwatch icon to create a key in the track.

Current Time indicator

Key

Figure 12.16 Creating an initial key in the layer mask position track of the Route layer

18. Click the Animation menu button in the upper-right corner of the Animation panel and choose Document Settings from the menu. Change the Duration to 0:00:05:00, or 5 sec (Figure 12.17). Leave the Frame Rate at 30 frames per second (fps) and click OK.

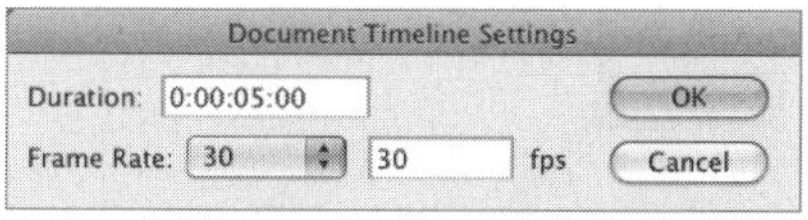

Document Timeline Settings

Duration: 0:00:05:00   OK

Frame Rate: 30   30   fps   Cancel

Figure 12.17 Changing the duration of the entire animation

19. Drag the Current Time indicator all the way to the right, to 4:29. There is actually one more frame (frame 0) in the total animation, making the duration 5 seconds exactly.

20. Press V to select the Move tool and verify that the mask on layer Route is still targeted. Drag the mask down and to the right so that the route is completely exposed. A key automatically appears in the Layer Mask Position track (Figure 12.18).

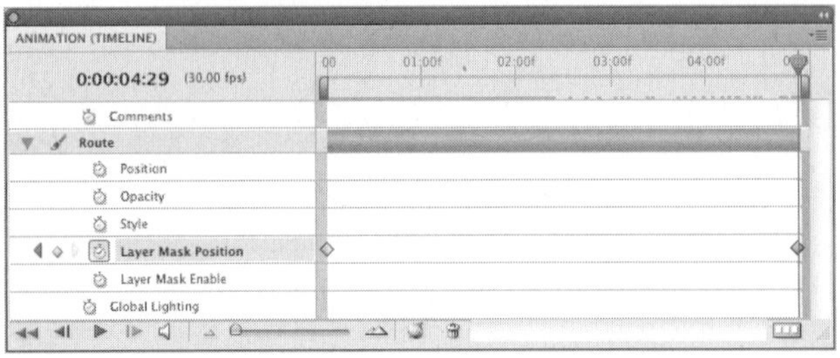

Figure 12.18 Keyframing a mask position change on the timeline

21. Preview the animation by using the playback controls at the bottom of the Animation panel. The route progressively appears as Photoshop interpolates the changing mask position over time.

22. Choose File > Export > Render Video. The terms *animation* and *video* are often used interchangeably, although video is arguably something shot in the real world with a video camera. Choose QuickTime Export and click the Render button. After a processing delay, a video file called `Map.mov` appears on your hard drive. Double-click this file and watch it in QuickTime (Figure 12.19). Playback is smoother in QuickTime than in Photoshop.

Figure 12.19 Watching the rendered output

23. Save the image as `Map.psd`.

This tutorial was just a small taste of what's possible with timeline animation. You can animate layer position and opacity, meaning things can move around and/or fade in and out. Anything in the Layer Style dialog box can be animated—in other words, a tremendous number of settings. You animated Layer Mask Position here, but also consider fading masks in and out with the Layer Mask Enable track.

> **Note:** If you don't have the free QuickTime player on your computer, you can download it from www.apple.com/quicktime/.

Altering Videos the Smart Way

You can alter video in two fundamental ways in the Extended version of Photoshop. You can either alter one frame at a time in a painstaking process called *rotoscoping* (which I avoid because there are 30 frames in each second of video), or encapsulate a video layer within a smart object and save loads of time.

Adjustment layers and/or filters applied to smart objects are assigned to the entire video clip all at once. If you want an adjustment layer or filter to affect only one portion of a video, animating a layer mask or vector mask is the more efficient approach.

Animating a Vector Mask

By animating a vector mask, you can cause an adjustment layer to follow an object in motion. You will use a Black & White adjustment layer to convert everything but the featured building (defined by a vector mask) to grayscale. Animating the vector mask keeps the featured building colorized as the camera slowly pans. Here is how to animate a vector mask:

1. Open the Dubai.mov video from the DVD (Figure 12.20). Press the spacebar to start and stop video playback.

Figure 12.20 Original video clip showing high-rise buildings rising above yachts in a Dubai marina

2. Rename Layer 1 to **Video Clip**.

3. Press P to select the Pen tool. Draw a path around the high-rise building on the left. Remember to drag when you want to curve the path, and simply click to create corner points. Click the last point on top of the first point to close the path.

4. In the Adjustment panel, click the Black & White adjustment icon. A Black & White adjustment layer is added that automatically has the path you drew in step 3 as a vector mask (Figure 12.21). However, the desired effect is reversed as the building is in grayscale and everything else remains in color.

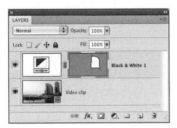

Figure 12.21 Creating an adjustment layer converts the path into a vector mask.

5. If there is no space padding the border between the edge of the video and the document window, drag the document window's lower-right corner down and to the right to expand the working space around the video. Press U to select the vector toolset and choose the Rectangle tool on the options bar. Draw a rectangle larger than the video clip but still fitting within the document window (Figure 12.22).

Figure 12.22 Drawing a rectangle larger than the video

6. Press Shift+A until the Path Selection tool is active. Hold down Shift and click the vector mask in the document window that you drew in step 3, so that both the rectangle and the mask are selected. On the options bar, click the Exclude Overlapping Shape Area button (Figure 12.23). The vector mask thumbnail inverts as the featured building appears in color while everything else in the video goes black and white.

Exclude Overlapping Shape Area

Figure 12.23 Reversing the vector mask

7. Choose Window > Animation to open the Animation panel if it isn't already open. Expand the Black & White 1 layer and click the stopwatch icon in the Vector Mask Position track (Figure 12.24) to set the initial key.

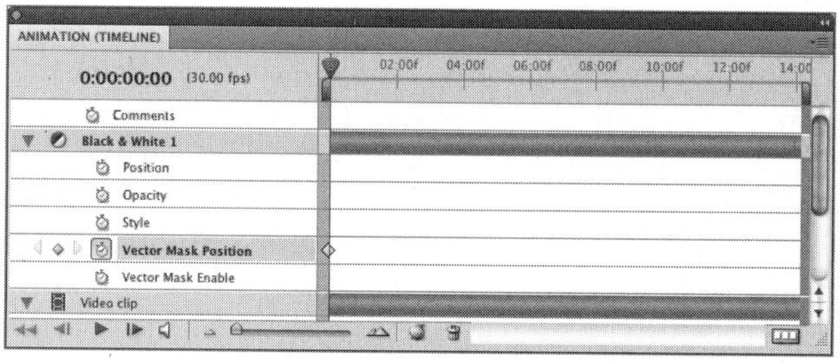

Figure 12.24 Setting the initial key in the Vector Mask Position track

8. Drag the Current Time indicator to the right end of the timeline (14:04). The video pans to the left, and the colorized portion inside the vector mask remains in the same position.

9. Press A to select the Path Selection tool. Drag the paths in the document window to the left and hold down Shift after you start dragging to constrain the movement horizontally. Use the arrow keys on the keyboard to nudge the paths into position over the building where the paths belong (Figure 12.25).

10. A narrow band of color appears on the right edge of the document window, where the vector mask has moved beyond the edge of the image. Press Shift+A to select the Direct Selection tool. Drag a window around the two path points on the right. Press and hold the right-arrow key to nudge these two points all the way to the right so the vector mask covers the entire image (Figure 12.26).

Figure 12.25 Keyframing vector mask movement

Figure 12.26 Changing the shape of the mask to cover the exposed portion of the image

11. Open the Paths panel. Deselect the Black & White 1 vector mask by clicking below it in the Paths panel. Play the animation by pressing the spacebar. The colorized region follows the high-rise building on the left, drawing attention to it. Toggle the spacebar again to stop playback.

12. Save the image as **Dubai.psd**.

Assigning Smart Filters to a Video Layer

By converting a video layer into a smart object, any filters you assign not only remain editable but also affect the entire clip. Here is how to alter videos the smart way:

1. Open Dubai.psd from the DVD if it's not already open.

2. In the Layers panel, right-click the Video Clip layer and choose Convert To Smart Object from the menu that appears. The layer thumbnail changes from a video icon to the smart object icon (Figure 12.27). The video layer still exists inside the smart object container.

Figure 12.27 Converting a video layer into a smart object

3. Choose Filter > Filter Gallery. Expand the Brush Strokes category and select the Accented Edges filter. Set Edge Width to 1, Edge Brightness to 15, and Smoothness to 3.

4. Click the New Effect Layer button at the bottom of the Filter Gallery. Expand the Texture category and select the Texturizer filter. Select Canvas from the Texture drop-down. Set Scaling to 100% and Relief to 4. Select Top from the Light drop-down (Figure 12.28). Click OK.

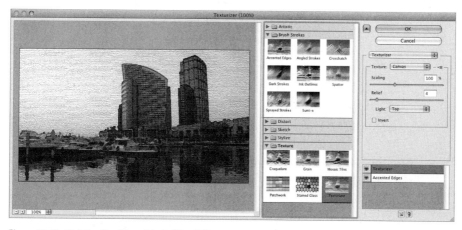

Figure 12.28 Stylizing the video with the Filter Gallery

5. Target the top layer and click the Vibrance button in the Adjustments panel. Drag the Vibrance slider all the way to the right.

6. Choose File > Export > Render Video. Choose QuickTime Export and change the output file to **AlteredVideo.mov**. Click Render, and after a processing delay, the file appears on your hard drive. Double-click AlteredVideo.mov and watch it in the free QuickTime player (Figure 12.29). The artistic possibilities are unlimited for editing video with Photoshop.

Figure 12.29 Watching the edited video in QuickTime. The building on the left is vibrantly colored while everything else is black and white. The camera pans while the ripples in the water dynamically reflect the scene.

Animating 3D Models on the Timeline

This section puts together what you've learned in earlier 3D chapters plus what you've learned so far in this chapter in regard to video. 3D layers have a number of tracks you can animate, including 3D object and camera positions, 3D cross sections, and various render settings. In this tutorial, you will animate a section plane dynamically cutting through a building. To make the animation more compelling, you will also keyframe the 3D camera position to get a better view of the building interior. The following steps show how to animate a 3D model:

1. Open House.dae from the DVD (Figure 12.30).
2. Click Continue if the warning dialog box appears (Figure 12.31).

Note: A warning appears if the model has more than a preset number of materials or lights, as set in Preferences. Models with fewer materials or lights load faster in Photoshop, so you should try to minimize the number of materials and lights defined in the model when creating models in 3D programs. This is not critical for the tutorial file because it loads very quickly (3 seconds).

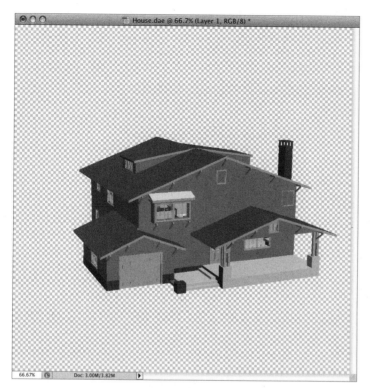

Figure 12.30 House 3D model

MODEL BY 3D WAREHOUSE USER J. WALLACE http://sketchup.google.com/3dwarehouse/
details?mid=43b45a47288d89df157ba9ba12ccda57&prevstart=0

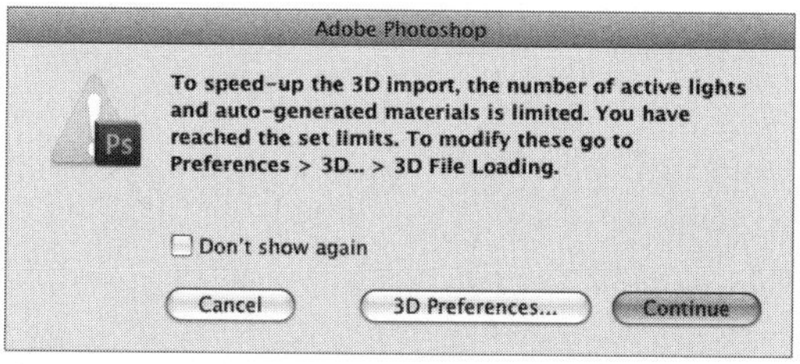

Figure 12.31 Potential 3D model importing delay

3. The building comes in rotated with respect to the document window. Press K to
select the 3D Object tools, type **-90** in the X Orientation text box on the options
bar, press Tab twice, type **45** in the Z Orientation text box (Figure 12.32), and
press Return/Enter. The building looks like Figure 12.30, shown earlier.

Figure 12.32 Changing the initial 3D object orientation

4. Rename Layer 1 to **House**. Choose Window > Animation if the Animation panel isn't already open. Expand the House track and click the stopwatch icon in the 3D Camera Position and 3D Cross Section tracks (Figure 12.33).

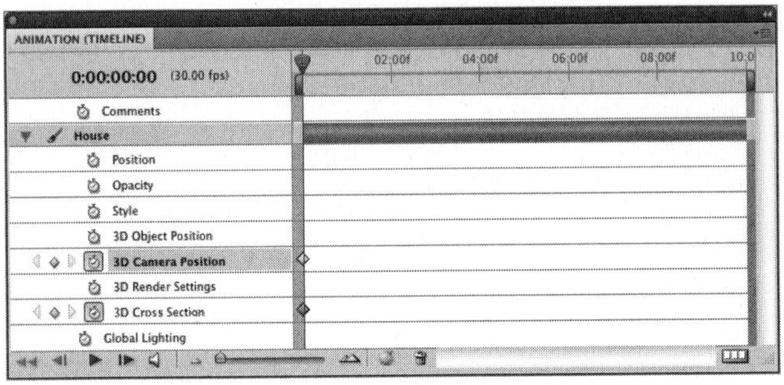

Figure 12.33 Creating initial keys in tracks you plan to animate

5. Choose Window > 3D to open the 3D panel. Click the Filter By: Whole Scene button at the top of the 3D panel if it is not already selected. Select Cross Section and deselect both Plane and Intersection. Choose the Y-Axis radio button, type -30 in the Offset text box, and press Return/Enter (Figure 12.34). The basement walls and the front porch are all that appear in the document window, as the cross section slices away everything above the cutting plane.

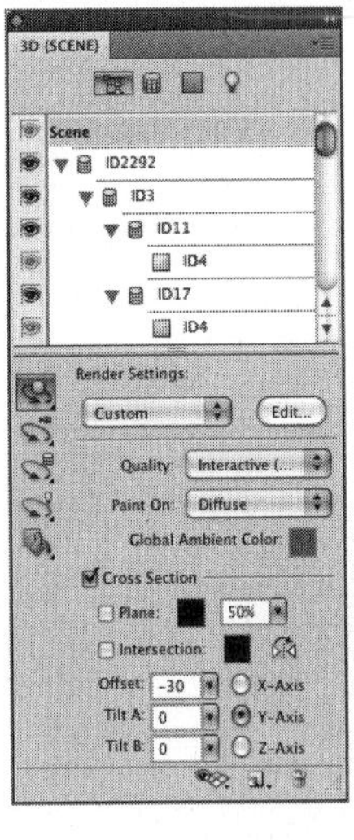

Figure 12.34 Configuring cross-sectional parameters

6. In the Animation panel, drag the Current Time indicator all the way to the end of the timeline (extreme right).

7. In the 3D panel, type +35 in the Offset text box and press Return/Enter. The section plane moves above the house, and everything is visible.

8. Press N to select the 3D Camera toolset. Drag up approximately 1 inch in the document window to orbit the camera and look down more on the house.

Observe that final keys appear in both of the tracks in which you placed initial keys in step 4 (Figure 12.35).

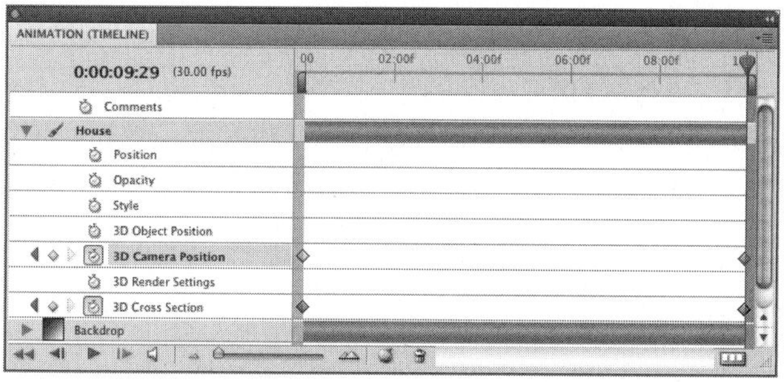

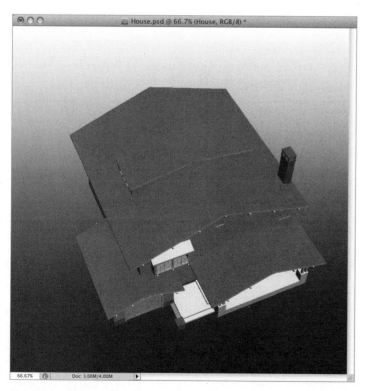

Figure 12.35 Changing the 3D camera position automatically creates an animation key at the end of the timeline.

9. Choose Layer > New Fill Layer > Gradient, type **Backdrop** in the New Layer dialog box, and click OK.

10. Select the Black, White gradient in the Gradient dialog box that appears and click OK. Press Cmd+[/ Ctrl+[to move the current layer below layer House. A gradient backdrop appears behind the house (Figure 12.36).

Figure 12.36 Adding a gradient backdrop

11. Save the image as **House.psd**.

12. In the Animation panel, drag the Current Time indicator to see the animation. The camera moves as the section plane dynamically moves through the house, revealing its interior. Choose File > Export > Render Video. Choose QuickTime Export and click the Render button.

13. After a processing delay, open House.mov on your hard drive and enjoy the animated 3D model in the QuickTime player (Figure 12.37). House.mov is provided on the DVD for your convenience.

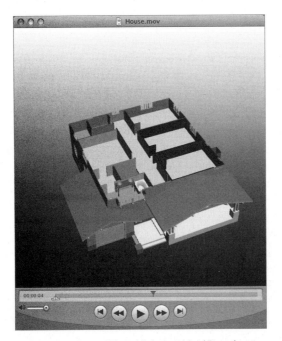

Figure 12.37 Animated 3D model playing in QuickTime player

In this chapter, you've been exposed to several techniques for creating animations and editing videos entirely with Photoshop. From frame-by-frame animation to sophisticated timeline animation to altering video footage and presenting 3D models, you have the tools to put designs into motion. Consider rendering compelling motion graphics with Photoshop the next time you present your architectural designs.

Appendix: About the Companion DVD

In this appendix:

What you'll find on the DVD

System requirements

Using the DVD

Troubleshooting

What You'll Find on the DVD

The following sections are arranged by category and provide a summary of the software and other goodies you'll find on the DVD. If you need help installing the items provided on the DVD, refer to the installation instructions in the "Using the DVD" section of this appendix.

Programs on the DVD fall into one of these categories:

Shareware programs are fully functional, free, trial versions of copyrighted programs. If you like particular programs, register with their authors for a nominal fee and receive licenses, enhanced versions, and technical support.

Freeware programs are free, copyrighted games, applications, and utilities. You can copy them to as many computers as you like—for free—but they offer no technical support.

GNU software is governed by its own license, which is included inside the folder of the GNU software. There are no restrictions on distribution of GNU software. See the GNU license at the root of the DVD for more details.

Trial, demo, or *evaluation* versions of software are usually limited either by time or functionality (such as not letting you save a project after you create it).

Tutorial Videos

For Windows and Mac

The DVD features a tutorial video for each chapter highlighting the techniques presented.

Example and Resource Files

For Windows and Mac

All the examples and resource files are located in the Chapter Files directory on the DVD and work with Macintosh and Windows 98/2000/Me/XP/Vista/7 computers.

Pano2VR Trial Software

For Windows and Mac

Pano2VR is a great application that converts spherical or cylindrical images into QuickTime VR and Flash formats. It also features customizable skins, hot spots, and directional sound. The DVD includes a demo of this cool software, and you can get more info at http://gardengnomesoftware.com/pano2vr.php.

System Requirements

Make sure that your computer meets the minimum system requirements shown in the following list. If your computer doesn't match up to most of these requirements, you may have problems using the software and files on the companion DVD. For the latest and greatest information, please refer to the ReadMe file located at the root of the DVD.

- A PC running Microsoft Windows 98, Windows 2000, Windows NT4 (with SP4 or later), Windows Me, Windows XP, Windows Vista, or Windows 7
- A Macintosh running Mac OS X
- A PC running a version of Linux with kernel 2.4 or greater
- An Internet connection
- A DVD-ROM drive
- The most recent version of QuickTime

Using the DVD

To install the items from the DVD to your hard drive, follow these steps:

1. Insert the DVD into your computer's DVD-ROM drive. The license agreement appears.

> **Note:** Windows users: The interface won't launch if you have autorun disabled. In that case, click Start > Run (for Windows Vista or Windows 7, Start > All Programs > Accessories > Run). In the dialog box that appears, type **D:\Start.exe.** (Replace *D* with the proper letter if your DVD drive uses a different letter. If you don't know the letter, see how your DVD drive is listed under My Computer.) Click OK.

> **Note:** Mac users: The DVD icon will appear on your desktop. Double-click the icon to open the DVD and then double-click the Start icon.

2. Read through the license agreement, and then click the Accept button if you want to use the DVD.

The DVD interface appears. The interface allows you to access the content with just one or two clicks.

Troubleshooting

Wiley has attempted to provide programs that work on most computers with the minimum system requirements. Alas, your computer may differ, and some programs may not work properly for some reason.

The two likeliest problems are that you don't have enough memory (RAM) for the programs you want to use, or you have other programs running that are affecting installation or running of a program. If you get an error message such as "Not enough memory" or "Setup cannot continue," try one or more of the following suggestions and then try using the software again:

Turn off any antivirus software running on your computer. Installation programs sometimes mimic virus activity and may make your computer incorrectly believe that it's being infected by a virus.

Close all running programs. The more programs you have running, the less memory is available to other programs. Installation programs typically update files and programs; so if you keep other programs running, installation may not work properly.

Have your local computer store add more RAM to your computer. This is, admittedly, a drastic and somewhat expensive step. However, adding more memory can really help the speed of your computer and allow more programs to run at the same time.

Customer Care

If you have trouble with the book's companion DVD-ROM, please call the Wiley Product Technical Support phone number at (800) 762-2974. Outside the United States, call +1(317) 572-3994. You can also contact Wiley Product Technical Support at http://sybex.custhelp.com. John Wiley & Sons will provide technical support only for installation and other general quality-control items. For technical support on an application itself, consult the program's vendor or author.

To place additional orders or to request information about other Wiley products, please call (877) 762-2974.

Index